9/13

HOLLYWOOD'S COPYRIGHT WARS

FILM AND CULTURE John Belton, Editor

Peter Decherney

HOLLYWOOD's

COPYRIGHT WARS

FROM EDISON TO THE INTERNET

COLUMBIA UNIVERSITY PRESS

NEW YORK

COLUMBIA UNIVERSITY PRESS

Publishers Since 1893
New York   Chichester, West Sussex
cup.columbia.edu

Library of Congress Cataloging-in-Publication Data
Decherney, Peter.
Hollywood's copyright wars : from Edison to the internet / Peter Decherney.
p. cm. — (Film and culture)
Includes bibliographical references and index.
ISBN 978-0-231-15946-3 (cloth : alk. paper)
1. Copyright—Motion pictures—United States—History. 2. Copyright—
Broadcasting rights—United States—History.   I. Title.
KF3070.D43   2012
346.7304'82—dc23   2011041745

Columbia University Press books are printed on permanent and durable acid-free
paper.

This book is printed on paper with recycled content.
Printed in the United States of America
c 10 9 8 7 6 5 4 3 2 1

References to Internet Web sites (URLs) were accurate at the time of writing.
Neither the author nor Columbia University Press is responsible for URLs that
may have expired or changed since the manuscript was prepared.

for Emily

CONTENTS

LIST OF ILLUSTRATIONS

ACKNOWLEDGMENTS

L IKE MANY BOOKS about copyright, I must start by thanking the inimitable copyright scholar Peter Jaszi. Peter has been my guide and guru throughout the research and writing of this book. He has generously spent many hours talking with me and reading drafts of every part of the manuscript. As others who know Peter will surely agree, he is like the eye of the copyright storm; things grow more confusing and tumultuous the farther away you get.

I also need to thank Peter Jaszi's college friend and my longtime mentor John Belton. Through Columbia University Press, John has assembled one the best book series in the history of media studies. John's secret, I have been privileged to learn, is not only selecting good books but tirelessly cultivating authors, sending relevant articles and thoughtful notes. Most importantly, he is always my toughest reader.

I was fortunate to write this book while many other scholars in a variety of fields were interested in similar questions. Writing the book has felt closer to a conversation than a monologue. Many people have offered invaluable comments on drafts or after hearing me present work in progress at conferences. In particular, I want to single out the incisive criticism of Patricia Aufderheide, Eric Hoyt, Paul Saint-Amour, Jessica Silby, Bob Spoo, Rebecca Tushnet, and Martha Woodmansee.

My colleagues at the University of Pennsylvania must feel like they have been listening to me talk about Hollywood and copyright forever. Yet they never cease to show up for more and to keep me on my toes. I greatly appreciate the friendship and intellectual support of Karen Beckman, Tim Corrigan, Michael X. Delli Carpini, Jim English, Nathan Enzmenger, Gerry Faulhaber, Nicola Gentili, Andrea Matwyshyn, Meta Mazaj, Sharrona Pearl, Monroe Price, Katherine Sender, Peter Stallybrass, Wendy Steiner, Joe Turow, Anu Vedantham, Kevin Werbach, Christopher Yoo, and Barbie Zelizer. And I hate to imagine what I would have missed without the research support of Tamar Lisbona and Gary Kafer.

Work on this book has been supported by a number of institutions, organizations, and publications. I received generous grants and fellowships from the Academy of Motion Picture Arts and Sciences, the American Council of Learned Societies, the Scholars Program in Culture and Communication at the Annenberg School for Communication, and the Penn Humanities Forum. The International Society for the History and Theory of Intellectual Property, the Penn History of Material Texts Seminar, the Wharton Media and Communications Colloquium, and the Annenberg Internet and Media Policy Working Group greatly enriched my work by allowing me to present in their intense and collegial forums. And King's College, London, where most of the book was written, offered an essential escape from distraction, while being right in the heart of London. Earlier versions of chapters or parts of chapters have been published in the journal *Film History*, the *University of Wisconsin Law Review*, and in Paul Saint-Amour, ed., *Modernism and Copyright* (Oxford University Press, 2011). Thank you for permission to reprint material here. My editors at Columbia University Press have shown enthusiasm for the project since I first mentioned it. In the final stages, Jennifer Crewe put up with far too many questions about rights, and I was fortunate to have Roy Thomas cast his famous eye over the manuscript.

As always, I am greatly indebted to my family for all of their support. Thank you mom and dad, Alec and Sharon, Natalie and Juliet, and Bob and Marilyn. And most of all, I must thank my brilliant and beautiful wife Emily, to whom this book is dedicated, and my inexhaustible kids, Sophie and Asher. More than anything in the footnotes, Sophie and Asher have taught me that existing culture is only the springboard for creativity, as we enact unauthorized sequels to our favorite movies and fill our walls with crayon-made derivative works.

HOLLYWOOD'S COPYRIGHT WARS

INTRODUCTION
THE THEATER OF COPYRIGHT

MANY FACTORS have shaped the development of the American film and television industries: the personalities of moguls, advances in technology, and changing social mores to name a few. One of the most important drivers of the media, however, is too often underemphasized or entirely overlooked by media historians.[1] Regulation—government policies, court decisions, and internal company policies—might at first seem to be an impossibly dry or specialized subject. But when put in context, regulatory struggles often reveal some of the most human tales of personal conflicts over power, politics, and art. Regulation has also been vitally important to both the structure of media companies and the art of making movies and television shows. Consider antitrust rulings, First Amendment cases, labor laws, media ownership rules, tax codes, wartime sedition acts, and international trade policy. These forms of regulation touch every aspect of media creation and circulation; they influence who makes films and television shows, what they look like, and ultimately who can see them.

At times, legal regulation has caused the entire film and television industry to turn in one direction or another. After the Supreme Court's 1948 antitrust ruling,[2] for example, the Hollywood studios sold off their theater chains. The entire system for distributing and marketing films changed. Studios stopped churning out weekly B films and short subjects to fill their theaters. They began to make fewer and more expensive films, and this one decision played a pivotal role in leading Hollywood on the path to the blockbuster-driven industry of today. Other forms of regulation affect Hollywood more subtly. Tax credits, for example, have become one of the most important factors that producers consider when they choose locations for a film or television shoot. Shooting in Louisiana instead of California can shave millions of dollars off of a production budget, because that state returns up to one third of the money that production teams spend there.[3] Regulation arises at almost every stage of production, distribution, and reception from manufacturing cameras to operating a theater to using a clip from a film in a YouTube parody video.

Copyright law is perhaps the most important form of media regulation. It guides filmmakers' artistic decisions; it underlies Hollywood's corporate structure; and it determines how audiences consume media. Since the widespread adoption of the internet in the 1990s, copyright law has begun to affect an ever-expanding range of media producers and consumers, including amateur video makers, file sharers, and internet entrepreneurs. As a result, interest in digital copyright law has moved beyond the realm of scholars and lawyers. Even high school students now hold strong opinions about copy protection, the public domain, and other areas of cultural policy that had previously been the obscure domain of legal experts.

Times have changed, but the issues themselves are not new. *Hollywood's Copyright Wars* historicizes the heated debates over copyright and digital media. Starting with Thomas Edison and continuing through the present, I address the long history of antipiracy campaigns, filmmakers' rights, and the legal environment for new technologies. I demonstrate that the film and television industries have struggled to influence and adapt to copyright law throughout their history. And many of our most valued Hollywood treasures, from *Modern Times* (1936) to *Jaws* (1975), we will see, cannot be fully appreciated without an understanding of their legal context.

But the legal battles are only half of the story. In contrast to (most) legal scholars who touch on some of the same issues, I focus on the industrial and cultural impact of copyright law. Legal historians often limit themselves to landmark decisions and key policy changes. But sometimes landmark legal decisions have surprisingly little effect. Other times, new copyright policies have revolutionary unintended effects. The most surprising thing that we learn from the history of Hollywood and copyright is that most of the time Hollywood's leaders have responded to intellectual property skirmishes through self-regulation. Rather than submit to Congress or judges and juries, studio heads and filmmakers have consistently brought copyright regulation "in house," as it were. Hollywood has a history of responding to other forms of legal regulation in the same way. Most famously, in the 1920s and 1930s Hollywood found itself subject to the whims of state censor boards and facing the potential threat of federal content legislation. The studios reacted by adopting the Production Code and allowing their trade association, the Motion Picture Producers and Distributors Association, to regulate violent, sexual, and political content in movies. Hollywood has, similarly, devised internal methods for controlling intellectual property. In the 1940s, for example, Hollywood's writers and moguls found themselves frustrated by decades of shifting court decisions about screenwriting credit and compensation. Rather than continue to pursue a legal resolution, they turned to Hollywood's talent guilds to arbitrate disputes over authorship. Similar stories of self-regulation, we will see, can be told about piracy battles in the 1900s, film studios' attempts to contain the disruption wrought by the VCR (video cassette recorder), big copyright holders' strategies for managing amateur and noncommercial uses of their content, and many other pivotal moments in the development of Hollywood. Indeed, much of what constitutes the history of Hollywood's engagement with copyright law has happened outside courthouses and congressional halls—in the larger theater of copyright—as well as inside them. *Hollywood's Copyright Wars* examines in great detail the court cases and policy battles that have shaped American media, but I also consider the often extralegal resolution to these conflicts.

COPYRIGHT WARS AND PIRACY

A common misconception about copyright is that its primary function is to protect authors and creators. It does protect creators but only as a by-product. At least in the United States, copyright's goal, as it is stated in the Constitution, is to "promote the progress of science." (Science, in this instance, retains its eighteenth-century meaning of knowledge or learning.) To serve this goal, copyright gives creators a limited monopoly on their creations before their work enters the public domain and becomes freely available to all. Since 1998, works enter the public domain 70 years after their creator's death. If the work was created for a corporation, as most films and television shows are, its copyright term expires 95 years after it is published (or 120 years after creation, whichever comes first). This assumes that the copyright term will not be extended, as it has been every time that works from the 1920s—including early Hollywood masterpieces—approach the end of their monopoly. Even before a work enters the public domain, however, there are many limits on a copyright holder's monopoly. Whole categories of creative work are excluded from copyright protection, including fashion design and culinary creations. Other limitations on copyrighted works exist to protect users, i.e., consumers or creators who need to use work still protected by copyright. A user may be a television writer who wants to remake a basic science fiction plot or an engineer with a brilliant new concept for a video player or a parent who simply wants to show a Warner Bros. cartoon to a group of children. As these examples suggest, copyright is not a watertight monopoly that protects against all forms of copying and reuse. It is designed to leak at the sides, and it has strategically placed holes throughout. As it is often said, copyright strikes a balance between copyright holders and users. It allows copyright holders to profit from and control their work, but only up to the point where society's needs outweigh those of the copyright holder.[4] At that threshold, the public domain, fair use, and other exemptions begin to take over. The ultimate goal of copyright is always to enrich society by encouraging the creation of art and ideas, so they can be consumed and built upon.

Hollywood is caught on both sides of this divide. Studios are in the business of creating and controlling intellectual property, but the creative professionals working in the film and television industries make new works by building on the storehouse of cultural ideas. The Walt Disney Company's tried-and-true business model is retelling public domain fairy tales, and George Lucas drew on a wide range of myths and allusions in order to create the *Star Wars* franchise. Yet Disney and Lucasfilm remain some of the most aggressive policers of their intellectual property. Throughout its history, Hollywood has been placed in the often-contradictory position of trying to protect filmmakers' rights to use copyrighted material as freely as possible while, at the same time, limiting others' use of the works created by Hollywood. To some extent, studios' positions on copyright have changed predictably over time. As the industry's archive of intellectual property has increased, studios have sought greater copyright protection. At least this is their public face. Behind the scenes, we will see, the industry has remained very pragmatic about intellectual property. Both Disney and Lucasfilm, for example, often remain quiet when fans reuse their work. And despite overinflated public rhetoric, studios have regularly been willing to accept compromises and creative solutions when new media—from the VCR to the internet—have challenged their business models.

For close to 300 years, two metaphors have been used dependably to explain the conflict over how to balance copyright law, and I think they are worth retaining. Since the eighteenth-century's "Battle of the Booksellers," critics have cast copyright debates as a "war," and they have referred to the side challenging the status quo as "pirates." There have been many attempts to abandon these metaphors over the centuries,[5] but they persist. And from a historical perspective, it is difficult to escape the conclusion that copyright has been shaped largely by militaristic and piratical thinking.[6]

The parties invested in copyright wars have changed over time, but copyright has consistently pitted incumbents who have grown too comfortable with the status quo against pirates who are pushing the boundaries of art and technology. To be sure, many pirates push too far and act maliciously. But just about every leading media company from the Edison Manufacturing Company to Fox Studios to YouTube have been labeled pirates at one time or another. Surely many pirates must be doing something that society values. Legal scholar Lawrence Lessig makes the important historical argument that most media technologies began as piratical instruments. Recorded music, radio, and cable television all exist today because copyright law was changed or reinterpreted in order to legalize practices that had previously been labeled piracy. Piracy, history tells us, is often just a name for media practices we have yet to figure out how to regulate.[7]

Debates about piracy are not only normal, they are actually a healthy aspect of a developing media industry and society. In chapter 1, "Piracy and the Birth of Film," I show that many forms of copying which we would now consider piracy were central to the emergence of both the art of film and the structure of the film industry. Filmmakers made exact copies of each other's films and sold them as their own; they remade competitors' films shot for shot; and Thomas Edison and his Trust built an industry on the unauthorized adaptation of books, plays, and newspaper cartoons. Early filmmakers, in other words, copied from each other and from other media without permission. Courts ultimately put an end to most of these types of copying, but not before the circulation of films and a culture of copying fostered the rapid growth of film as an art form. Moreover, the courts took decades to devise effective methods for regulating the new technology of films. I argue in this chapter that what we now see as piracy in the pre-1911 debates about regulating film were simply a function of society's attempts to explore, understand, and assimilate the new technology.

Claims of piracy did not end in 1911. They have continued throughout the history of the entertainment industries, and there are no doubt new copyright wars on the horizon. These wars take place in the press as well as in courts and congressional hearings, and consumers make themselves heard through purchases. Piracy debates are a form of indirect public negotiation, another part of the theater of copyright. The debates often drag on for decades, as they did with Edison and his rivals, and the ongoing debates about piracy are a necessary part of the regulatory process; they build in a valuable element of deliberation. The length of a particular copyright battle alone can sometimes be the key to determining its outcome. In a telling interview, intellectual property lawyer Fred von Lohmann described his many years' work for the digital rights advocacy organization the Electronic Frontier Foundation. Von Lohmann suggests that the longer a new consumer media technology remains on the market, the more consumers become accustomed to it and the harder it is for Hollywood studios or other companies to have legal limits placed on its use. As a consumer advocate, von Lohmann saw his job, in part, as prolonging debates until watching your TV remotely via the web, for example, became so routine that it could not be taken away. Conversely, a swift end to a piracy battle can often help incumbents.[8] It is easier to deny the importance of new technologies or new artistic practices while they still seem strange and potentially transgressive. From the Battle of the Booksellers to the copyright disputes of Edison and his rivals to the lawsuits against YouTube, piracy battles denote the most innovative periods in media history. And where we see claims of piracy, we are seeing a vital part of the regulatory process.

NEW TECHNOLOGY AND AUTHORSHIP

Each chapter of *Hollywood's Copyright Wars* addresses a different technological or institutional transformation that has affected the American film industry: the invention of movies, the development of the studio system, the challenge of airing films on television, the rise of home video, and the impact of the internet. At the same time, each chapter also addresses new challenges to the definition of authorship. The Constitution does not actually provide for the grant of a monopoly to "creators," as I have been suggesting. The framers of the Constitution used the much narrower term "author." But conceptions of authorship are constantly changing, and copyright has expanded to protect a much wider group of creators than we think of when we use the term *author*. "Author" conjures up images of a lone writer sitting at a café, but film editors, producers, and camera operators are all potential authors or coauthors of a film or television show.

In fact, the invention of motion pictures and the development of media industries have posed many new challenges for legislators and judges grappling with the continually evolving idea of the author.

Even before the invention of movies, as we will see in chapter 1, photography proved to be a conundrum for policymakers and courts. Could pushing a button really make someone an author? Or did cameras take humans and art out of the process of representation, making objective images of the world? The question became even more complicated when moving pictures were added to the equation. Were movie camera operators taking multiple photographs, judges wondered, or a single moving picture? Films resemble plays as well as photographs, and judges soon began to struggle with the problem of deciding whom to hold responsible for the public performance of a film when the actors, directors, and producers were not physically present. These issues reveal not only the challenge that film posed for late-nineteenth and early-twentieth-century policymakers, they also suggest the difficulty of determining when a new technology can be governed by the regulations already in place and when authorship has been so entirely remade that it requires a new set of rules. It is a question that persists in the regulation of media technology. In the two landmark cases that I examine in this chapter, courts defined film as an extension of photography and theater rather than pushing Congress to create new regulation for the new medium. Because these decisions failed to fully address the changes wrought by the new technology, they left vacuums for film companies to fill. And in both cases, I show, the failure to regulate film as a new medium opened the door for a few large companies to control the entire industry. First the Edison Trust and then the vertically integrated independents, who went on to form the Hollywood studios, erected large oligopolies in the vacuum left by courts.

After the independents moved out west, they developed new storytelling conventions. Filmmakers both built on existing art and literature, and they diverged from them. Chapter 2, "Hollywood's Golden Age of Plagiarism," examines filmmakers' and film studios' legal battles to protect their right to borrow liberally from literary and dramatic stories. In cases involving Charlie Chaplin, Harold Lloyd, James M. Cain, Billy Wilder, the Marx Brothers, Jack Benny, and many others, U.S. courts addressed filmmakers' use of old narrative devices and stock characters. Copyright allows creators to use ideas from earlier works, but not their expression. It is a distinction, we will see, that needed to be rethought in the context of Hollywood. In the process, judges helped to define the Hollywood genre system, determining which elements belonged to all westerns, for example, and which were the sole property of a particular novelist, playwright, or filmmaker. In the end, Hollywood studio heads were determined not to let the capricious decisions of judges run their industry. And in a process I have already hinted at, they took over the regulation of originality, credit, and compensation, establishing internal registration, arbitration, and contract systems.

A technological upheaval, the advent of television, forced another reappraisal of the idea of film authorship. Chapter 3, "Auteurism on Trial," turns to the changing nature of film authorship as a result of Hollywood's grudging embrace of television. The Hollywood studio system created a class of artists who were celebrated as auteurs but who, for the most part, did not hold the copyrights to their work. Ever since studios began to release films to be aired on television in the 1950s, auteurs have consistently sought the right to preserve the integrity of their work. They have fought against the "mutilating" and "emasculating" edited versions (as some court decisions read) created for television. From Douglas Fairbanks and Otto Preminger to George Lucas and Terry Gilliam, auteurs have sued studios and lobbied Congress for greater control over how their films are adapted for new media. Judges and legislators have been surprisingly sympathetic to film directors' plight, and the law has gradually grown to safeguard a romantic vision of the besieged film director who needs protection from the commercial desires of the studios. Although directors initially fought for control from the studios, the studios have learned to use the image of the defenseless director as leverage in their attempts to control new home video technologies.

Chapters 4 and 5 examine the challenges that home video and the internet posed for the regulation of media distribution, consumption, and authorship. Home video and the internet are, in a way, two acts of the same drama. Home video created new tools for amateur and independent media creators; the internet offered film and video makers networks for distributing their work and forming larger communities. Chapter 4 begins with a revisionary history of the rise of the VCR, and it chronicles Hollywood's slow but ultimate acceptance of the new machine. The cautionary tale of the VCR offers a blueprint for Hollywood's approach to new technologies—an approach that relies much more on public relations campaigns and licensing deals than on the high-profile legal cases so often covered in the press. The chapter then goes on to show how off-line communities of video artists, fans, and documentary filmmakers forged fair use conventions. They did not read statutes or court decisions. They listened for stories about filmmakers encountering resistance from rights holders, and they were even more attentive when film studios remained silent about brazen demonstrations of fair use. Studios, in turn, learned how to communicate with these fair use communities through alternate shows of strength and tolerance. Mythologies about fair use rather than the law, I suggest, have governed many pockets of media creation.

Once these fair use communities began to move online, however, they became subject to increased surveillance and scrutiny. Chapter 5 examines two aspects of the 1998 Digital Millennium Copyright Act (DMCA), and how the new law continues to change media production, distribution, and consumption more than a decade after it was passed. First, I examine the impact of the DMCA's anticircumvention provisions, which forbid users to bypass the copy protection—the locks—on DVDs and other digital media. I place the DMCA in the long history of copy protection going back to Edison (and further). In its historical context, we can see why Congress and the courts have historically rejected legally backed copy protection systems. The anticirumvention provisions demonstrate what happens when a watertight and unbalanced copyright system is put in place: it drives media production and use underground, and it bypasses the natural process of assimilating new uses of technology. It also creates the kind of unchecked monopolies that copyright was originally designed to limit.

The second section of the chapter examines the "safe harbor" provision of the DMCA, the part of the statute designed to shield internet service providers from liability for the infringement—the piracy—that takes place on their networks. Through sites like YouTube, video fair use communities stopped being local. Fans, artists, critics, and every other video creator were thrown together in the same venues. At first, they were subject to the capricious moves of film studios. But through recent case law, more subtlety is being built into the system for regulating noncommercial work on the web. This chapter ends by asking whether technology can solve the problems that it created.

Finally, in the conclusion, I chronicle the rise of the copyright reform movement. In the wake of the DMCA and the Napster trial, a grassroots movement has arisen among the ranks of students, activists, and artists. Facilitated by the blogosphere and social networks, this community has emerged as an influential voice in the making of copyright policy. I place the growth of the copyright reform movement in the context of the larger sphere of political activism and online organizing that stretched across the first decade of the twenty-first century, from protests against the World Trade Organization in Seattle in 1999 to the financial crisis of 2008. In the short term, the media reform movement and big content companies, including Hollywood studios, have reached an impasse. The polarization of positions and the volume of the debate have caused most copyright legislation to stall since 1998. But, I suggest, the plurality of voices in copyright debates can only be good in the long run. And there are signs to suggest that widening the sphere of influence over copyright policy will help restore balance to the system, perhaps just as it is time for it to be shaken up again by a major technological, political, or cultural revolution.

1

PIRACY AND THE BIRTH OF FILM

WRITING IN 1926, film historian Terry Ramsaye described the first decades of the U.S. film industry as a "lawless frontier." He dismissed the many piracy battles that consumed the first filmmakers, claiming that "ethics seldom transplant. They must be raised from seed, in each new field."[1] Ramsaye's conclusion may have been right—new media require new ethics—but he overlooked the process through which media ethics are updated and rethought when he swept piracy battles under the carpet. It is in the debates over piracy that we see new media breaking away from the old. Piracy wars veil contests to control innovation and new avenues for creativity. Where we encounter piracy claims in new media, we find incumbent businesses trying to protect their investment in older media by resisting the new. On the other side, today's pirates are often tomorrow's moguls, who are simply pushing the limits of new technology in directions that have yet to be assimilated (or condemned) by the law or society. To be sure, many pirates simply take advantage of the temporary lawless frontiers that accompany the diffusion of new media. Whatever their motivation, most early filmmakers were pirates of one stripe or another.

Copyright law is the battlefield on which media piracy battles are fought; it is the official engine for distinguishing piracy (or, more innocuously, "infringement") from the many legal forms of copying, distributing, performing, and building on art and culture. Judge Joseph Story (later a Supreme Court Justice) famously referred to copyright as the "metaphysics of the law." We could add that copyright law is also the metaphysics of new media.[2] Through copyright law, courts and Congress decide when existing laws are sufficient to regulate the aesthetic and commercial upheavals brought by technology and when new laws are needed to meet the novel demands of new technology.

Throughout the history of copyright and new media, the law has regularly domesticated new forms of copying and distribution. Radio, the VCR, cable television, and other new media all grew out of forms of communication that moved from the unstable category of piracy to a legal and socially acceptable status.[3] But the early history of film in the United States is different. It is the story of a business built on two forms of copying that we would now consider piracy: selling exact copies of competitors' films as if they were your own (a process known as *duping*) and making unauthorized adaptations of novels and plays. Unlike the law's assimilation of the forms of piracy enabled by so many other media, both of these forms of copying were eventually declared illegal in landmark court cases, one in 1903 and one in 1911. This chapter examines those two cases and how they gave birth—for better or worse—to the American film industry.

The history of the emergence of film does not, however, suggest that piracy can be or should be stopped, even if that were possible. As we will see, piracy is a natural part of the development of new media. The metaphysical questions that legislators and judges struggled with were not how to stop piracy. Rather, they struggled with the question of whether film was a new medium that required new regulation or whether it was simply the extension of existing media. In both of the cases that determined how film would be regulated by copyright law, courts decided that film should be considered an extension of earlier media. Film was simply moving photography and virtual theater. I argue that both cases led to the further monopolization and vertical integration of the American film industry. Declaring film to be a new medium and drafting new legislation might have better served the art of film by developing a richer and more competitive market for film production, rather than the vertically integrated oligopoly that developed.

PHOTOGRAPHY: AN UNSTABLE BASE

What are movies? Just a lot of photographs strung together, right? That is what Thomas Edison's lawyers argued at first. And the story of copyright law's impact on the development of the U.S. film industry begins with Edison's successful, though short-lived, attempt to monopolize the film business. The Edison Manufacturing Company and later Edison's trust, the Motion Picture Patents Company, were involved in every landmark copyright case leading up to the 1912 Townsend Amendment, which officially added motion pictures to the Copyright Act.[4] Edison and his confederates were slow to realize the centrality of copyright law to their endeavors, and, as we will see, they generally clung to old laws when new ones might have been more beneficial to their business. Until 1903, for example, the Edison Company campaigned to have films defined and protected as photographs. As a result of Edison's successful campaign, the law defined films as photographs from 1903 to 1911—some of the most important years for the development of film style and the film industry.

The Edison Manufacturing Company began registering its films for copyright protection as photographs in 1894. While looking for an illustration of its new motion picture technology for a promotional article in *Harper's Weekly*, the Edison Company printed the entire film of laboratory assistant Fred Ott's sneeze on a single sheet of paper (fig. 1.1). It then must have occurred to someone in the company that they had transformed their film into an object that could be protected by copyright law: a photograph. In accordance with the current copyright regulations, the Edison Company proceeded to register the photograph, pay the registration fee, and deposit two copies with the Copyright Office of the Library of Congress.

Over the next eighteen years (until 1912), Edison and his competitors experimented with different methods of copyright deposit. It is often thought that early film companies only deposited films printed on long strips of photographic paper known as "paper prints," but occasionally they also deposited complete celluloid film negatives and positives; in some cases, they even tried depositing representative frames from every scene of a film. Several major film companies of the time, including the dominant French company Pathé Frères, went for long stretches without registering any films with the Copyright Office. The changing methods of applying (or not applying) for copyright reflected the battles to define what film is, to define standards of originality in filmmaking, and to stem the tides of piracy.

From the perspective of copyright history, one of the most fascinating things about the filing of paper prints is that this widespread practice went unchallenged and unverified for almost a decade. The practice of registering films as photographs is particularly troubling, because the status of photographic copyright was itself far from settled in the 1890s.

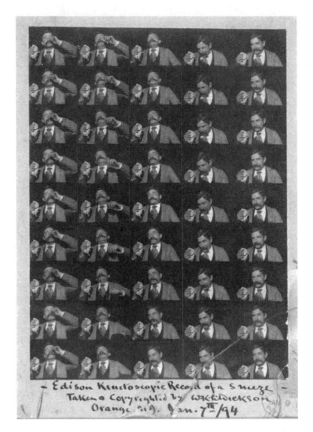

FIGURE 1.1 *Edison's Kinetographic Record of a Sneeze*, aka *Fred Ott's Sneeze* (1894), the first film registered for copyright. It was registered as a photograph.

Congress added photographs to the copyright statute as early as 1865 to accommodate the growing market for artistic photographs established by Matthew Brady and other photographers. Brady's Civil War photographs, which were exhibited in New York galleries, helped to legitimize the medium, conveying aesthetic value and historical significance.[5] England had also added photography to its copyright laws just three years earlier, and U.S. copyright laws frequently follow on the heels of British law, even today.[6] The amendment to the Copyright Act, however, did not satisfactorily draw a line between photographs eligible for copyright registration and those that fell outside of the copyright system. Which photographs, for instance, were truly original and therefore deserving of copyright protection and which did not have enough of a spark of originality to fall under the copyright umbrella?[7] Copyright, after all, protects originality, not artistic or historical significance. In determining whether photographers could be considered authors for merely pushing a button, copyright law came up against a strong and very long tradition in the theory of photography, articulated most famously by Oliver Wendell Holmes Sr. in the 1850s. This line of accepted wisdom held that the genius of photography—Holmes called it "sun-painting"—is precisely its ability to capture unbiased reality free of human mediation.[8]

A second line that remained to be drawn would separate photographs that could be considered original expressions from those photographs that belonged so firmly to the field of commerce that they forfeited copyright protection. In the 1879 *Trade-Mark Cases*, the Supreme Court made clear that the commercial purpose of many symbols and signs used for advertising disqualified them from the scope of copyright. And the ability of courts to see art in commerce has been a very gradual process. In the late nineteenth century, it was not at all clear where the line should be drawn for mass-reproduced postcards or other commercial photographs.[9]

As a result of these unanswered questions, photographic piracy remained rampant in the decades after the 1865 addition of photography to the Copyright Act. In the early 1880s, two cases directly questioned the constitutionality of adding photographs to the statute. In both cases the defendants claimed that they could not be considered pirates, because photographs were neither writings nor works of authorship, two constitutional criteria for copyright protection.[10] The Supreme Court eventually heard both cases.

In the first and now very famous case, a well-known portrait photographer, Napoleon Sarony, sued the Burrow-Giles Lithographic Company for duplicating and selling copies of his portrait of Oscar Wilde (fig. 1.2). Sarony had built a successful business making *cartes-de-visite*, small photographic portraits that celebrities frequently distributed to enhance their fame. Oscar Wilde had yet to publish any of the works that made him an internationally known literary star, and he used the cards from Sarony to boost his profile on his first trip to America. A retail store in New York City, Ehrlich Brothers, decided to take advantage of the sartorial trends Wilde was bringing to America, and the store commissioned the Burrow-Giles company to print an advertisement for hats using the Wilde photograph (although, strangely, Wilde was not wearing a hat in the image in question). Over 85,000 copies of the ad were made by the time Sarony brought the printers to court in the case of *Burrow-Giles Lithographic Co. v. Sarony*, 1884. The number of copies helps to indicate the scope of piracy at the time, almost twenty years after Congress had added photographs to the list of media covered by copyright law. When the Supreme Court decided

FIGURE 1.2 Napolean Sarony's photograph of Oscar Wilde, the subject of the Supreme Court case *Burrow-Giles Lithographic Co.* v. *Sarony* (1884). Can a photographer be an author?

the case, moreover, they did not exactly settle either of the burning questions. Did pushing a button constitute authorship? Did the commerce in photographic portraits negate their inclusion in the scope of copyright law?[11]

The Court did not doubt that images could be protected as writings, since the original U.S. Copyright Act of 1790 included maps and charts. But was a photograph different? Was it "simply the manual operation . . . of transferring to the plate the visible representation of some existing object, the accuracy of this representation being its highest merit?" The Court found that "this may be true in regard to the ordinary photograph, and, further that in such case a copyright is no protection. On the question as thus stated we decide nothing." In other words, they sidestepped the pushing-a-button-as-authorship question entirely. The justices refused to rule on whether pushing a button constituted authorship, because they found another method for defining Sarony as an author. Sarony had posed Wilde, arranged his costume and the decor, and generally composed the image before the camera passively recorded it. As such, the photograph could be protected as the record of the arrangement of a creative scene. But this standard was very far from acknowledging that photographers were artists, whose creations were original works of art.[12]

Four years after the *Sarony* case, the Supreme Court decided a similar case, *Thornton v. Schreiber*, which had originally been launched two years before Sarony's. The inconvenient death of one of the defendants and some confusion about whom to prosecute delayed the case's route to the Supreme Court. In this case, Schreiber and Sons, a publisher of postcards and stereopticon views, sued Edward B. Thornton, an employee of the Charles Sharpless and Sons dry-goods company in Philadelphia. Without permission, Thornton had duplicated and published 15,000 copies of Schreiber and Sons' photograph "The Mother Elephant 'Hebe' and her Baby 'Americus,'" using the elephant photograph on packing labels for Sharpless's merchandise (fig. 1.3).[13]

The *Thornton* case was very similar to the *Sarony* case. But this time, the court's decision focused largely on how to award damages properly. At the opening of the case, Justice Miller, who had written both the *Trade-Mark* and the *Sarony* decisions, seemed simply to assume that the photograph of the two elephants was eligible for copyright protection with no further scrutiny. But had the photographer posed the elephants? Was the photograph, which was made by a company that specialized in commercial postcards and stereopticon views and used by the infringers in the production of labels, worthy of copyright protection despite its commercial nature? Had something changed between the two cases that suddenly expanded the law to include even advertising photographs? The Supreme Court did not signal a clear method of interpreting the copyright status of photographs, and confusion continued to reign.

An article in the *New York Sun* that was reprinted in *Scientific American* in February 1900 cataloged the variety of interpretations that confused lower courts, publishers, and photographers alike. Many editors thought the *Sarony* precedent existed so that celebrities like Wilde could protect the circulation of their images; the author of the *Sun* article favored this interpretation. Moreover, the awarding of damages in copyright cases was so severe ($1 for each infringing copy with a cap of $10,000) that it caused most cases to be settled out of court; one innocent mistake could topple a small newspaper. When cases did make it to the courts, judges inconsistently

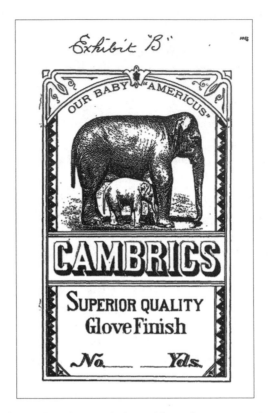

FIGURE 1.3 "The Mother Elephant 'Hebe' and her Baby 'Americus,'" a subject of the Supreme Court case *Thornton v. Schreiber* (1888).

applied the *Sarony* standard of authorship. In one case, a landscape photograph had been deemed to have no human author, because nature alone could be thought responsible for its own arrangement. In another case, a printer of advertisements claimed that he could use nonartistic photographs without permission.[14]

The following year, in 1901, legislators attempted to put an end to the public and judicial confusion over which photographs met the conditions for copyright protection. Congress clarified the copyright statute by extending the scope of copyright from the ambiguous "photographs" to the all-inclusive "any photograph." This clarification might have settled the debates about photographic art and authorship, but the law could not keep up with technology. One of the first major cases to be tried under the new "any photograph" statute, *Edison v. Lubin* (1903), asked a particularly difficult question: were motion pictures photographs or not?

AN INDUSTRY BUILT ON COPYING

Unauthorized copying was a staple of the early film industry, as it was for early book printing, photography, and recorded music, and as it would be for digital intellectual property on the internet. But as with those other media, separating the good piracy from the bad was an unenviable task. Which new methods of copying were really positive features of the new medium that had yet to be understood, and which forms of copying simply took advantage of the lawless frontier of new media? Film pioneers, including the Edison Company, had built their businesses on the practice of copying each other's films—that is, duping. After obtaining a print of, say, Georges Méliès's A *Trip to the Moon* (1902), a rival company would create its own negative from the positive print and then begin printing and selling the film as if it were its own.

Dupes circulated rapidly and globally, and they fed an international system of filmmaking based on copying and imitation. As film historians Georges Sadoul, Jay Leyda, David Bordwell, and Jane Gaines have all shown, filmmakers around the world were engaged in a project of rapid, fluid exchange of ideas that contributed to the fast-paced global growth of film art. Duping was only one part of a much larger culture of copying.[15]

Some companies indiscriminately duped their competitors' films. The industry leaders like Edison and American Mutoscope and Biograph (Biograph), however, set some ground rules. They freely duped films that had not been registered as photographs with the Copyright Office, but for the most part they respected the copyright notices on films that had been registered. It had yet to be determined that films could be registered as photographs, and these companies were clearly taking a gamble by forging their own legal practices, even if they set fuzzy boundaries. By adhering to this model, however, Edison and others helped entrench the position that business could proceed unhampered under the existing copyright law—the law, that is, that already governed the reproduction and distribution of photographs.

Even for these industry leaders, it is important to note, duping was a large and integral part of their business. Duping European films that were less likely to have U.S. copyrights, in particular, was a major part of every early U.S. film company's strategy, and the fastest dupers were also the market leaders. As Charles Musser observes, "To a remarkable degree, Edison's competition with its rivals revolved around the rapidity with which newly released European story films could be brought to the United States, duped, and sold."[16] Although Biograph was careful not to dupe films that had copyright notices, Biograph itself did not begin registering its films until 1902, which suggests that the company was unconcerned with competitors copying its films before that point.

This was not a case of honor among thieves, however. The Edison Company may have publicly led the move to establish a copyright system for film, but privately Edison contracted out the duping of films made by the Lubin and Amet companies to the Vitagraph Company.[17] Musser also recounts the elaborate deceptions Edison had to create just to purchase Georges Méliès's films. Once the French filmmaker became aware of Edison's prodigious duping, he refused to sell to Edison or his subsidiaries. Edison was forced to use multiple layers of intermediaries to acquire Méliès prints undetected.[18]

The decision to protect film content at all was gradual and born out of experience with the medium and the cultures of copying. Many of the first film production companies were principally equipment manufacturers, who were not immediately concerned about who copied their films. For years, films were made primarily to sell equipment, where the real money was to be made.

Moreover, each machine had a proprietary format. No Edison film, for example, could be shown on a Lumière projector without modification, because the sprocket holes were in different places. Indeed, much early film duping was the direct by-product of the technological format wars; distributors used duping as a method of bypassing technical limitations. A Lumière film, for example, could be transformed into one playable on Edison projectors through duping, or vice versa. Edison had already experienced widespread duping in the phonograph industry before he entered the film market; phonograph records were regularly duped to bypass technologies that tied phonograph disks to players.[19] And this pattern is repeated today, where attempts to bypass technical protections result in film, music, and software piracy—copying iTunes videos for playback on a non-Apple media player or copying a DVD encoded for one geographic region to a format playable in another. As it does today, tying content to technology encouraged rather than deterred piracy. (This early form of copy protection is discussed in more detail in chapter 5.)

It was only during a brief window when patent disputes began to be settled and the technology platforms stabilized that concepts like originality and authenticity in moviemaking registered with producers, who then needed to protect their content as well as their technology. In 1903, we will see, the patent environment became clearer for a moment, and content and copyright became more important. In that year, a Pennsylvania court decided the first major copyright case involving the new medium of the movies; first the circuit court and then an appeals court weighed the arguments for and against protecting films as photographs. The story of the case reads like a soap opera, with switched loyalties, filmmakers on the lam, and dramatic court reversals. In the end, the decisions came down to a systematic interpretation of how to answer this question: was film a new medium or the extension of an old one?

EDISON V. LUBIN

Edison's campaign to control the entire film industry by controlling the technology rose and fell quickly. In 1901, Edison won a patent suit against his major competitor, Biograph. The decision stunned the industry, because Biograph seemed to be in the best position to oppose Edison. The technical wizard behind Biograph's camera, W. K. L. Dickson, had originally developed Edison's own motion picture technologies, the Kinetograph and Kinetoscope. If anyone understood how to avoid infringing Edison's patents, it was Dickson.

The same month that the court handed down the Biograph decision, Edison also gained the upper hand against his most brazen competitor, Philadelphia filmmaker Siegmund Lubin (fig. 1.4). Edison successfully wooed away Lubin's cameraman, J. Blair Smith, at a very high price. Smith now sat in a position to testify that Lubin had been using equipment protected by Edison's patents. More than any other early film producer, Lubin knew that film technology had changed the rules of art and business. And Lubin resented the advantages Edison enjoyed simply because he already ran an established business with a trusted brand.

Where Edison tried to establish rules that would favor his company, Lubin acted as if there were no rules at all. Lubin's biographer, Joseph Eckhardt, captures the filmmaker's dismissive attitude in a description of his reaction to Edison's first suit against him:

> Annoyed that Edison, who he felt had no more invented the motion picture than he had, would, nevertheless, have the chutzpah to sue him for infringement, Lubin angrily told his lawyers, "I want nothing to do with that man!" "Well, Mr. Lubin," his lawyers advised him, "He wants something to do with you."[20]

FIGURE 1.4 Siegmund Lubin (1851–1923), king of the film pirates.

With the combination of the Biograph decision and the Smith defection, Lubin weighed his options and quickly decided to flee to Berlin, where he (but not Edison) had been registering patents on motion picture technology.

The following March, the appeals court overturned the earlier Biograph decision and presented a crushing blow to Edison, finding that his patent claims far exceeded his accomplishments. The judge gloated, adding, "It is obvious that Mr. Edison was not a pioneer, in the large sense of the term, or in the more limited sense in which he would have been if he had also invented the film."[21] The Edison Company consequently changed its strategy. Edison's lawyer, Howard Hayes, resubmitted Edison's patent applications with considerably restricted claims (which were eventually granted), and he began to devise the licensing agreements and alliances that led to the creation of the Edison Trust. Hayes also added copyright to the company's legal arsenal, controlling the content in addition to the motion picture hardware. During the next year, the Edison Company launched copyright suits against Biograph in New York, against the Selig Company in Chicago, and against Lubin in Philadelphia.[22]

The cases began to set legal parameters for film duping, but, equally important, the onslaught of suits announced a new front of attack on Edison's competitors. After launching its case against Lubin, for example, the Edison Company took out an ad in the *New York Clipper*, warning producers and distributors that anyone making or exhibiting a dupe of an Edison film would be prosecuted. At the last minute, the Edison Company decided to remove the line, "Who will be the next man to be sued?" fearing that it might be bad business to threaten all of its customers directly.[23] Edison and Lubin would continue to fight their battle through advertisements as well as in the courts. The advertisements may have been more important than the lawsuits, since the ads helped to control the interpretation and impact of the technical court decisions.

After the courts overturned Edison's patent claims and subsequently dismissed the patent case against Lubin, the Philadelphia optician returned to the United States with a new vigor for duping films. Among other subjects, the Lubin Company copied a popular film, *Christening and Launching Kaiser Wilhelm's Yacht "Meteor"* (1902), which showed the Prussian Prince Henry and U.S. president Theodore Roosevelt engaged in the titular ceremony on an island off the coast of New York. The Edison Company had paid a high price for the exclusive right to record the widely publicized, invitation-only event, and Edison prosecuted Lubin for his audacious copying and advertising of the film. In the lawsuit, the Edison Company defended its method of registering films for copyright protection. Nearly a decade after Edison submitted the film of Fred Ott's sneeze to the Library of Congress's Copyright Office, a court would consider the process of registering films as photographs. Did the thousands of copyright confirmation notices given to filmmakers by the Copyright Office have any value? Could filmmakers afford to continue making films without the limited monopoly offered by a copyright? The answers to these legal and business questions hung on the interpretation of a number of philosophical questions about the nature of film and the role of courts in shaping copyright law.

THE ARGUMENTS

Neither Edison nor Lubin disputed the details of the case. Rather than filing separate briefs, the two sides filed an agreed statement of facts. Edison's and Lubin's lawyers explained that Lubin's old cameraman, Smith, had shot the film for Edison, choosing the angle and then cranking the camera. The rest of the filmmaking process, the court document stated, was "automatic." Once the film had been processed, Edison's lab made prints of the film to be sold, and his secretary submitted two positive prints to the Library of Congress. Thorvald Solberg, the recently appointed Register of Copyrights, recorded the deposit, and responded with a note officially confirming the granting of the copyright. The Edison Company, as it had for years, then affixed a copyright notice to the beginning of the film.

Lubin, for his part, freely admitted purchasing a copy of the film, making dupes, and reselling it. According to Lubin, the copyright notice had been removed from the copy he purchased, and he did not know that Edison had registered the film. Lubin's plea of ignorance is hard to believe since one of his former employees, Fred Balshofer, has written in a memoir that Lubin first employed him to snip off copyright notices and block out trademarks from films to be duped. But this claim did not matter in the end. The burden of determining if a film had been registered with the Copyright Office lay with the copier, who was obligated to check registrations before making a copy. If Lubin had checked, he would have found Edison's registration.[24]

From both Edison's and Lubin's perspectives, this was a cut-and-dry case. Edison's lawyers argued that Lubin illegally copied the film without permission. Lubin's lawyers responded with a very simple argument: films are not photographs, and they did not fall within the scope of the then current copyright statute, which read "any photograph" but did not bother to mention motion pictures of any kind. On June 27, 1902, Judge George Mifflin Dallas denied Edison's request for an injunction against Lubin, thus allowing Lubin to continue selling the Edison film. Both sides regrouped to prepare for the trial, suspecting that the scales tipped toward a Lubin victory.

After a decade of registering films as photographs, the Edison team briefly considered suspending its practice altogether. But they decided that the costs of registering and depositing films were so minimal that it was not worth curtailing the practice just yet. Instead, they left it up to their lawyer, Howard Hayes, to strengthen their legal case.

In the new brief Hayes prepared for the case, he made several arguments about the nature of the new art of film. First, he reconsidered the earlier arguments about authorship he had constructed on Edison's behalf. Hayes worried that the film did not meet the *Sarony* standard of original authorship, so he expanded on Smith's role as a photographer. "Does the photograph in question show such artistic skill as to make it the subject of copyright?" Hayes asked rhetorically. He responded by enumerating the many artistic decisions Smith had made in choosing the placement of the camera, although he could only come up with two: lighting and angle. The brief went on to describe the growing market in artistic photographs as evidence of the artistry—and by extension originality—that went into their production. Finally, just to cover all bases, Hayes cited the case of *Bolles* v. *Outing* (1899), in which the copyright of a photograph of another yacht had been upheld, just in case photographs of boats were somehow outside the sphere of copyright. The *Sarony* precedent, after all, still suggested that photography was the art of recording an arranged scene.[25]

Hayes's concluded his discussion of photographs and aesthetics by citing several cases in which the scope of copyright had been liberally construed, including one in which a judge declared a single sheet of paper containing a dress design to be a book in order to bring it within the scope of the current copyright statute. According to Hayes—and this was really the larger issue at hand—in the past U.S. courts had expanded copyright law to include a new medium if it could be stretched that far. But Hayes himself could not quite decide if he was looking at a photograph or something new. In the brief, he alternated between calling the Edison film a "photograph" and a "photographic view," sometimes crossing out one and writing the other (with no apparent logic) in his draft.

Another argument proposed that projection was an integral element of the film, actually weakening his attempts to draw correspondences between film and photography. Now that Edison's diminished patent claims had been granted, Hayes returned to the argument that films were part of the machine (the hardware) rather than works of art and the product of human authors (the software). Hayes still held out hope that Edison could monopolize the entire market through the control of technology, and he claimed boldly that "this art of reproducing motion is the product of the genius of Thomas A. Edison." Further, each frame of film "is worthless. . . . It is only when the photograph is used in connection with an apparatus like the magic lantern that it is useful."[26] Edison's genius, in other words, lay behind every film, regardless of who shot it. As a result, Edison alone owned the exclusive right to create moving images. It did not seem to bother Hayes that the diminished patents simply granted Edison the very limited claim on his sprocket mechanism—hardly a claim on the entire apparatus.

At first, this argument about patents seems to reveal little more than the frustrations of the Edison Company. It had no direct bearing on the case at hand. Yet, as we will see below, this argument went to the heart of the issue, one that complicates the copyright policies of many new technologies—where to draw the line between hardware and software. In another landmark case, five years after *Edison* v. *Lubin*, the Supreme Court faced a similar decision when confronted with player piano rolls. They decided that player piano rolls—really just perforated pieces of paper—belonged to the machine that read them; they were not a form of software like sheet music.[27] Since the 1980s, courts have continually had to move the line between computer hardware and software, first granting copyright protection to computer applications and eventually to the short bits of code embedded in microprocessors.[28] When new technology necessitates the development of a new recording medium, it generally takes time for the recording medium to appear independent from the technology. Needless to say, this further complicates judges' decisions about whether a new media technology is truly new or not.

In a final argument, Hayes got greedy. Copyright law, after all, is about money as well as protecting original expression. He argued that the phrase "any photograph" in the copyright statute should be interpreted liberally when considering the scope of copyright, not only extending the copyright in photographs to films but allowing an entire film to be registered as a single photograph. This argument was key to defending Edison's method of registering film as photographs because it required only a single copyright fee on the part of the production company. But, Hayes argued further, the phrase "any photograph" should be interpreted strictly when awarding damages. In this scenario, when infringers paid damages, they would have to suffer as if each frame were an individual photograph even though the work had only been registered once as a single photograph.

DUPING BECOMES LEGAL

While Judge Dallas considered the arguments, Lubin kept on duping Edison films to the great consternation of Edison's staff.[29] Still awaiting legal restitution, the Edison Company adjusted its business practices to counter Lubin. Edison realized that the high price of his films drove many exhibitors to use cheap, poor-quality dupes. His refusal to adjust film prices to the demands of the market had actually stimulated the traffic in pirated films. Lubin capitalized on this by advertising the "reasonable price" of his films, whether they were dupes or original Lubin films. Now a bit desperate, Edison finally capitulated and adopted a new pricing scheme. The Edison Company divided its films into two classes (A and B), lowering the price of its older and less ambitious films to compete with the cheap Lubin dupes.[30]

At the same time, the Edison Company began to register its films with the Copyright Office as dramas, in addition to registering them as photographs. This new registration method also indicated the growing importance by 1903 of longer, narrative, multishot films. The first case to consider films as dramas was decided in 1905, although it would take until 1911 for courts to put together all of the pieces necessary to adapt copyright law to encompass the dramatic and performance elements of film. *Meteor*, the film in question in *Edison v. Lubin*, however, was composed of one long shot, perhaps much closer to a single photograph than other films being made in 1903. Regardless, the decision in the case would govern the copyright status of all films, whether they were short "actualities" or multishot narrative films.[31]

On January 13, 1903, Judge Dallas handed down his decision, siding with Lubin as he had done in the initial injunction hearing. Brushing aside all of the arguments Hayes made on Edison's behalf and the nine years of film copyright registrations, Judge Dallas decided the case in two succinct paragraphs. The entire case, he argued, hinged on one very simple question: how to interpret the phrase "any photograph." "The question is," he explained, "is a series of photographs arranged for use in a machine for producing them in a panoramic effect entitled to registry and protection as a photograph?" His answer: "[the revised copyright statute] extended the copyright law to 'any . . . photograph,' but not to an aggregation of photographs."[32] Judge Dallas bought Lubin's argument completely: films and photographs are different, and it is just too complicated for the law to consider them to be equal. As even Hayes had argued on Edison's behalf, photographs and films function differently. A single photograph has value and can be experienced as a whole where a film requires the rapid display of a series of frames to create both the experience of film and its value in the marketplace.

Judge Dallas was not endorsing piracy. As many judges have done when considering new technologies, Dallas took the position that court decisions are blunt instruments, declaring one winner and one loser. Judges cannot always accommodate the new worlds opened up by technology. The task of extending copyright to new media, he suggested, should fall to Congress, which can sculpt subtle laws. And with Dallas's decision, for a brief period film duping was legal.

Edison immediately appealed the case, which the court heard three months later, overturning Dallas's decision and finding for Edison. How did Dallas's decision and the legalization of duping affect the film industry in the interim? The Edison Company continued to make short-term decisions while the case worked its way through the court system. Edison's studio suspended its production of original films and took advantage of the window for legal duping. Many other companies continued their duping practices as well.

French magician-filmmaker Georges Méliès, like many European film companies, continued to be hurt by the mass duping of his films in the United States. In response, Méliès sent his brother Gaston to New York that March to set up shop and control the expanding market for unauthorized duplication and reselling of his films. In the new U.S. catalog of Méliès films, Gaston threatened American dupers: "we are prepared and determined energetically to pursue all counterfeiters and pirates. We will not speak twice; we will act." Those sentences were clearly aimed at Edison and Lubin, who had both been prodigious dupers of Méliès's films. According to some accounts, Gaston visited Lubin's studio posing as a potential buyer in order to expose the film pirate. When Lubin tried to pass off Méliès's famous film A Trip to the Moon as a Lubin creation— renamed A Trip to Mars—Méliès jumped to his feet and harangued the rival filmmaker. But after Judge Dallas's decision, Méliès had little legal recourse.[33]

Edison's lawyers worried that Gaston Méliès had actually come to the United States to take advantage of the new court precedent and dupe Edison films rather than protect those of his brother. To deter this suspected pirate, they sent Gaston a note informing him of the cases against Biograph, Selig, and Lubin. They did not mention, of course, that they had lost the first round of the Lubin case.[34]

Not only did duping proceed unabated, but producers also withheld new films from the market or cut back production in the unstable environment. The Edison Company shelved one of its most ambitious and expensive productions to date, Edwin S. Porter's Jack and the Beanstalk, while they waited for the court to ensure copyright protection. When Dallas refused to grant the initial injunction stopping Lubin's duping, the Edison Company took a chance and released the film anyway. With the court on his side, Lubin duped Jack and the Beanstalk and advertised it as his own. Still infuriated by Edison's bullying, Lubin impishly suggested in the same ad (fig. 1.5) that Edison had in fact duped his creation. "We are aware of the fact," Lubin's ad read, "that our films are copied by unscrupulous persons,

FIGURE 1.5 Advertising Lubin's short-lived court victory over Edison.

but the Copyright Law contains many loopholes through which they make their undignified escape." After Porter completed *Jack and the Beanstalk* and Lubin duped it, the Edison Company gave its top director a hiatus from directing. The company set Porter to work remaking Biograph's films rather than investing the time and effort in creating original films, which could so easily and legally be duped.[35]

In his compelling cultural history of U.S. copyright law, Siva Vaidhya-nathan speculates that if Judge Dallas's decision were allowed to stand, it would have exacerbated the chaos of the early film industry. And the decision certainly created a brief window of chaos. But it is also possible that Congress would have heeded Dallas's warning and stepped in to calm the storm by revising the copyright statute to encompass films rather than waiting another nine years. It is often when judges throw up their hands and put the burden on Congress that new solutions are found for new media. That is what happened with the 1908 Supreme Court *White-Smith* v. *Apollo* piano-roll case mentioned above. The Court left it to Congress to find a method for compensating composers and musicians for recorded music. It was a complex problem that a court decision probably could not have addressed adequately. Congress's solution was to introduce statutory licensing in the 1909 Copyright Act the following year. The licenses not only compensated the music creators; they leveled the market and helped to prevent one company from gaining a monopoly on music copyrights. Film, in contrast, was left out of the 1909 Copyright Act, in part because the appellate court stepped in to reverse Dallas's decision and find a court-made solution.[36]

EDISON WINS

On April 20, 1903, the Third Circuit Court of Appeals overturned Dallas's decision, siding with Edison over Lubin. Only a few months separated the two cases, but between the two decisions the Supreme Court released a landmark copyright decision that signaled a change in court-made approaches to copyright. On February 2, Supreme Court Justice Oliver Wendell Holmes Jr., a newcomer to the bench, wrote the first of several copyright decisions that dramatically changed the field. In *Bleistein v. Donaldson Lithographic Co.*, Justice Holmes overturned lower-court decisions that found circus posters to be unworthy of copyright protection because they were used as advertisements (fig. 1.6). In his decision, Holmes made clear that neither mass reproduction, nor commercial use, nor lowbrow or risqué subject matter could disqualify a work from copyright protection. "It would be a dangerous undertaking," Holmes wrote sagely, "for persons trained only to the law to constitute themselves judges of the worth of pictorial illustrations."[37]

In the appellate decision in *Edison* v. *Lubin*, Judge Joseph Buffington took his cue from Holmes. Citing the *Bleistein* decision, Buffington easily found the *Meteor* film to be a work of original authorship. But more than that, the *Bleistein* decision empowered Judge Buffington to use case law to expand the scope of copyright rather than throw the ball into Congress's court. When Congress expanded the Copyright Act to include "all photographs," he reasoned, it certainly did not expect the technology and art to stand still. As a result, it fell to the court to expand on the intention of the legislators rather than ask Congress to revisit the issue. Looking at the *Meteor* film, Buffington concluded that motion pictures advanced the art of photography rather than creating a new medium.[38]

FIGURE 1.6 One of the posters considered in *Bleistein v. Donaldson* (1903). Too commercial or lowbrow to be protected by copyright?

How is film like a photograph? Judge Buffington found a solution in one of the arguments Hayes had offered in the brief he wrote for Edison. It was Hayes's rant about the centrality of the technology that spoke to Buffington. The argument seemed to have little to do with the case at hand, but it tapped into the greater philosophical question: what is cinema? Hayes argued that motion picture photography only gained value when presented through a projecting or viewing machine. Buffington agreed that film created a complete experience when projected or displayed and that the experience of the whole should be protected, not the individual frames, which were effectively worthless. In his pithy formulation, Buffington overturned Judge Dallas's decision and logic. "To require each of numerous undistinguishable pictures to be individually copyrighted, as suggested by the court, would, in effect, be to require the copyright of many pictures to

protect a single one." Edison's method of depositing films, which began
with the film of Fred Ott's sneeze in 1894, was finally sanctioned. Filmmakers could register an entire film as a single photograph—one that just
happened to move. Buffington had been empowered by Holmes's decision in *Bleistein* v. *Donaldson*, and he probably was not surprised that the
Supreme Court decided not to hear the case, finally resolving the issue in
November 1904.[39]

FILMS AS PHOTOGRAPHS

With Edison's method of registering films as photographs upheld, Edison's
staff immediately resumed film production. But did defining film as a new
form of photography rather than as a new medium either stop piracy or
stabilize the market? Legal histories often enumerate precedents and stop
there. But like any landmark decision or new law, this one needed time to
be digested and diffused. The decision was the beginning and not the end
of the process of defining and controlling film piracy.

Edison won, but Lubin still had a card up his sleeve. Lubin's lawyers
had convinced the Edison Company to sign an agreement preventing it
from advertising the decision.[40] Both sides knew that the public perception of piracy was as important as its legal definition. Even Edison could
not afford to sue every duper if the practice continued on the same massive scale. In order to enforce the decision, Edison needed to instill fear
of retribution into potential pirates and the exhibitors who bought their
wares. Advertising had been the main forum both Edison and Lubin used
to inform others about the law and to create norms in the marketplace.
With that important means of communication closed off, Edison had little
chance of implementing his new legal protection. Of course, the agreement not to advertise the decision would have hurt Lubin too if he had
won. It does not seem to be a stretch to speculate based on Lubin's history
that he might have found some way to get out of the deal. Edison, however,
honored the agreement, although he continued to use ads to intimidate his
competitors, without mentioning the case directly.

Even after the decision and Edison's advertisements, widespread confusion about duping's legality remained. To begin with, the Edison Company did not interpret the Buffington decision as having created a black-
and-white ethical or legal standard. Rather than condemning all duping in
its advertisements, which might have helped clarify the impact of Buffington's decision, the Edison Company approached the Buffington decision

as having created a technical distinction, separating legal from illegal duping. It still was not clear to anyone, even Edison, if duping was in itself a
form of piracy that should be outlawed.

The Edison Company tried to take advantage of the precedent by creating a market for *legal* duping, continuing to copy European films as it
had in the past. Some members of Edison's staff, including the company's
manager, William Gilmore, thought the process was unethical. The legal
department disagreed, and, in the end, the bottom line dictated that duping continue. "I understand that personally you are averse to the copying
of our competitors' films," Edison lawyer Frank Dyer wrote Gilmore, "but
at the same time there must be a good profit in that business as it does
away with making an original negative."[41] By "making an original negative," Dyer meant the writing, acting, directing, and filming. And it does
seem to be cost-effective to skip those steps.

On Dyer's advice, Edison's staff then set out to develop a system for
duping unregistered films. They first identified four European films that
had commercial potential in the American market. Then they hired a law
firm to track down copyright registrations for the films. When every effort
to find U.S. registrations for the films failed, the Edison Company duped
the films and released them to exhibitors, only to learn that Biograph had
already duped and registered the films under different titles. Tracking
down copyright registrations proved to be expensive and difficult. Creating a technical distinction between legal and illegal duping created even
more confusion.

Lubin did not waste his time trying to find loopholes. He had been
sued many times before, and he knew that the tides of motion picture law
would continue to change. If the past had taught him anything, it was to
ignore the capricious mandates of judges—apparently even those on the
Supreme Court. Lubin just went on duping. According to Terry Ramsaye,
an Edison partisan to be sure, Lubin skirted the law by developing political
connections. "Philadelphia's master film duper," explained Ramsaye, "is
wealthy and so well bulwarked politically that prosecutions have proven
impractical and he has seldom been annoyed by indictments." Perhaps this
is the image of Lubin that Edison liked to circulate: a slick, savvy business-
man who skirted the law. But in reality, both patent and copyright suits
against Lubin continued. Indeed, Lubin was back in court for copyright
infringement even before the Supreme Court decided not to hear *Edison
v. Lubin*—this time for duping Biograph films. Only a few months later,
the Edison Company was sending cease-and-desist letters to Lubin, adding
trademark infringement to its ongoing patent and copyright battles.[42]

Nevertheless, Lubin remained an irrepressible duper. Lubin's old employee Fred Balshofer remembered Lubin duping films until 1906, and Richard Abel has shown that Lubin's duping continued to frustrate the French production company Pathé Frères. In turn, Lubin's competitors in the United States and Europe duped his original films. Lubin only seems to have curtailed his duping when he joined the Edison Trust in 1906. Duping, however, remained a standard industry practice. The market for new films turned over quickly, and prosecuting every case of duping was not a practical solution. Moreover, the film industry had been built on duping, and it was very difficult for companies to give up a practice so central to their livelihood. A 1907 issue of *Show World*, four years after the *Edison* v. *Lubin* decision, sounded the familiar alarm, "'Duping' of Fine Pictures Condemned."[43] Despite the expensive court battles, little had changed. Declaring duping to be piracy was easy; enforcing the decision was virtually impossible.

Another reason that declaring films to be a new form of photography did not put an end to piracy is that in 1903 film style was changing. Films began to look less like moving photographs than they had just a year before. Buffington's decision came on the cusp of a transition in filmmaking, and his landmark decision appeared relevant to only a fading genre of film. Buffington's decision clearly protected single-shot, panoramic films, like the film of the Kaiser's yacht *Meteor*. But 1902–1904 saw the rapid displacement of this type of film with multishot, narrative, fiction films such as *Life of an American Fireman*, *Jack and the Beanstalk*, and *The Great Train Robbery*, to name only a few Edison titles.[44] Films began to look more like a new form of drama and less like animated photographs. It was not clear how Buffington's decision applied to these films, which were already prevalent by the time he decided the case.

Edison's company led the transition to story films, and even his lawyers were confused about how to implement Buffington's decision. Did it apply to the new films they were making? The lawyer who had won the *Edison* v. *Lubin* copyright suit, Howard Hayes, died shortly after the case was decided. The Edison Company, which was now in the business of fighting lawsuits as much as manufacturing technology and entertainment, started its own in-house legal division. Edison appointed the young and brilliant Frank Dyer as its head. Dyer had a special interest in film, and he would eventually oversee much of the Edison film business. New on the job, Dyer was justifiably frustrated by film copyright law and by the *Lubin* decision in particular. In October 1905, Dyer wrote to the Register of Copyrights, Thorvald Solberg, asking how the *Lubin* decision applied to multishot films. Should each shot be registered separately? Or could the entire film be registered as a single photograph, a process that would cut down on paperwork and expense? Dyer also suggested that registering just one representative frame from each scene might satisfy the requirement. Once the films were registered, Dyer continued to wonder, how would the multishot films be protected: as a series of distinct moving photographs or as a single photograph?

Solberg offered a bureaucratic and unhelpful response: "This opens up legal questions of some difficulty, which should receive very careful consideration before action is taken."[45] There is no further correspondence on the subject in the Edison archive, but this question was decided later that year in a case involving Biograph and Edison. In the decision, Judge Lanning reasoned, "I am unable to see why, if a series of pictures of a moving object taken by a pivoted camera [as was the case in the *Meteor* film] may be copyrighted as a photograph, a series of pictures telling a single story like that of the complainant in this case, even though the camera be placed at different points, may not also be copyrighted as a photograph."[46] As a result, the legal doctrine that defined films as photographs became broader and more entrenched.

THE AFTERMATH OF *EDISON V. LUBIN*

Although *Edison v. Lubin* clearly set a legal precedent, I think it is fair to say that the quick fix of declaring film to be a new form of photography rather than a new medium did not solve any of the existing problems. On the contrary, the decision exacerbated the problems. Duping continued and the confusion over how to implement the new standard contributed to the monopolization of the film industry.

With no end to duping in sight, Edison and other companies changed the way they did business. The high price of films had always driven exhibitors to buy cheap dupes. In response, producers began to rent rather than sell films to exhibitors—a model that allowed for greater price differentiation. The move to rentals also allowed the producers to institute restrictive licensing agreements, exerting greater control over their prints. Finally, the expense of legal cases and the inability of the courts to stabilize the market led Lubin and other companies to sign exclusive licensing agreements with Edison and join his cartel, the Motion Picture Patents Company (fig. 1.7). This was not a case of the industry fixing a problem that the courts failed to solve. Edison's cornering of the film industry was, in part,

FIGURE 1.7 Members of the Motion Picture Patents Company (c. 1908–1909); Edison is at center front, with white hair, and Lubin is standing in the back (*center*). Edison's lawyer, Frank Dyer, is on the far right. (Courtesy of the U.S. Dept. of the Interior, National Park Service, Thomas Edison National Historical Park)

the disastrous outcome of the court's failure to recognize film as a new medium rather than as a new form of photography.

ANOTHER FORM OF PIRACY: UNAUTHORIZED ADAPTATIONS

Edison's Motion Picture Patents Company may have curtailed duping, but it built its oligopoly on another form of unauthorized copying, one that would eventually come to be defined by both the law and society as piracy. Before 1911, film companies freely adapted works from other media (literature, theater, comic strips, etc.) without permission. Today, licensed adaptations are the cornerstone of Hollywood's output, the very fount of creative material. Studios regularly option books and Broadway shows long before they are released or performed. The deal to film a popular series like the *Harry Potter* novels can be the foundation for a monopoly on a billion-dollar franchise. Hollywood has relied on such adaptations and franchises since the 1910s. But for most of the first decade and a half of film history, U.S. law freely allowed film producers to adapt works from other media without permission or payment. Not only could a film company adapt a novel or play without asking, other companies could, and often did, film their own versions of the same work.

As we have already seen, the decision to classify film as a new type of photography left many questions unanswered. In addition to being a new form of photography, film also built on the traditions of drama and performance. The Edison Company recognized this even as it fought to have film defined legally as photographs. While the *Lubin* case was pending, the Edison Company began to register its films with the Copyright Office as dramas as well as photographs. One year later, in 1904, Biograph began to register its scenarios, the descriptions on which films were based.[47] Nevertheless, it was very difficult to subsume the dramatic and performance aspects of film under existing copyright law. Ultimately, it took a landmark 1911 Supreme Court case involving a film adaptation of the novel *Ben-Hur* for the law to hold filmmakers responsible for adapting other media.

As we will see in the remainder of this chapter, the decision in the *Ben-Hur* case by Justice Oliver Wendell Holmes Jr. transformed both the structure of the film industry and film style. Within a few years of the decision, a series of independent production companies—the independents who would go on to form the Hollywood studios—displaced the Motion Picture Patents Company, which had previously enjoyed a near monopoly on the U.S. film industry. Holmes's decision enabled the independents' novel and successful business model. Moreover, the decision led to changes in the kinds of stories that filmmakers told and the way they told them. Unlike *Edison* v. *Lubin*, which left enough ambiguity for the major companies to jump in and control the interpretation and effect of the law, the *Ben-Hur* case effectively remade the film industry and contributed to the creation of Hollywood as we know it today.

PUBLIC PERFORMANCE AND THE CINEMA OF ATTRACTIONS

Edison v. *Lubin* established that film is a photographic medium, but is it also a performance medium? Does it represent action in a way that can infringe on the exclusive rights of authors and publishers to authorize performances of their works? A number of legal and conceptual obstacles made this question difficult to answer in the first decades of U.S. film exhibition.

A public performance right existed in U.S. law as early as 1856, but both film technology and film content made it difficult to define early film screenings as public performances under the law. In particular, the characteristics of the period that film scholars refer to as the "cinema of attractions" (pre-1908) made it unlikely that publishers or theater producers would bring a suit against film companies who adapted their works without permission. Authors, performers, and theater producers were frustrated by unlicensed film adaptations, and they unsuccessfully lobbied Congress to change the law and make film companies liable for infringing plays and books, but no significant lawsuits were brought until the 1911 *Ben-Hur* case.

The first reason that copyright holders were unlikely to sue filmmakers for adapting their works without permission is the *virtual* nature of film presentation. If film is a performance, it is a strange kind of virtual performance—one often performed by actors in a distant place and at another time. The law regulated public not private performances, and the question of who publicly performs a film is difficult to answer. Is it the actors, who perform semi-privately before the camera but are only distant shadows on the screen? Are the producers responsible for the performance, even though they might not have been present at either the filming or the theatrical screening of the film? The projectionist is the most directly responsible for physically displaying the film to an audience, but it would seem ludicrous to hold the lowest person in the hierarchy responsible. The sticky question of whom to hold accountable for performing the film was as difficult to solve in the 1910s as are problems we face today about how to regulate virtual environments and media distribution on the internet.

The complications posed by film's virtuality were not limited to the law; filmmakers, audiences, and even law enforcement officials were confused about how to treat this new form of representation. Many of Edison's early films, for example, were simply recordings of vaudeville stars performing their acts in his studio, the Black Maria (fig. 1.8). Bodybuilding pioneer Eugen Sandow (fig. 1.9), dancer Annabelle Moore (later Annabelle Whitford), and many other vaudeville stars traveled to West Orange, New Jersey, to be filmed by the great inventor. How were the performers compensated? They were paid once for their performance in the studio, but they did not receive royalties for subsequent screenings of the films. (Sandow apparently did it simply for the chance to shake Edison's hand.) The performers were not present at the screenings, and it was not clear what they contributed after their first performance—certainly not their labor.[48]

To take another example, boxing films, one of the most popular genres of early films, exemplify some of the contradictions introduced by the new virtuality of film. In the early 1890s, boxing was illegal in all U.S. states. Some states, however, did permit what they called "boxing performances," upscale versions of the bloody, pugilistic displays that took place outside

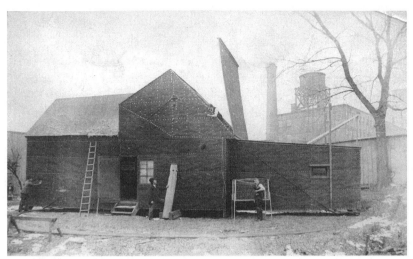

FIGURE 1.8 The Black Maria: Edison's studio, where vaudeville performers would come to have their acts captured on film. (Courtesy of the U.S. Dept. of the Interior, National Park Service, Thomas Edison National Historical Park)

FIGURE 1.9 Sandow the strong man posing for Edison in Black Maria (1894). He asked only to shake Edison's hand as compensation.

of the law. Even where authorities allowed boxing performances, however, it was considered improper for women to attend. Not only were the performances violent, but they starred half-naked men, often of varied racial and ethnic backgrounds. And yet boxing films traveled freely across state borders, regardless of differing social norms and local laws. Moreover, as newspapers liked to report, both men and women regularly enjoyed boxing films in mixed company and in the open.[49]

Both of these examples—of performer compensation and the regulation of boxing films—point to the complex relationship between films and the reality they represent. A film image is not the thing that it represents, and performers, producers, and audiences clearly treated the image as something different than the physical reality. As a result, there was no consensus on whom to hold responsible for the showing of a film if one happened to violate copyright law.

There is a second reason that it took so long for either publishers or theater producers to sue a film producer for infringement is that during the pre-1908 cinema-of-attractions period. It continued to be unclear whether the content of many films, especially those that were records of vaudeville acts, belonged on the moral or aesthetic radar of copyright law at all.

The Constitution explains that the goal of copyright law is to "promote the progress of science," where science refers generally to knowledge in the eighteenth-century sense of the word. Today, "promote the progress of science" is frequently thought to delimit the length of copyright terms (i.e., after how many years does the monopoly that copyright bestows begin to harm the promotion of progress?). But in the late nineteenth and early twentieth centuries, judges took the "promote the progress" phrase as license to censor work that they thought immoral; for how could something immoral aid progress? In perhaps the most extreme case of the progress clause being used to justify moral censorship, a Bert Williams ragtime song, "Dora Dean," was declared immoral simply because it referred to an African-American woman as "hot" in the sentence, "She's the hottest thing you've ever seen."[50]

Vaudeville performers regularly ran into the same problem when they tried to defend the copyrights in their acts, especially when the acts contained women in revealing or suggestive dress or situations. Copyright law so frustrated vaudevillians' attempts to protect their new art that, as historian Kerry Segrave explains, vaudeville performers learned to set professional norms in place of legal regulation: "Artists were more likely to try and act together to limit piracy by bringing pressure to bear on theatrical bookers, using trade papers to inform each other about infringements and to shame alleged lifters and copyists and so on, as opposed to launching copyright suits."[51]

When performances did successfully pass courts' moral censors, they were frequently dismissed because they failed to meet another constitutional criteria for copyright protection: they were not "writings." As we saw in *Burrow-Giles Lithographic Co.* v. *Sarony*, the case involving the photograph of Oscar Wilde, the term "writings" had been stretched very far by Congress and courts; the first U.S. Copyright Act of 1790 included maps and charts as writings. Today, "writings" is understood very broadly as encompassing anything "fixed in a tangible medium." As early as the 1860s, drama and nonverbal action (pantomime) were considered forms of writing by the law. But, significantly here, spectacle was not protected. Courts' interpretation of the Constitution held that for drama or action to be protected, it needed to have language, and spectacle was where judges drew the line. When Edison and others started to show films publicly in the United States in the early 1890s, the kind of spectacle that films presented were clearly beneath the purview of copyright law.

In an 1867 case, for example, a judge decided that *The Black Crook*, often credited as one of the first true Broadway musicals, was "mere spectacle" and therefore beyond the scope of copyright law. "The principle part and attraction of the spectacle," wrote Judge Deady, "seems to be the exhibition of women in novel dress or no dress." Ironically, the codes of representation changed so much over the next half century that in 1916 the Kalem Company (a film company that will feature prominently in the remainder of this chapter) adapted *The Black Crook* to film in an effort to bring "the high class legitimate house . . . to the cinema."[52]

A slightly later case took up a subject that would prove to be very popular among filmmakers: the Serpentine Dance. In 1892 the choreographer Loie Fuller (fig. 1.10) attempted to protect her signature dance routine from its many knockoffs. But in this case the judge found the performance to be mere spectacle. "Surely, those [movements] described and practiced here," wrote Judge Emile Lacombe, "convey and were devised to convey, to the spectator, no other idea than that a comely woman is illustrating the poetry of motion in a singularly graceful fashion. Such an idea may be pleasing, but it can hardly be called dramatic."[53] Again, spectacle and immorality seem fused. If the dance can be described as the "poetry of motion," then it seems to approach the legal definition of action that has language. It must then be the "comely woman" that changes the equation.

FIGURE 1.10 Loie Fuller performing the Serpentine Dance, which a judge thought unworthy of copyright protection.

The *Black Crook* case, the Serpentine Dance case, and others all reveal that moral censorship in the form of copyright law was imposed because of the feelings and ideas that works were thought to stimulate in audiences. Judge Deady worried about the "attraction to the spectacle," and Judge Lacombe decided the Serpentine Dance case by taking up the perspective of the "spectator." These legal cases were about social control more than the metaphysics of the law.

The Serpentine Dance was one of the first vaudeville acts recorded by Edison's Kinetoscope, although Fuller acolyte Annabelle Moore and not Fuller herself performed for Edison. And it is indicative of the types of films that comprised the cinema-of-attractions period. Anyone familiar with early film will immediately recognize in the above-mentioned court descriptions of vaudeville acts the content of early films: short, attention-grabbing subjects designed to evoke immediate, visceral responses from audiences.[54] Many if not most early films would have been beneath the threshold of the law because their subjects (often taken directly from vaudeville) would have been classified as immoral or mere spectacle. Even when films adapted copyrighted works, the style of film presentation—boiling down a novel or play to a few important moments—would have classified the work as spectacle. As a result, film adaptations of literature and theater remained under copyright law's radar until 1911.[55]

1907–1909

Things changed between 1907 and 1909; spectacle gave way to narrative and bourgeois respectability. First, films changed. Film style began to develop in ways that allowed filmmakers to tell longer, more complex, and more psychologically revealing stories. Visual codes were developed for camera placement, staging, acting, lighting, and editing, all of which put the image at the service of telling richer stories that drew film spectators deeper into the world within the frame. Movies also became significantly longer, and filmmakers began to poach more from middle-class plays and novels for source material. Previous adaptations generally represented a few simple highlights from a well-known book or play, often staging only a handful of tableaux—posed still scenes that offered visual reminiscences of books or plays. When moviegoers went to see Edison's 1903 adaptation of *Uncle Tom's Cabin*, for instance, they were expected to know the basic story outline, as they were for any adaptation. When Lubin made his own version of *Uncle Tom's Cabin* following Edison's success, with Lubin himself playing Simon Legree, the advertisement announced: "The most beautiful production in 24 life motion tableaux." Film adaptations were really just visual interpretations of key scenes, similar to the illustrations in a book.[56]

During this 1907–1909 shift, films started to re-create more of the drama and action of the world they adapted. While books and plays had always been borrowed for film content, adaptations, especially adaptations of middle-class literature and theater, became much more prevalent after 1907. In addition, more of each story—more in terms of both narrative detail and psychological depth—could be incorporated into films using the new visual grammar.[57]

Publishers and theater producers took notice right at the beginning of this transformation, and they lobbied both Congress and international legal bodies to stop the film pirates and give book and play copyright holders the exclusive right to license film adaptations of their works. In a series of congressional hearings leading up to the 1909 revision of the U.S. Copyright Act, theater professionals made a very strong case against film companies' practice of adapting plays without permission. At one hearing, theater producer William A. Brady claimed that "if this thing [unauthorized film adaptations] is not stopped it means the ruination of us [theater producers] and the men who write for the stage." Brady and others made the case that their plays were losing money because unauthorized film adaptations told the same stories, sometimes just a few blocks away from the original play.[58]

Edison's top lawyer, Frank Dyer, attended every round of the hearings in order to defend the Motion Picture Patents Company and the entire film business (in addition to Edison's phonograph business). Dyer's improbable response to the complaints of theater producers was to deny the existence of the problem entirely. According to the *New York Times*, at one point Dyer made the outrageous claim that "there was only one company surreptitiously acquiring the play of any author and representing it in a series of moving pictures, and [Dyer] was under the impression that that company was simply using historical plays," by which he seems to have meant plays in the public domain.[59]

It is not entirely clear why, but Congress chose not mention film at all in the 1909 Copyright Act. Copyright scholars often claim that the film industry was too young,[60] but films had been shown publicly in the United States since 1894 and had developed into a major industry by 1909. Perhaps Congress overlooked film because there were too many other major issues on the table during the drafting of the 1909 Act, including the adoption of compulsory licensing for recorded music. It may be that Congress was still not ready to take on the philosophical questions brought up by film: who was responsible for the public showing of a film? Does film have language? Can silent moving images copy words on a page? Or it may be, and I suspect this is most likely the reason, that Dyer convincingly argued that the film industry was healthy and developing nicely without regulation or government intervention.

After Congress passed the new act, Dyer and the Edison team tried to determine how the revised laws of dramatic copyright applied to film, if they applied at all. If Edison registered the short scenarios on which films were based, Dyer wondered, would that protect the underlying story of the film? Dyer exchanged letters with Register of Copyrights Thorvald Solberg as he had after the *Edison* v. *Lubin* case, but neither the Edison staff nor Solberg seemed to know just what to do with films, which were more than photographs but not exactly dramas. The new Copyright Act did not seem to apply. Nevertheless, Dyer began to protect the Edison Company from possible litigation by insisting that scenario writers sign contracts stating that their stories were original, potentially shifting responsibility for infringement from Edison to the writers.[61]

Publishers and theater producers found much more sympathetic ears in legislators outside the United States. During the 1908 Berlin conference to revise the Berne Convention, the international copyright treaty, the delegates took account of both film adaptations and the rights of film artists. Members of the conference updated the treaty to include protection for dramatic and literary works adapted to film; filmmakers now needed permission to adapt books or plays. The treaty then granted protection to films as both a series of photographs, as they were protected in the United States, and in some cases as "personal and original" dramatic works themselves.[62] The members of the Berne Convention adopted the policy that publishers and theater producers had been campaigning for in the United States. The United States, however, was not a member of the treaty, and it would not become a member until 1989. At least in America, Congress continued to allow unauthorized film adaptations.

THE *BEN-HUR* CASE BEGINS

By failing to include film in the 1909 Act, Congress left it to the courts to figure out the relationship between film and other art forms, and the unauthorized adaptation of *Ben-Hur* became the test case.

The novel *Ben-Hur*, written by General Lew Wallace, was an international phenomenon. It sold over 2 million copies in the first two decades following its 1880 publication. Before Wallace died, he sold the publishing rights to the large publishing house of Harper and Brothers (today a part of the News Corporation's HarperCollins) (fig. 1.11), and he sold the theatrical rights to the major Broadway producers Marcus Klaw and A. L. Erlanger. Wallace took an active interest in the adaptation of his work, and he waited a long time to sell the theatrical rights; he worried, specifically, about the impact of giving Christ a physical form on stage. Klaw & Erlanger solved the problem and satisfied Wallace by using a beam of light rather than an actor for the role. For the first theatrical version of *Ben-Hur* in 1899, Klaw & Erlanger created a spectacle on an unprecedented scale. They spent $75,000 to stage the performance, and the elaborate sets included live horses running on treadmills during the climactic chariot race. The play was an enormous success, grossing over $5 million and spawning myriad professional and amateur productions across the United States.[63]

In 1907 the Kalem Company, a member of the Edison Trust, created a film version of *Ben-Hur*. This adaptation appeared right at the beginning of the 1907–1909 transition in film style and just as publishers and theater producers were becoming more concerned about film companies stealing their readers and audiences. The *Ben-Hur* film, however, belonged more to the fading style of adaptations than to the new narratively and psychologically complex films that were beginning to appear. Following a standard pattern of development, Kalem paid Gene Gauntier—both

FIGURE 1.11 The Harper Brothers, whose lawsuit against the Kalem Company brought an end to unauthorized film adaptations.

the company's top actress and screenwriter—to read *Ben-Hur* and write a brief treatment on which the final film was based. The film ran only about 15 minutes, and like adaptations from an earlier period, it simply staged sixteen key scenes from the lengthy 560-page novel. There was no effort to hide the source of the film. On the contrary, Kalem depended on the reputation of the novel. Kalem's advertisements openly declared that the film was "based on Lew Wallace's book." The ads further described the film as a "spectacle" and listed the titles of the scenes from the book that were illustrated in the film. As always, audiences were expected to be familiar with the story before they came to see the movie. In the Kalem film it is difficult to identify the important action and characters without some knowledge of the story, and without the aid of the titles that preceded each scene it would be difficult even for someone familiar with the book to follow the film. Movie spectators might be able to enjoy the spectacle on the screen alone, but they would find it impossible to infer a story from the elliptical, disjointed scenes.

Harper and Brothers, Klaw & Erlanger, and Lew Wallace's son, Henry Wallace, joined forces and sued Kalem, although with its outdated adaptation style, *Ben-Hur* may not have been the best film on which to hang such a weighty and long-overdue legal, aesthetic, and commercial inquiry. Despite the appearance of the author's heir on the docket, this was a clash of major American industries. The lucrative *Ben-Hur* franchise was at stake, and so was the much larger issue of unauthorized film adaptations. Big business lined up on either side of the case. The major publisher and theatrical producer teamed up to stop the film industry from continuing to poach its art and audience. The film industry, in turn, recognized that both its business model and the foundation of its art were on trial, and Edison's trust, the Motion Picture Patents Company, supported Kalem by paying the legal fees. Although the future of three major industries—publishing, theater, and film—were at stake, the underlying question of the case would be how to regulate new media.[64]

THE SUPREME COURT BRIEFS 1: CAN FILM COPY LITERATURE?

Two lower courts granted and upheld an injunction, permanently barring the *Ben-Hur* film from further showings. Yet the case was sufficiently novel and the details sufficiently complicated for it to remain likely that the Supreme Court would eventually hear it. When Congress failed to address film in the 1909 revision of the Copyright Act, the Supreme Court intervened and took on the *Ben-Hur* case. Film had grown into a major industry, and someone needed to negotiate between the publishers, the Broadway producers, and the film companies. Finding a solution required a sophisticated understanding of the art of film and the state of American popular culture in addition to legal doctrine. The seasoned and accomplished film and entertainment lawyers[65] for both sides made a range of fascinating arguments about the nature of art and the state of American jurisprudence. Their arguments were obviously pragmatic, but the arguments in the case also reveal the many complications of regulating new media, even when the medium at hand is well over a decade and a half old. The biggest hurdle is often simply to conceptualize the similarities and differences between established and new media.

The first question the lawyers tackled was whether film could infringe a work of literature. In order to answer this question under the then-current copyright statute, the lawyers had to demonstrate that film either does or does not have a language analogous to literature. In addition, they had to persuade the court that the law governing drama could or could not be stretched to encompass film.

Kalem first responded by claiming that its film was just spectacle as it had very plainly proclaimed in its advertisements. The law, as we have seen, was clear that spectacle could not infringe the language of literature or drama. Kalem's film neither told the story of the book nor did it use any of the specific phrasing or expression of the novel. Copyright law protects expression but not the underlying ideas of a work. By creating "Roman Spectacles" inspired by the novel *Ben-Hur*, Kalem's lawyers maintained, the filmmakers were simply building on Lew Wallace's ideas, not copying the expression—the words and narrative—used to clothe those ideas. Kalem's lawyers explained how images could tap into the underlying subject without copying the text: "In writing a book, details must necessarily be subordinated, if not omitted altogether, to avoid interference with the general plan or story. . . . But, with photography, every detail must be realized before the penetrating eye of the camera can be turned upon it. . . . Each reader, each artist, has a different realistic conception of the subject of the text." Film filled in the details left out of the book.[66]

Not only did the film speak in a language incompatible with literature, but, Kalem's lawyers argued, defining film as dramatic performance simply stretched the commonsense definition of that term too far. "If [Harper Brothers and Klaw & Erlanger's] argument is correct," they wrote, "there can be a dramatic performance or representation without stage, scenery, curtain, without a theater itself and without actors, the machine and the white screen upon which its light is focused becoming a substitute for all." In other words, the law, as it existed, could not encompass film. Film was a new medium that needed to be defined and regulated differently. This was something Congress could do—create new law—but not a court, which had to decide the case based on the existing law.

In another argument, Kalem invoked fair use. (Fair use had existed in U.S. common law since the mid-nineteenth century, although it would not enter the Copyright Act until 1976.) As part of their fair use claim, Kalem argued that its film actually stimulated rather than diminished book and play ticket sales; the film was, in effect, free advertising for the novel and the play. Because the film did not hurt the market for the book, the lawyers reasoned, it was a fair use of the novel. Defendants regularly make this claim in copyright cases involving new technologies, but in most cases it misconstrues the doctrine of fair use. Adaptations are derivative works, and copyright holders generally have the right to authorize derivative works, especially when the adaptations serve the same purpose as the original (entertainment, in this case). The fair use exception enters into the equation when the adaptations parody or comment on the original, or when the context is significantly different. The fact that a new medium helps the sales of an old one, however, is not enough to make an adaptation a fair use. On the other hand, diminishing the market for a work does not necessarily negate fair use either; successful parodies, for example, often hurt the market for the original by criticizing it. When it comes to new technologies, the question is generally whether the copyright holder has the right to exploit that particular new market. Lew Wallace or his heirs had the right to authorize dramatic performances of his novel. Did they also have the right to authorize film adaptations?[67]

A final argument is worth noting, if only because it seems to indicate just how radically film transformed the definition of "performance." Kalem's lawyers called the entire premise of the case into question by claiming that the Kalem Company had not staged a chariot race at all; it had simply filmed a real chariot race. Even the nature of this claim is not immediately apparent. Had the Kalem film crew gone back in time? Were the lawyers claiming that all film had an inherent documentary quality? The case brief does not elaborate on the claim, but, as it turns out, the claim was factually accurate. The Kalem crew did not stage the chariot race. Klaw & Erlanger's Broadway version of Ben-Hur had been so successful that local performances of the chariot race became commonplace. These races were an accepted form of unauthorized imitation. Rather than stage its own race, the Kalem crew saved some time and money by filming the Brooklyn Fire Department engaged in a re-creation of the Ben-Hur chariot race for a charity event in Manhattan Beach, Brooklyn. The filmmakers may not have staged the scene, but the firemen had. It was clearly a dramatization. By shifting the blame, Kalem's lawyers looked for a technical loophole. The argument, however, also points back to the question of virtuality. If the Kalem Company had not staged the event itself, was it responsible for recording it, and displaying it to an audience?

In the responses of the book and play copyright holders, lawyers combated these claims with traditional property arguments. Harper Brothers and Klaw & Erlanger had paid for the right to publish and adapt Wallace's novel, and someone could not take for free what they had paid for. But were movies different? Did they require new laws, or could the laws that regulated dramatic adaptation encompass recorded moving images as well? At first, Harper Brothers's brief dismissed the suggestion that film was new and different. This is what pirates always do, the brief stated; they claim that what they are doing is so new that it is beyond the law. "It has ever been the answer of people who endeavor to appropriate the property of others to set up that the method of annexation was new and original and not within the purview of the law."[68]

In the end, however, the lawyers for the publishers and theater producers had two answers to the question "how is film like a play?" The lawyers first drew a correspondence between film and theater through an examination of the motivation for making a film of *Ben-Hur*. The filmmakers, they argued, made a film adaptation in order to reduce production costs and reach a less affluent audience, who could not afford to see the stage play. That audience, they claimed, belonged to the rights holders. How then was a film like a play? According to this argument, the major distinction was that film did not require actors to be present at each performance. Film was not a new art form; it was a cheaper one.

Harper's lawyers then very literally addressed Kalem's argument that calling a film a performance stretched the commonsense definition too far. They agreed that films and plays had different physical properties. To begin with, films could reveal action across a greater space, through crowd scenes for example. But, the lawyers speculated, with the use of mirrors reflecting offstage action, a theatrical stage could potentially encompass everything shown on film. What about the fact that the movie actors performed in a theater long before the showing of the film? Again, the mirror analogy held up. "Films," the brief theorized, "are mirrors which have been perpetually impressed with the reflections of a great play."[69] The analogy drawn by the lawyers was strained, yet, as we will see, it turned out to be a crucial step for the Supreme Court justices trying to conceptualize the relationship between theater and film.

Like *Edison v. Lubin*, this case demanded that the line be drawn between new and old media, and the lawyers invoked a wide range of copyright doctrines to explain how film changed the nature of adaptation. Were films only taking the idea and not the expression of the novel? Was it a fair use to adapt a book to film? Were plays and films significantly different media or could they be governed by the same laws? The Supreme Court justices had to consider these legal arguments, but they were also influenced by the social norms and business environment. The film industry had been built on the practice of adapting works from other media without permission. Filmmakers had forged a distinct visual style that relied on a symbiotic relationship with other media, expecting viewers to have knowledge of the stories they illustrated. Would ending the artistic process of adaptation also destroy the American film industry, which was now a major business and form of American leisure activity?

THE SUPREME COURT BRIEFS 2:
WHO PERFORMS A FILM?

Before the Court could render a decision about whether filmmakers needed permission to adapt books and plays, there was a second question for the lawyers to address: who performs a film? If the court found that films could in fact infringe the rights of book or play copyright holders, then who should be held responsible? How could the law account for the virtual nature of film?

The lower court had adopted a novel approach to the problem, one suggested by the Harper Brothers and Klaw & Erlanger attorneys. The appeals judge considered whether Kalem could be held responsible for the display of the film, even though the company did not seem to be directly responsible for showing the film to an audience. The court borrowed the doctrine of "contributory infringement" or "secondary liability" from patent law. The appeals court decision reasoned that Kalem had made a product, a film, that could only be used for an infringing purpose, display before an audience. Kalem had thus contributed to the infringement and could be held legally responsible. In the Supreme Court briefs, the two sides returned to this question of contributory infringement.[70]

Kalem replied by explaining the process of distributing films. Kalem had made the *Ben-Hur* film, but then it sold the film to a distributor, who in turn sold it to a theater owner or exhibition chain. As a film producer, Kalem sold the film outright to the distributor and was not responsible for how the film was used later. Not only was Kalem two steps removed from screening the film to an audience, but the producers did not even profit from screenings. Moreover, Kalem claimed, there was nothing wrong with filming its adaptation within the confines of the studio. If the film adaptation was illegal, it only became illegal when publicly performed. Kalem pushed for a literal translation of the statute that would hold the projectionist responsible for performing the film before the audience.

Harper and Klaw & Erlanger attempted to demonstrate that Kalem was much more responsible for the exhibition of its films than its picture of the industry would suggest. First they repeated the finding in the lower court decision: Kalem made a product, the film, which had no other purpose other than its display before an audience. Any other potential use for the film seemed unlikely. Moreover, Kalem actively "induced" and "seduced" exhibitors into showing *Ben-Hur*. As Klaw & Erlanger's lawyers wrote:

> The Kalem Company is not a "contributory infringer" but much worse. It seduces others into becoming infringers. . . . The innocent proprietor of a "moving picture" theater may have had no intention of infringing *Ben Hur*, but is induced to do so by the advertising cards of defendant.[71]

This is an argument that the Supreme Court considered again almost a century later when deciding if the creators of file-sharing software contributed to the infringement of peer-to-peer music distribution on the internet.[72] Here, the lawyers argued that the Kalem Company did more than violate a technical standard that had yet to be applied to copyright infringement. The brief accused Kalem of acting in bad faith, moving the case to a battle between right and wrong rather than one about interpreting the statutes.

THE DECISION

Oliver Wendell Holmes Jr.'s opinion in the case was his first majority copyright opinion since *Bleistein* v. *Donaldson* in 1903, although he had written a concurring opinion in the 1909 *White-Smith* v. *Apollo* (piano-roll) case. His decisions in all three cases reveal Holmes's pragmatic view of judicial reasoning, his willingness to use the Court to legislate where Congress failed, and his ability to see a continuity of artistic practice in the face of technological or cultural change.

Holmes neatly summarized his own judicial philosophy in his popular book, *The Common Law*. "The life of the law," he wrote succinctly, "has not been logic; it has been experience." And throughout his career, Holmes believed that legal principles were malleable and always served experience. In Holmes's view, judges did not draw on personal experience but collective and social experience. At their best, he thought, courts strove to reflect mass opinion. The construction of sound constitutional arguments followed rather than led decision-making. As Supreme Court historian Jeffrey Rosen characterizes Holmes, he was a "majoritarian legal realist." Holmes used the court to speak for the people and the times.[73]

Holmes's copyright decisions point to a perspective derived primarily from his populist sensibility. Holmes preferred the classics to vaudeville, but as a student of history he knew that today's popular amusements form tomorrow's canon. As Holmes wrote in *Bleistein* v. *Donaldson*, "Certainly works are not the less connected with the fine arts because their pictorial quality attracts the crowd."[74]

Five years later, in his concurring opinion in *White-Smith* v. *Apollo,* Holmes showed that he thought technology did not fundamentally alter the scope or function of copyright law. *White-Smith,* discussed above, asked whether the piano rolls used to control player pianos were copies of musical scores. The case had some remarkable similarities to the *Ben-Hur* case. In both cases, the justices had to decide whether a new medium of reproduction and performance copied an old medium or not. In *White-Smith,* the Court found that piano rolls were so different from musical scores that they required legislative intervention. Holmes agreed with the legal principles of the decision, but he bristled with the feeling that it defied common sense. "The result," he wrote, "is to give to copyright less scope than its rational significance." Holmes grappled with the transformations that mechanical reproduction wrought on intellectual property. Technology, he admitted, changed the relationship between author and audience. As a result of copying technologies, a copyright "may be infringed a thousand miles from the owner and without his ever becoming aware of the wrong." Holmes did not agree, however, that technology alone should be a deciding factor. "On principle," he concluded in *White-Smith,* "anything that mechanically reproduces that collocation of sounds [the sounds captured on a score] ought to be held a copy."[75]

The same logic drove Holmes's approach to the *Ben-Hur* case. The appeals court had been persuaded by the argument that film took only the idea and not the expression of the novel. After all, one was composed of words, the other of images. Holmes, in contrast, reasoned that the law already protected action as language. Why couldn't moving images have language as well? "Drama," he wrote, "may be achieved by action as well as by speech. Action can tell a story, display all the most vivid relations between men, and depict every kind of human emotion, without the aid of a word."[76] But were moving images somehow different? To answer this question, he borrowed the mirror metaphor from the plaintiffs' brief. If a mirror could be used to display action, then so could a film. "The moving pictures," Holmes stated poetically, "are only less vivid than reflections from a mirror."[77] Film could have a language and that language could be compared to the language of a book or a play. Moving images could certainly infringe words.

The second issue in the case, however, required a technical answer. Who was responsible for the exhibition of the film? Here again, common sense seems to have guided judicial reasoning. Actors were hired to perform roles. Distributors and exhibitors bought films by the foot to quench the weekly thirst of audiences. Projectionists ran the films they were given.

But producers decided which films to make and how to make them. The producers also profited greatly from successful films. It only made sense to find the producers liable. Since Congress had not intervened as European legislatures and the drafters of the Berne Convention had, the Supreme Court expanded the law. Holmes agreed with the reasoning of the appeals court, and he corroborated the position that Kalem had made a film that could only be used for one purpose: public exhibition before an audience. Moreover, the company advertised the film for that purpose. Holmes invoked the law that governed the sale of liquor. If a clerk had knowledge that liquor was being purchased for an illegal purpose, the clerk could be held secondarily liable for the infringement. Like a clerk selling liquor to a minor, Kalem had sold a product to distributors that it knew would be used illegally.

In a few short paragraphs, Holmes and the Court banned the business model on which the American film industry had been built. Film producers needed to obtain permission in order to adapt works for the screen. What happened to the American film industry? It certainly was not destroyed.

NOW A MAJOR MOTION PICTURE: THE IMPACT OF THE BEN-HUR CASE

Holmes had not written a watertight decision. It took some time to work out the legal details. Just four years after the case, the two winners, Harper Brothers and Klaw & Erlanger were back in court, this time battling each other to determine if Klaw & Erlanger's license to dramatize Ben-Hur also gave it the right to film the novel. Only a few months after the decision, both theater producers and film studios were back in congressional hearings. Edison convinced his hometown congressman, Edward Townsend, to introduce an amendment to the three-year-old Copyright Act limiting the damages filmmakers would have to pay if they were caught making unauthorized (and now illegal) adaptations of novels and plays. Broadway producers objected, seeing no reason why film companies should have special treatment. Congress had decided not to include motion pictures in the Copyright Act just a few years earlier, but now that the Supreme Court had taken on the philosophical burden of determining the relationship between film and other arts, Congress was happy to pass the Townsend Act, as the amendment was called. Motion pictures were finally added to the Copyright Act.[78]

Despite the legal ambiguities, the movie moguls responded quickly to the case, and Holmes's decision caused a direct and rapid reshuffling of the film industry. Within two years of the *Ben-Hur* decision, the Edison Trust began to be displaced by a handful of companies—the independents—that had established exclusive alliances with theater producers and publishers. A few years later, in 1915, the Edison Trust would be found to be in violation of the Sherman Anti-Trust Act, but the Supreme Court had already sealed the Trust's fate with the *Ben-Hur* decision.[79]

Some members of the Edison Trust began to license literary and dramatic material, but none were able to give up their old ways and adapt to the new business model dictated by the case. Trust member American Mutoscope and Biograph established one of the most promising agreements, licensing all Klaw & Erlanger plays, but Biograph only managed to produce films for a few more years before closing its production division. Edison, Selig, Vitagraph and others began to buy rights to magazine stories, and even Lubin capitulated and began to buy rights to adapt plays, though he was—like many other Edison licensees—forced to sell his studio before the end of the 1910s.[80]

New and independent companies formed much more successful alliances. Popular Broadway producer David Belasco, for example, created an alliance with the Jesse Lasky Feature Play Company. Through an exclusive agreement with Belasco, Lasky produced Cecil B. DeMille's first films and went on to help form the Paramount studio. The Bosworth Company, which also became a part of Paramount, acquired the exclusive rights to Jack London's work. The Éclair Company, which was allied with Universal, licensed all of O. Henry's short stories. By 1918 every publisher had established a film rights department with a cadre of agents. And within a few years of the *Ben-Hur* decision, film companies were funding Broadway shows in order to obtain exclusive licenses to create the film adaptations. The film companies that formed the strongest alliances with publishers and theater producers, like Lasky and Éclair, moved to Los Angeles and became the major studios and eventually multinational media conglomerates.[81]

The exclusive relationships between publishers, theater companies, and movie studios became a staple of the new film market. This vertical integration of media industries allowed for the creation of franchises, series, and authorized adaptations. But something was also lost with the *Ben-Hur* decision. Before the decision, there was a competitive market for adaptations. Many companies would adapt the same novel or play, and the best one would emerge as the more popular and the more successful version.

Of course, book and play authors were not properly compensated for the exploitation of their work, but it is a problem that Congress might have solved without creating monopolies on adaption rights. Congress could have imposed a compulsory license for film adaptations, as it did with song performances and recordings. Many companies could then have adapted the same novel as long as they paid the author the price determined by the statute. Compulsory licenses revolutionized the music industry after the 1909 Copyright Act, and it protected composers from a monopoly that threatened the music industry. A compulsory license for film adaptations might have promoted more competition among filmmakers, and it might have lowered the barrier for new independent producers to enter the market.

In one of the first books of screenwriting advice, Frances Taylor Patterson wrote about what she called the new "copyright age." She warned budding screenwriters not to adapt works in the public domain, because production companies were unlikely to make a film if they knew that a competitor could quickly put out its own version. Indeed, most screenwriting books began to contain similar copyright advice for aspiring screenwriters, who needed to understand the legal intricacies of adaptation.[82] Cross-media monopolies on content replaced the competitive market for adaptations that existed before the *Ben-Hur* case, and film companies did not even want to adapt the classics for the screen if they could not be assured of a monopoly on the story.

The *Ben-Hur* decision not only created a new market for licensed adaptations, it initiated a rush to find original stories, what Edward Azlant has called "scenario fever." Today's culture, in which everyone has a script or at least a script idea to pitch, is another remnant of the *Ben-Hur* case. As studios began to search for original scenarios and scripts that would be less expensive to option than successful books and plays, schools began to appear across the country offering training for aspiring screenwriters who wanted to sell their stories. Columbia University established one of the most prominent of these schools, underwritten by two of the producers who led the path to licensed adaptation, Jesse Lasky and Adolf Zukor.[83] The move to find and tell original stories also contributed to a change in film style. When audiences were expected to know the plot beforehand, filmmakers only needed to illustrate and remind. Now that films were telling longer, original stories, filmmakers needed to narrate as well as illustrate.

The *Ben-Hur* decision effectively transformed the American film industry. Where *Edison v. Lubin* helped push the industry into the hands of the Motion Picture Patents Company, Kalem led to the trust's downfall. But one oligopoly was replaced by another. The decision resulted in the immediate alliances and eventual vertical integration of publishing, theater, and film industries. The *Ben-Hur* decision is one—though not the only—parent of the entertainment conglomerates of the twentieth century.

CONCLUSION

Edison v. *Lubin* and *Kalem* v. *Harper Brothers* not only remade the film industry, they also transformed copyright law and, inevitably, the regulation of future new media. The two cases have much in common and together they blazed a new path for copyright law. In both cases, judges creatively interpreted the emerging art and technology of the cinema through the lenses of existing media (photography and theater, respectively). Both cases went far beyond regulating the content of movies to theorize the nature of communication technology, the structure of the entertainment industry, and the experience of spectators.

The last ingredient in that list—experience—was, I would argue, the most important element in both decisions. Judge Buffington in *Edison* v. *Lubin* and Justice Holmes in *Kalem* v. *Harper Brothers* both located the consistency between old and new media in the spectator's experience. Film, Buffington reasoned, resembled photography because spectators viewed both as complete images, one still and one moving. Similarly, Holmes found that spectators experienced film as both an expanded and limited theater, one that could create realistic settings and action but lacked the immediacy of live theater, appearing merely as its reflection. The emphasis on audience experience was not entirely new. Since the nineteenth century, judges had used copyright law to regulate the moral experience of theater audiences, using copyright law as a tool of social control. Also, in copyright cases that compared the similarity of two works, judges frequently reached their decisions by speculating about the experience and perception of an average reader, viewer, or listener. As a result of these two film cases, however, copyright began to regulate the aesthetic experience created by new technologies in addition to the audiences' reaction to specific works.

Interestingly, the Supreme Court had a chance to revisit the legal status of film spectatorship four years after the *Kalem* case. The Supreme Court seemed to pluck film out of the mire of immorality and spectacle in the *Kalem* case, acknowledging that the art of film is comparable to literature and theater. But in *Mutual* v. *Ohio* the same court qualified its opinion.

In the *Mutual* decision, the Court decided that film was "a business pure and simple," not worthy of First Amendment protection, and therefore an appropriate subject of state censorship. As the decision makes clear, the Court worried about the social space of the theater, specifically the mixing of men and women, children and adults. Where Justice Holmes had reduced judges' power to use copyright law to regulate spectacle and immorality in his *Bleistein* and *Kalem* decisions, *Mutual* v. *Ohio* transferred that power to state censor boards.[84]

Finally, these two landmark film cases, *Edison* v. *Lubin* and *Kalem* v. *Harper Brothers*, helped solidify the role of piracy in the birth of new media. Piracy was, we have seen, absolutely central to the birth of the film industry. Early filmmakers relied on several methods of copying and borrowing, including dupes, remakes, and unauthorized adaptations. But when and how should these forms of copying be declared piracy or made legal? Congress considered regulating the film industry many times as it heard testimony leading up to the rewriting of the 1909 Copyright Act. But Congress consistently decided to allow the early film industry to regulate itself.

Duping and unauthorized adaptations were ultimately outlawed as piracy, but not until after the film industry had been given decades to experiment with the new art form and develop its business. The question of film piracy, however, was not and indeed could not be settled. Courts and Congress regularly return to consider new questions of film borrowing, distribution, and consumption, from the recording of television programs with VCRs to internet film sharing. Piracy is not something that you can put your finger on. It is not something that you can be for or against. Piracy is an ever-shifting concept, there to be fought over endlessly in the development and cultural integration of new technologies.

2

HOLLYWOOD'S GOLDEN AGE
OF PLAGIARISM

COPYRIGHT LAW protects original expression. Of course, many critics of copyright law have argued that originality is overrated or that it does not exist at all. But even if we accept uncritically copyright's claim on originality, we might wonder how the law can regulate the creative output of an industry like Hollywood, which has, throughout its history, actively worked to standardize its products, to keep things relatively unoriginal. Since the earliest narrative films, the majority of movies have been adapted from literature, drama, cartoons, news stories, or some preexisting idea. Starting in the mid-1910s, Hollywood standardized its film output by cultivating repeatable studio styles, fixed genre tropes, and stable star characters that could all be used across films. The studio system was designed, in other words, to promote predictability and homogeneity and to keep originality in check. All of these systems of standardization and reliability, which were intended to stabilize the film business, carried over relatively seamlessly to television. Although it is not generally recognized, copyright law has been a key force driving the design of the studio system. The legal definitions of originality, creativity, and authorship have been interwoven into both Hollywood film and television style and into the structure of the entertainment industry, from the genre and star systems to the functioning of the talent guilds.[1]

To say that copyright law protects originality, however, is only half of the story. Copyright law may protect original expression, but the ideas expressed remain free to be borrowed and used. As Supreme Court Justice Louis Brandeis once famously put it, "the noblest of human productions—knowledge, truths ascertained, conceptions, and ideas—become, after voluntary communication to others, free as the air to common use." As another justice, Sandra Day O'Connor, once explained, the detangling of ideas from their expression keeps copyright law from hampering free speech. No one can own an idea, only a specific manner of expressing it.[2] At times, the distinction between ideas and expression can seem as meaningless or arbitrary as the notion of originality. We can, for example, imagine paraphrasing another author's words to express the same idea differently. But how can anyone decouple the underlying idea of an image or a musical phrase from its expression? Fortunately, like many elements of copyright law, the idea/expression dichotomy does not exist as some Platonic ideal. It is a living concept that changes over time. The idea/expression dichotomy is a sort of valve that responds to the influence of artists, the economy, and popular culture. Like any valve, it can be turned to increase or decrease the flow of creative ideas.

The history of film genres, television formats, and moving image authorship can all be seen as an ongoing attempt to adhere to shifts in the interpretation of the idea/expression dichotomy. In more colloquial terms, Hollywood spent decades defining the limits of film plagiarism. Plagiarism, like piracy, is a term whose definition is bound up with the forging of new media. Borrowing from previous work is essential to any artistic endeavor. As copyright scholar Peter Jaszi sagely describes the creative process, "Some conscious or unconscious borrowing from past works is inevitable, if only because the store of words and phrases available to express particular ideas is finite, and no writer is a truly 'naïve' artist. . . . These are immutable facts of artistic enterprise; only attitudes towards them change."[3] Plagiarism is the barometer we use to understand the legal, ethical, and cultural codes that separate acceptable methods of creative borrowing from illegal and unethical kinds. As a result, the definition of plagiarism is always upset by the introduction of new media, like film or television.

Throughout the twentieth century, the term *plagiarism* was used frequently in copyright decisions. Plagiarism, however, is a broad ethical and professional category and not a strictly legal one, though it does overlap with copyright law.[4] Plagiarism can be monitored and punished by extralegal authorities—teachers and contest judges—as well as by court-appointed judges. In the process of defining the codes of plagiarism that govern U.S. film and television, Hollywood used internal methods of policing the creative flow of ideas as well as court battles. Talent guilds, in particular, preempted legal intervention by registering ideas and scripts, negotiating contracts, and settling authorship disputes rather than allowing the courts to intervene.

Hollywood also invested tremendous time and resources in forging new legal doctrines that favored its profligate borrowing from popular culture. During the first half of the twentieth century, as we will see in this chapter, Hollywood studio leaders fought to enlarge the range of acceptable borrowing—of plagiarism—so that film and television producers could freely use the storytelling traditions that preceded the invention of film. The Hollywood studio system was built on plagiarism just as the early film industry had been built on piracy.

BEFORE HOLLYWOOD

Before the invention of film, vaudeville comedians and comic performers had all but given up on using copyright to protect their material. As we saw in the previous chapter, in a series of late-nineteenth-century cases, vaudeville performers attempted and failed to protect the copyrights in their performances. When copyright law proved to be a dead end, vaudevillians began to rely on the self-policing of their industry. Performers and their managers took out ads in trade papers to call out and shame other performers who unabashedly stole their material. Vaudeville theater owners regularly pledged that they would not hire copied acts, although this may have been a sop to performers and managers rather than a real commitment. And a series of short-lived institutions arose to accept documentation about acts or arbitrate disputes. In some cases, these ad hoc copyright offices or grassroots courts would establish royalty-sharing agreements between the original performer and the copycats.[5]

But these were extreme solutions. For the most part, vaudeville performers simply permitted and expected a certain amount of imitation from their peers. Live vaudeville performers could only cover so much territory, so there was more room for duplication. It was very common, for example, for European performers to copy acts they had seen on the American vaudeville circuit and for American performers to repeat acts they had seen in Europe.[6]

Even in instances where performers sought to protect their acts, they often found the task impossible. Celebrated vaudeville dancer Loie Fuller, who was mentioned in the previous chapter, vigilantly protected her performance style. She held patents on her use of color in stage lighting and on her design for a dancer's skirt frame (fig. 2.1). She sued lithographers, ultimately unsuccessfully, for distributing her image. And in 1892, Fuller attempted, also unsuccessfully, to protect her signature "Serpentine Dance" from imitation in a copyright suit. *Fuller* v. *Bemis* is one of the cases in which a judge found a vaudeville act to lack sufficient narrative or drama to be protected by copyright.[7] As a result of the decision, Fuller could not prevent dozens of dancers from using her Serpentine Dance routine across the United States and Europe. In her autobiography, Fuller recounts several instances in which she thought the presence of emulators or counterfeiters would ruin her career. But she consistently performed her original dance to sold-out crowds even when rivals performed the Serpentine Dance at nearby theaters. There were many stages on which to perform, and audiences were willing to pay in proportion to the dancers' levels of talent and acclaim. The Serpentine Dance eventually grew into a widely performed genre of dance rather than the property of a single performer, and it remained popular in the United States and in Europe for more than three decades.[8]

FROM VAUDEVILLE TO EARLY FILM

Unlike vaudeville performers, early filmmakers were not content to allow self-policing alone to govern their industry. And in the first years of the twentieth century, legal decisions began to set parameters on imitation and copying in the film industry. Film companies eventually proved to be more successful than vaudeville performers in convincing judges to recognize their copyrights, but the early case law continued to preserve the culture of imitation that pervaded vaudeville.

Market leaders Edison and Biograph initiated most of the early film copyright cases. Frequent rivals in patent disputes, the two firms threatened each other with copyright lawsuits as well. All of these were settled out of court until Edison's company remade Biograph's *Personal* (1904) without permission—a standard practice at the time. Edison and other companies often made their own versions of competitors' films, which were frequently shot-for-shot copies of the original. But several factors led to the 1904 standoff. First, the case of *Edison* v. *Lubin* (1903) had outlawed film duping, the practice of taking a competitor's film, making a negative from that film, and then striking new prints from the

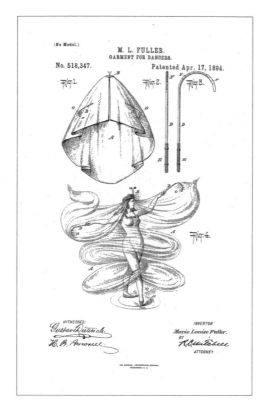

FIGURE 2.1 Loie Fuller's dress frame patent.

new negative. Now that courts had frowned on duping, remakes became an even more important part of the film business. Also, in 1903–1904, fictional narrative films began to replace reality-based genres such as travel films and films of newsworthy events. With the turn to fictional narrative, remakes suddenly had much more value, and for the first time in a copyright dispute, Biograph's lawyer, Drury Cooper, and Edison's, Frank Dyer, failed to come to an agreement after months of negotiations.

Biograph v. *Edison* asked whether the common practice of remaking a competitor's film violated copyright law. But how could courts or filmmakers determine if and when remakes took too much from the original?

Biograph's *Personal* tells the story of a European nobleman who takes out a personal ad asking potential brides to meet him in front of Grant's Tomb. When more than one willing prospect arrives at the assigned hour, the nobleman runs. The suitors pursue him until the fastest woman gets her man. The film merged comedy with a chase format, two popular genres at the time. Exhibitors clamored for copies when they read the description of *Personal*, and Biograph immediately sold the film to its licensed distributors. Following its usual practice, however, Biograph refused to sell the film to Edison's distributors or to other competitors. Biograph wanted their circuit of licensees to enjoy some exclusivity.

When the Edison Company failed to obtain a copy, the head of production followed standard procedure and instructed the company's top director, Edwin S. Porter, to remake the film. Edison was not the only company to remake *Personal*; Siegmund Lubin and the French company Pathé also made their own versions. But Porter's quickie remake, which the Edison Company entitled *How a French Nobleman Got a Wife Through the New York Personal Columns* (fig. 2.2), reached the market before Biograph's original version, and audiences much preferred it to *Personal*. Biograph's management was infuriated, and they petitioned the New Jersey District Court for an injunction against Edison, asking that Edison surrender all prints and negatives to Biograph.[9]

In a series of affidavits, Edison's staff admitted having seen and copied the Biograph film. In Edison's own testimony, he suggested that they were operating in an extralegal realm. "As far as I am aware," he told the court, "it has never been considered that a copyright upon a moving picture photograph covers the plot or theme which the exhibition of the moving picture portrays." Porter, the director, had a more nuanced interpretation of what happened. He saw the Biograph film and immediately recognized it as a genre film, a "chase picture." Moreover, *Personal* was not much more than the elaboration of a joke, something so basic that it could not be protected. "It occurred to me after seeing the exhibition of the complainant's film *Personal*," Porter stated for the record, "that I could design a set of photographs based upon the same joke, and which, to my mind, would possess greater artistic merit. My conception of the principal character representing the French Nobleman was entirely different from that of the complainant's film, as regards costume, appearances, expression, figure, bearing, posing, posturing and action."[10] Porter had had his own films remade by Biograph and other companies for years. He had, in turn, remade many films. Remakes had been a standard of the industry; improving on another director's film was how an international industry of filmmakers exchanged ideas and contributed to the growth of their art form. Porter had not duped any scenes—a practice now out of favor and illegal—and he felt entitled to take Biograph's ideas as long as he expressed them differently.

FIGURE 2.2 *How a French Nobelman Got a Wife Through the New York Herald Personal Columns* (1904), a non-infringing remake of Edwin S. Porter's film *Personal.*

As Porter suggested in his testimony, *Personal* might best be characterized as the visual representation of a joke. And in the court statements, Edison's lawyers accused Biograph's director of having taken the story from a newspaper cartoon, although no one involved in the case was able to produce the original cartoon. The film does have the quality of a live-action cartoon. It sets up a situation that leads to an unexpected result and then turns into a slapstick chase. Like any other work of art, the underlying ideas of jokes, gags, and other kinds of comic routines are part of the public domain, but copyright law may protect the specific expression of a joke. Jokes and gags, however, pose some extra difficulties when one tries to separate the original contributions of individual performers from the underlying ideas that they are building upon.[11] Jokes and gags are generally short; they fall into a few broad structural categories; and they often circulate widely. Frequently, jokes and gags respond to cultural trends or political events, and, as a result, jokes come in waves: different comedians often create similar jokes about similar circumstances. Part of *Personal*'s humor, just for example, came from the fact that it responded to a cultural phenomenon, the trend of European nobility marrying American money. Jokes and gags also tend to draw broad characters in order to remain socially relevant (a rabbi, a priest, and a blonde walk into a bar). Because of their simple structure, broad characters, and brevity, jokes and gags have always been difficult to protect legally.

Both Edison's and Porter's testimony indicates that an interpretation of the idea/expression dichotomy guided many early filmmakers' creative decisions. That did not make the judge's job any easier. It is always difficult—especially when a medium or genre is new—to separate the generic tropes of an art form from the nuances and individual contributions of a particular work. In 1868, for example, playwright and producer Augustin Daly successfully defended his copyright in the staging of a last-minute rescue from an oncoming train. How would the judge in the Daly case have known that such scenes would become a stock fixture of professional and amateur plays around the world and eventually the stuff of children's cartoons?[12]

Chase films and comedies were already common by 1904, and filmmakers remade each other's films regularly. There was no legal or normative consensus about acceptable and unacceptable borrowing. Judge Lanning made his decision by closely analyzing the two films; he even requested a shot-by-shot description of *Personal* from Biograph. In Judge Lanning's reading, "the two photographs [as he referred to the films] possess many similar and many dissimilar features." The plotlines were uncannily similar, but the framing and some of the backgrounds were different. Despite the similarities, Lanning concluded, Porter's remake "is not an imitation . . . [he] took the plaintiff's idea, and worked it out in a different way."[13] Moreover, the two films had significantly different titles, so exhibitors and audiences were unlikely to mistake one for the other from the advertisements. An appeals court agreed with Lanning, and as a result remakes remained a common practice of production companies during the early years of narrative film development.[14]

The high judicial tolerance for remakes fostered an international culture of creative exchange among filmmakers. This open creative environment, as Jay Leyda and others have shown, allowed the nascent art of narrative film to develop extremely rapidly. In one example, suggested by Leyda and elaborated by Tom Gunning and Charles Musser, D. W. Griffith's great masterpiece of crosscutting, *The Lonely Villa* (1909), turns out to have been the result of an international dialogue among writers, dramatists, and filmmakers. Pathé Frères made a film, *A Narrow Escape* (1908), inspired by a French Guignol play, *Au Telephone*, about a man who receives a phone call and listens to his family being attacked by robbers. Six months later, Edwin S. Porter made a film, *Heard Over the Phone* (1908), based either on the English version of *Au Telephone* or on the Pathé film. The narrative, now too widely circulated to pinpoint the exact chain of influence, was remade and altered by both Russian filmmaker Yakov Protazanov and by Griffith, whose version remains a touchstone of film history.[15]

Biograph v. *Edison* sanctioned an environment of creative exchange in which plots and themes could be repeated, and this environment helped to solidify early film genres. More than twenty years after *Biograph* v. *Edison*, Buster Keaton remade *Personal*—or perhaps he remade Porter's remake of *Personal*—as a feature-length comedy, *The Seven Chances* (1925). Some of the simple ideas in Biograph's film became the building blocks of film comedy; they were ideas that no one could own.

"LEGALLY UNIQUE": CHAPLIN VERSUS APLIN

Vaudeville and early film comedians accepted the liberal legal standards of ownership. In the mid-1910s, however, the loose conglomeration of small film companies began to merge into vertically and horizontally integrated film studios (i.e., Hollywood), with more rationalized models of production, distribution, exhibition, and marketing. The star system was one such form of rationalized marketing, and when some of the vaudeville comedians emerged as slapstick film stars in the 1910s, they began to push for much greater protection of their images and their material. Several of the new stars turned to copyright law, and they fought to redefine the idea/ expression dichotomy. The case that transformed comic authorship for the age of mass media and finally broke with the imitative cultures of vaudeville and the early film industry involved Charlie Chaplin.

Chaplin had been an unexceptional member of the British music hall and vaudeville troupe Karno's Speechless Comedians before Mack Sennett invited him to perform in a film in 1911. After that, Chaplin's star rose quickly in Hollywood, and only six years later he enjoyed an almost unparalleled degree of creative autonomy, having established his own studio where he wrote, produced, directed, and starred in all of his films. After cofounding United Artists in 1919, the multitalented Chaplin had a hand in distributing his films as well and even began scoring them after the adoption of sound. In a collaborative medium, Chaplin enjoyed a degree of individual authorship that only a few other filmmakers have ever achieved.

Chaplin helped to redefine the idea of the filmmaker, giving rise to a mythic conception of the director as lone artist. According to one story, he was known to go off on a short fishing trip in the middle of shooting a film just to look for inspiration in the stillness of a lake or stream. Art and film theorist Rudolf Arnheim helped to propagate the Chaplin-as-solitary-genius myth, describing him as "a man who, in the middle of the Hollywood film industry, where every day in the studio costs thousands and art is produced with a stopwatch, sometimes disappears suddenly and for days paces in solitude with his plans."[16] Indeed, it became a rite of passage for every modernist cultural theorist in the 1920s and 1930s to write a profile of Chaplin as the exception within the commercial sphere of mass culture, as the artist who could work within the capitalist machine of mass production, at the pinnacle of the system, yet remain apart from it. The Frankfurt School theorists, in particular, seemed determined not to break ranks in their unified defense of Chaplin as the last vestige of a Romantic authenticity. Walter Benjamin, building on an essay by Surrealist writer Philippe Soupault, called Chaplin the "poet of his films."[17] Siegfried Kracauer, in his own obligatory Chaplin portrait, performed great contortions to argue that money and success had not changed Chaplin. "Rather than letting himself be changed by money, like the majority does," Kracauer wrote, "he changes it; money loses its commodity character the moment it encounters Chaplin, becoming instead the homage which is his due."[18] Even the Frankfurt School's severest critic of Hollywood, Theodor Adorno, who elsewhere described laughter as "a disease" of "the false society," made Chaplin an exception by celebrating the actor's imitative genius.[19] As many admirers claimed, Chaplin was simply able to become the characters he mimicked. Only the American cultural critic Gilbert Seldes contested Chaplin's singularity by putting him "wholly in the tradition of the great clowns" and tracing the origins of his style to his film apprenticeship in Mack Sennett's Keystone studio. The "Keystone touch," Seldes wrote, "remains in all [Chaplin's] work."[20]

Was Chaplin a Romantic poet of the screen whose inspiration came only from his own genius? Or was he more like Homer, fixing on film a comic performance style that had been developed over decades or even centuries by court jesters, traveling comics, and vaudeville performers? The question of Chaplin's originality grew increasingly important as his films gave rise to thousands of professional and amateur Chaplin imitators. Were the imitators taking and remixing the same ideas that Chaplin had himself lifted from other comics, or were they looting his individual expression?

In July 1915 alone, more than thirty New York City movie theaters sponsored Chaplin look-alike competitions (fig. 2.3).[21] Future professional comedian Bob Hope won one such competition, and Walt Disney, who would draw heavily on Chaplin to create Mickey Mouse, entered dozens of Chaplin impersonation contests, eventually being ranked the second best in Kansas City.[22] Professional imitators were also plentiful. The well-known Chaplin imitator Billy West (fig. 2.4) made over fifty films as a Chaplin-like character. Actress Minerva Courtney made three films cross-

FIGURE 2.3 A Chaplin lookalike contest promoting *The Idle Class* (November 5, 1922). (Photo by J. W. Sandison; Whatcom Museum, Bellingham, WA)

FIGURE 2.4 An advertisement for Chaplin imitator Billy West.

dressing as Chaplin, and former Chaplin understudy Stan Laurel developed a Chaplin stage act years before his success as part of the film duo Laurel and Hardy. The Russian clown Karandash ultimately had to give up his Chaplin routine because he was overwhelmed by competition from other Chaplin imitators.[23] There were both authorized and unauthorized Chaplin cartoons; the most prominent, *Charlie*, was animated by future *Felix the Cat* creator Otto Messmer and had an unofficial nod of approval from Chaplin, who sent ideas to Messmer (fig. 2.5). Even superstar silent

FIGURE 2.5 *Felix the Cat in Hollywood* (1923). A parody of Chaplin's pursuit of impersonators.

comedian Harold Lloyd began as a Chaplin imitator, making fifty-seven films as a Chaplin-like character named Lonesome Luke. Some companies took Chaplin's image more directly than did the imitators, selling dupes of Chaplin films or taking excerpts from his films and mixing them with stock footage, creating "mashups" (to use an anachronistic term). Other Chaplin mashups mixed footage from Chaplin films with footage of imitators.[24]

Modernist and avant-garde writers, artists, and performers were also obsessed with Chaplin. The Dadaists, the Surrealists, Fernand Léger, T. S. Eliot, James Joyce, Gertrude Stein, and countless others copied Chaplin and his Tramp character in a variety of ways. Critics have made strong cases that Joyce's Leopold Bloom and several Wyndham Lewis characters were, at least in part, explicitly modeled on Chaplin.[25] Eastern European poets used Chaplin and the Tramp character as figures in their poetry during the 1920s and 1930s. The tradition included poems by German-French writer Yvan Goll and by Russians Osip Mandelstam and Anna Akhmatova, the latter imagining herself sitting on a bench in conversation with Chaplin and Kafka. Cubist painter Fernand Léger, who had a deep obsession with Chaplin, illustrated an edition of Goll's *Chaplinade*. Léger went on to animate a dancing Charlot—the French diminutive for Chaplin—in his 1924 avant-garde film *Ballet mécanique*, which premiered in New York on a program with Chaplin's *The Pilgrim* (1923).[26]

FIGURE 2.6 Chaplin in *The Champion* (1915), which another company mashed up with undersea footage.

Neither Chaplin nor his attorney, the legendary copyright and entertainment lawyer Nathan Burkan, was happy about the massive proliferation of imitators and derivative works. Their first attempt to contain the spread of Chaplin's image was to go after a company that mixed Chaplin's film *The Champion* (1915) (fig. 2.6) with underwater footage to create a new film. (It is difficult to imagine how boxing footage might have been mixed with undersea shots, but that is what the accounts describe: the film isn't extant.) Chaplin had made *The Champion* for the Essanay Film Manufacturing Company, and he did not own the copyright. When Essanay failed to take action, Burkan sued the company responsible for the new film, claiming that the filmmakers had unfairly adopted Chaplin's Little Tramp character.

It was a novel argument at the time, but one would expect no less of Burkan, a pioneering lawyer and lobbyist who had previously led the campaign for compulsory licensing to be included in the 1909 revision of the Copyright Act. The judge in the first Chaplin case eventually rejected the argument that one performer could own a character independent of a particular work, but he did force the Crystal Palace Theatre in New York to stop misleading the public by advertising the film as if it were a real Chaplin film.[27] It is not clear, however, that the decision accurately assessed the situation or that it had the intended effect. According to Terry Ramsaye, writing in 1926, the Crystal Palace's attendance dropped by half when it attempted to pass off a Chaplin imitation as an original, which suggests that filmgoers were not as susceptible to misleading advertising as the judge thought. And if audiences knew the difference between Chaplin and his imitators, devoted fans were nonetheless willing to watch imitators' work in between the star's sporadic releases. Despite Chaplin and Burkan's partial victory, Chaplin biographer Joyce Milton notes, the decision led to even more imitators, who could now legally borrow the Tramp character as long as they did not mislead the public through advertising.[28]

But Chaplin and Burkan were not deterred. In a lawsuit against Mexican actor Charles Amador, who made several films under the name "Charlie Aplin," they reprised the argument that Chaplin owned his Little Tramp character. Burkan spent three years trying to settle with Amador before the case went to trial. But Amador and his lawyers were stubborn, maintaining that they had a right to use the comic elements that Chaplin used, too. Hollywood insiders and movie fans paid close attention to the case, which dragged on for six years, garnering dozens of op-ed pieces and occasionally making front page news.[29]

When the trial court heard testimony in the case in 1925, Amador's lawyers bravely let the charismatic celebrity take the stand and discuss his creative method. In a later copyright case involving the 1918 film *Shoulder Arms*, the opposition's attorney would try to stop Chaplin from swaying the court with his charm and wit.[30] But in the Amador case, Chaplin's testimony may not have helped him. Chaplin adopted an aloof and aristocratic tone. "My inspiration," he explained to the court,

> was from the whole pageantry of life. I got my walk from an old London cab driver, the one-foot glide that I use was an inspiration of the moment. A part of the character was inspired by Fred Kitchen, an old fellow-trouper of mine in vaudeville. He had flat feet." When Amador's lawyer, Ben Goldman, cross-examined Chaplin about his costume, Chaplin was dismissive. "Where did you get that hat?" Goldman asked.
>
> "Oh, I don't know. I just conceived the idea of using it," replied Chaplin.
> "Did you ever see anyone wear pants such as you wear?" Goldman continued.
> "Sure," replied Chaplin, "the whole world wears pants."[31]

Chaplin's answers had both a dismissive and a mystical quality. Ideas just came to him, or he extracted them from his observations of life.

Goldman and Amador, however, had another theory. Goldman called a vaudeville reviewer, Joseph Pazen, to the stand, and asked him if Chaplin

FIGURE 2.7 Charles Amador (aka Chalie Aplin) outside the courtroom where he defended himself against claims of using Chaplin's tramp character. (Courtesy Getty Images)

imitated any of the comics who had preceded him. Pazen named dozens of performers who had used similar elements in their routines. George Beban, for instance, had a similar moustache; Chris Lane had a similar hat; Harry Morris had baggy pants; Billy Watson used the same combination of baggy pants, big shoes, and a glide walk. A member of the Les Petries Brothers used the same makeup and a similar costume in his tramp character. This actor had even performed as a tramp in a film for Chaplin's old employer, Mutual. As later critics have noted, Chaplin's costume also invoked circus clowns and real tramps, who rode railway cars and took odd jobs.[32]

When Amador took the stand, he was as unsympathetic as his opponent, shiftily claiming that his contract engaged him to imitate the Chaplin look-alike Billy West, not Chaplin (fig. 2.7). Amador, however, did have one powerful argument: if Chaplin won, the precedent would create a new monopoly on performance. Amador's team made the case that Chaplin was only the most famous in a long tradition of comic tramps, and he could not be given a proprietary right in staples of the trade.[33]

When Burkan attempted to respond to the specifics of Amador's criticisms, he fell into rhetorical quicksand, fumbling in the attempt to name Chaplin's original inventions. Reporters following the case had the same problem as they combed the testimony for some element that Chaplin had contributed to the art of comedy. "Chaplin Pants Real Issue," read one headline.[34] But Burkan stuck to his larger strategy by insisting that Chaplin was a unique genius, endowed with an ineffable quality that people could see for themselves. Chaplin's genius, Burkan maintained, could not be described or broken down into distinct elements. In one show of court-room theatrics, he claimed that a clip from a Chaplin film would have to be placed in the court's decision, because words could not describe him.[35] The Romantic vision of the solitary artist is always compelling, but it was a particularly powerful part of the Chaplin myth. In addition to the German theorists mentioned earlier, writers as varied as Winston Churchill, Graham Greene, Edmund Wilson, and Dwight Macdonald had perpetuated the myth of Chaplin as an individual genius—perhaps the sole individual genius—working in the collaborative and commercial Hollywood system.

But the prevailing argument would end up being a humbler, more prag-matic one. In addition to calling for the protection of Chaplin's unique genius, Burkan argued that the Charlie Aplin name and appearance con-fused potential filmgoers because they resembled Chaplin's own name and iconic image too closely. This argument carried more weight with Judge John Hudner, who enjoined the distribution of Amador's film *The Race Track* and prohibited Amador from further misleading the public by advertising his films as if Chaplin had made them. By focusing not on the proprietary right in character but instead on the confusion that imitators unleashed in the market, Judge Hudner's decision itself sowed confusion: the press and the film industry were not sure who had won this round of the case. The *Los Angeles Times* declared "Chaplin Legally Unique." The *New York Times* agreed at first, running the headline "Chaplin *Wins* Suit to Protect Make-Up." But after revisiting Judge Hudner's final ruling with its limited emphasis on Amador's deceptive intent and advertising, the paper reevaluated its conclusion and ran a new headline, "Chaplin *Loses* Fight on Exclusive Make-Up." Chaplin had successfully prevented Amador from using his image, but he had failed to protect his character from imitation.[36]

Amador's lawyer, Goldman, claimed victory: "we can continue to pro-duce pictures featuring Amador in the characterization as long as we spe-cifically state in the titles that Amador is playing the character . . . [Chap-lin] has no patent or copyright on the character."[37] The decision raised more questions about originality and ownership than it answered. While Chaplin waited for an appeals court to rule on the Amador case, he was himself sued for copyright infringement—twice. The legal skirmish over the exchange of comic ideas had begun to heat up.

When the appeals court heard the case, it refined Judge Hudner's decision, giving more weight to the idea that Chaplin owned the Tramp character. As Judge H. L. Preston stated plainly in his decision, "the record reveals that Charles Chaplin . . . originated and perfected a particular type of character on the motion picture screen." Elements of Chaplin's character may have been in the public domain, free to be used by other comics. But Chaplin owned this particular expression of the Tramp character; he was the first to use it on screen; and he could prevent others from confusing the public by adopting his look and actions.[38]

The appeals court in *Chaplin* v. *Amador* did not entirely adopt Burkan and Chaplin's model of Romantic authorship, but Chaplin had succeeded in forging a new and greatly expanded legal definition of comic authorship and, indeed, of authorship and performance in general. The stated goal of both the trial and the appellate decisions was to protect the public from confusion, and both decisions used copyright to control unfair competition. In his decision in the Chaplin appeal, for example, Judge Preston made it clear that Chaplin had the right to protect his character from "the fraudulent purpose and conduct of [Amador]" and "against those who would injure him by fraudulent means; that is by counterfeiting his role."[39] There is no indication, however, that the existence of counterfeit Chaplins injured the original, at least not by deceiving his audience into misspending their ticket money. In a statement that Chaplin submitted ostensibly in support of his case, Lee Ochs, the former president of the Motion Picture Exhibitors League of the State of New York, told the court that Amador's film "is very poor and failed to embody the elements of comedy and pathos that so aptly distinguish the Chaplin pictures. Nevertheless, to the casual observer, it might readily be mistaken for a Chaplin picture." Yet as we saw in the wake of the trial court decision, audiences were not easily deceived. On the contrary, vaudeville had taught theater owners and audiences of popular amusement to expect repetition and imitation. The box-office dips when imitators' films were shown at the Crystal Palace demonstrate that audiences were well aware of the differences between Chaplin and pseudo-Chaplin films. The limits that *Chaplin* v. *Amador* placed on imitation did not serve to clarify the options available to audience members; it only limited their choices.[40]

By protecting Chaplin the great artist from cooptation by average screen comics, both the 1925 and the 1928 decisions made unprecedented levels of protection the reward for reputation and standing. Although the courts did not announce this innovation explicitly in their decisions, it became clear in the cases that adopted *Chaplin* v. *Amador* as precedent. Lawyers began to invoke the case, often successfully, to protect performers from defamation, trademark infringement, unfair competition, and lower-echelon imitators who tarnished their clients' reputations. The Chaplin precedent emerged as a tool for policing performers' reputations rather than for protecting their originality.[41]

Chaplin v. *Amador* also inaugurated the development of character protection in copyright law, but Chaplin's Tramp character didn't resemble the kinds of characters that copyright has since come to protect. As Judge Learned Hand would write in 1930, character copyright protects the specific traits of "sufficiently developed" characters. Chaplin, however, used a stock vaudeville figure, the tramp, and made it his own. Although the individual elements of the Chaplin's Tramp remained part of the public domain, Chaplin's global celebrity so identified him with the figure of the Tramp that it became impossible for other performers to play a tramp without evoking Chaplin. As a result, the new precedent of character protection gave a significant advantage to pioneering media stars who drew, as Chaplin did, on centuries of stage tradition to create their characters.[42]

Chaplin v. *Amador* signaled a cultural shift from vaudeville to Hollywood, from live to recorded performance, and from local celebrity to global stardom. Many other vaudeville performers, especially comics, were confounded by the new limits on imitation. Former vaudeville stars the Marx Brothers, for example, were mired in lawsuits over comic authorship after they made the transition to film.[43] Because film fixed performances permanently on celluloid and circulated exact copies rapidly and globally, the nature of imitation had undoubtedly changed. The vaudeville model of peer policing and tolerance for some degree of imitation no longer provided enough control and protection to satisfy performers, and the courts responded with new tools that constricted the flow of ideas between artists. The casualties of this change were future Bob Hopes, Stan Laurels, and Harold Lloyds, who were no longer free to learn their trade through emulation. The vaudeville circuit could house droves of clowns and tramps, but on film there was room for only one.

HAROLD LLOYD: UNINTENTIONALLY GUILTY?

While the appeals court considered the Chaplin case, former Chaplin imitator Harold Lloyd became embroiled in a copyright dispute of his own. It was the first of several important copyright cases that Lloyd would fight during his career, cases that were pivotal in the larger legal battle being fought over Hollywood authorship and genres.

Like Chaplin's copyright battles, Harold Lloyd's cases were about redefining the limits of originality, imitation, and comedy in the age of mass media. Lloyd, however, portrayed himself as a different kind of artist than Chaplin. Where Chaplin thought of himself as a Romantic genius, Lloyd described his process as that of a craftsman. Lloyd freely admitted that his filmmaking process involved collaboration from beginning to end. Lloyd owned his own studio, like Chaplin, but, unlike Chaplin, Lloyd happily acknowledged the teams of writers, gagmen, directors, editors, and many others who all labored in Lloyd's shop. Lloyd did not find inspiration in a pond, like Chaplin. His films were hammered out along the way. Writers made outlines, but the stories were collectively shaped during filming. The gagmen scripted some gags ahead of time, but many more were discovered while experimenting on the set. Lloyd's films were often shot in the order of the story's chronology (a very expensive indulgence), so that the team could develop the character and plot during production. Even after a film was "in the can," the entire project could be remade in the editing room, where intertitles and dialogue were added and retakes were ordered to ensure story continuity. This collaborative method, in which a team of artists sculpted the film as it progressed, offered a new challenge for the courts.[44]

Lloyd v. *Witwer* involved Lloyd's most successful film, *The Freshman* (1925), the second-highest-grossing film of the silent era after Chaplin's *The Gold Rush* (also 1925). In the early1920s, it had not yet become commonplace for every successful film to become the subject of a million-dollar plagiarism lawsuit. But the phenomenon would soon take off. In the next two decades, hits from Cecil B. DeMille's *King of Kings* (1927) to Josef von Sternberg's Marlene Deitrich vehicle *Blonde Venus* (1932) to the Marx Brothers' *A Day at the Races* (1937) to Frank Capra's *Mr. Smith Goes to Washington* (1939) were the subject of lawsuits by writers who claimed the studios had stolen their ideas. The phenomenon was novel enough in the 1930s and 1940s that the *New York Times* reported on dozens of cases in which people submitted story ideas or scripts to studios then sued after the same studio produced a similar film.

The vast majority of these cases were quickly dismissed by courts or never even made it to trial. Not only are ideas unable to be protected by copyright law, but since the days of Edison, studios have taken steps to protect themselves from such suits through contracts. When plagiarism involves the taking of expression in addition to ideas, however, copyright law can become implicated. In *Lloyd* v. *Witwer* both sides were willing to pursue a court solution over many years, and, as a result, the case set the terms for future film plagiarism suits.

Lloyd had been considering making a film about football and college life for almost a decade when he asked his writing team to begin working on an outline for the project that would become *The Freshman*. The writing staff was at work on the story when Lloyd's uncle arranged for him to meet with H. C. Witwer, a popular writer of the time who had sold many stories to film companies. Lloyd mentioned his current project to Witwer over dinner, and Witwer suggested that Lloyd look at a magazine story he had published called "The Emancipation of Rodney." The magazine piece tells the story of an academic overachiever, Rodney, who only wants to be a football star. Rodney eventually works hard, achieves success on the field, and gets the girl.[45]

Lloyd never read the story, and when the plot was described to the writing staff they rejected it as not suitable for a Lloyd film. The writers returned to work and completed their own outline. At around the same time, according to one member of the Lloyd production team, playwright Owen David threatened to sue Lloyd over his earlier film *Safety Last* (1923), which David claimed copied his Broadway hit, *The Nervous Wreck* (1923). The Lloyd team decided to be cautious with their new project, and before filming they described the outline to Witwer. According to several accounts, Witwer said that the Lloyd team's outline did not resemble his story, and Lloyd was free to take elements from his story if he wished. Apparently with Witwer's blessing, Lloyd and his team set off to shoot their "original" film.[46]

When the Lloyd Company finished *The Freshman*, it told a story similar to Witwer's, about a boy self-nicknamed Speedy who dreams of being popular in college. Although ridiculed at first, Speedy eventually achieves success on the football field and gets the girl in the end. The film earned $4 million during its initial run, and Witwer had second thoughts about his generosity. He claimed that the story had been changed since the version that had been presented to him, and the final version clearly borrowed too much from his story. Witwer died while his lawyers attempted to settle the case, and his widow took his place as plaintiff. The case finally went to trial in 1930, four years after the initial complaint had been filed and without Witwer to tell his side of the story.

For *The Freshman* to have infringed on the motion picture rights of "The Emancipation of Rodney," the Witwer lawyers needed to demonstrate two things: they first needed to prove that the creators of *The Freshman* had access to the original work, and, second, they needed to prove that the film and the Witwer story were "substantially similar." Not all material in the original story, it is important to note, could be protected by copyright. The generic and universal elements belonged to the public domain. There have been countless stories of unathletic college students who are thrown in the big game at the last minute and save the day. But determining where the public domain elements ended and the original contributions began was neither clear-cut nor a problem with great historical precedent, at least as it concerned the film industry. Courts had, however, developed a short-hand method for deciding if one work was substantially similar to another. A judge or jury was to assume the position of a common reader, listener, or viewer and deduce whether a lay audience member would be likely to recognize the second work as an infringement—a plagiarism—of the former.[47]

District Court Judge George Cosgrave compared the story and film as he imagined an average audience member might, and he sided unequivocally with Witwer. "From a comparison of the two," he wrote, "I am convinced that plaintiff's charge of plagiarism is well founded." There were, of course, a few differences, but Judge Cosgrave thought them insubstantial. "The humor of Harold Lloyd," Cosgrave noted, "does not appear in the magazine story, and much is added in *The Freshman* that furnishes a vehicle for this element." So, all that Lloyd had added was the comedy! This seems to be an important addition, one that clearly transformed the original story. And, as we will see, this small point of comparison that Cosgrave brushed aside would seem relevant to judges who heard the case on appeal.[48]

Although it seemed clear to Cosgrave that *The Freshman* was substantially similar to "The Emancipation of Rodney," the question of access and authorship proved more complicated. Cosgrave could only imagine Lloyd to be the sole author of the film, despite all of the testimony that *The Freshman* had been a collaborative effort. But Lloyd claimed never to have read the story. Witwer may have given Lloyd a copy of the magazine, but if so Lloyd had misplaced it and never read it. Lloyd had never heard the story description either, although his writers had. Witwer did travel to the Lloyd studio at one point and attempt to tell Lloyd the story, but on that occasion Witwer turned out to be too drunk to assemble coherent sentences. Lloyd was also absent the day that his writers described their plot outline to Witwer—the day that Witwer attested to the great differences in the two stories.[49]

Did Lloyd really have access to the Witwer story? Cosgrave could not find any direct proof. He agreed, "Lloyd personally had no knowledge of the actual plagiarism." But, nevertheless, there were so many connections that Cosgrave felt sure an exchange of more than ideas had occurred. Because Cosgrave was not willing to acknowledge that *The Freshman* was a collaborative work with many authors, he had to attribute the copying—if it did occur—to Lloyd. As the *Los Angeles Times* reported, Lloyd had been found "unintentionally guilty of plagiarism."[50]

The claim of unintentional plagiarism was not invented for the *Lloyd* case. Courts had gradually been considering a new doctrine of unintentional plagiarism for a decade and a half before the *Lloyd* case, but judges and juries had almost unanimously rejected it. Unintentional plagiarism was an idea that seemed particularly relevant to film and popular literature. Films were collaborative endeavors, and with so many authors in the mix it was not easy to tell how ideas and their particular means of expression entered into the final product. Moreover, popular literature, plays, and films circulated widely, and even people who had never read or seen the original book or play might still be familiar with the specifics of its story. New York Judge Emile Lacombe—the same judge who had decided in 1892 that Loie Fuller's Serpentine Dance could not be protected by copyright because it did not contain drama—first applied the test of unintentional plagiarism. In two cases, one involving a David Belasco Broadway play and the other a Biograph film, Lacombe evaluated works that clearly resembled works of literature. In both cases, it was difficult to prove access and direct copying, and in both cases Lacombe considered the possibility of unintentional plagiarism. In both cases, however, he found that the similarities ran much deeper than the books, plays, and films in question. The stories were all variations on timeless plots and themes, things that copyright did not protect. It was inevitable that the emerging medium of film would take up well-worn plots and themes and give them new visual expression. Even if the ideas had circulated widely in popular literature, the law did not entitle authors to a monopoly on their plots, only on the much narrower original details they had added to the plots. In the majority of subsequent cases in which filmmakers had been accused of unintentional plagiarism, judges looked for deeper similarities of structure and theme.[51]

But the Lacombe cases did not stop authors from assuming that filmmakers were taking their stories directly rather than simply drawing on the same basic plots and themes. In a series of cases, filmmakers defended their right to make westerns, Christ stories, comedies about ethnic intermarriage, and other common subjects. In almost every case, judges rejected the notion of unintentional plagiarism in order to stake out filmmakers' right to retell old stories and use common themes. And in almost every case, judges affirmed that average viewers would not be confused by the similarities between the films and the books or plays they were accused of copying. Audience members, the courts found consistently, are wise enough to see that the similarities between popular works often stem from the fact that they are constructed of the same cultural building blocks.[52]

The district court's decision in *Lloyd v. Witwer*, however, threatened to alter the development of the film industry and formalize a new test for plagiarism—unintentional plagiarism—which could have opened up a torrent of litigation and sent the film industry into a panic of overprotection. How could studios know if their products were the result of unintentional plagiarism?

Commenting on the Lloyd case, popular *Los Angeles Times* columnist Harry Carr warned of the dangers of plagiarism suits devolving into witch hunts, and he defended the process of borrowing that underlies all art and the Hollywood genre system specifically. "It is absolutely impossible to follow the life story of an idea," Carr wrote.

> Generally speaking all ideas are borrowed. All murder mystery stories are built upon the models of Edgar Allen Poe's "Gold Bug" or "The Murders in the Rue Morgue." There never was but one western. Told endlessly.[53]

When an appeals court reviewed *Lloyd v. Witwer* three years later, two of three judges on the panel felt the same way as Carr. They analyzed Lloyd's artistic method and the idea/expression dichotomy in much greater detail than the district court had. The majority opinion and dissent ran close to 200 pages combined, and the document contains extremely detailed, close analyses of the story and the film. The opinion completely reversed the earlier decision, developing a very different account of film authorship and denying the charge of plagiarism, either unintentional or deliberate.

Judge Curtis Wilbur, who wrote the majority opinion, questioned the practice of judges speaking for average viewers. "After having read the critical analysis of the story and the play contained in the briefs and argument," he wrote, "it is not easy to place oneself in the attitude of a fairly indifferent and disinterested spectator of the moving picture play." Judge Wilbur went on to analyze the two works with the close eye of a critic rather than lay viewer, and he also interrogated the methodology courts had adopted for dealing with plagiarism in film and literature.[54]

Wilbur reasoned that Lloyd's filmmaking process made it unlikely that *The Freshman* could have copied any other work. Lloyd's films grew organically from start to finish; the story was worked out at each stage of production and revised continuously. Gags, in particular, were not planned, but spontaneous, technical, and site-specific. Moreover, the final film bore little resemblance to the original outline composed by Lloyd's writers. Wilbur located the lion's share of authorship in the editing stage; for *The Freshman*, Wilbur noted, the Lloyd Company had shot over 100,000 feet of film and used only 7,000 feet in the final product. Some of the ideas in the shooting script may have made their way into the final film, but such an improvisational style surely created new forms of expressing those ideas. Finally, Judge Wilbur turned to the money invested in the production for proof. Witwer had sold the motion picture rights of his other stories for approximately $1,000. Lloyd invested $330,000 in *The Freshman*, including $40,000 paid to his writers. "Men must be judged as reasonable beings in appraising their conduct," Wilbur stated. And he concluded that no reasonable filmmaker would risk millions to save $1,000.[55]

In fact, the major studios had long made a practice of carefully documenting sources for their films by buying rights to books, newspaper stories, or other source material for just about every film made by Hollywood. By the mid-1920s more than half of Hollywood's output was ostensible adaptations of works in other media. Lloyd, too, thought he had covered himself by asking Witwer for his approval, but the status of the verbal agreement between writers and filmmakers would not become binding until the 1950s (in a case discussed below).

If any similarities between the magazine story and the final film existed after the Lloyd Company's arduous process of film production, then the connections would have to be subconscious, Judge Wilbur reasoned. Yet he rejected the idea of subconscious plagiarism—in this case, at least. "There are inherent difficulties," he wrote, "in the application of this proposition of subconscious memory to the facts in the case at bar." A much more compelling explanation for the similarities between "The Emancipation of Rodney" and *The Freshman* is that both stories shared generic plot structures, which are freely available and part of the public domain. "There is nothing novel," Wilbur summarized the overarching theme of both stories, "in the idea of achieving success or popularity by being true to oneself and avoiding temptation to imitate others who have achieved popularity." The plot that the two works share is an old one: the story of the college loser who attains success on the sports field. Witwer and the Lloyd Company had given the same basic idea very different expression. And through his drawn-out and expensive defense, Lloyd helped to protect the film industry

FIGURE 2.8 Harold Lloyd in *The Freshman* (1925), which courts briefly held to be the product of unintentional plagiarism.

FIGURE 2.9 Adam Sandler in *The Waterboy* (1998), a film that Harold Lloyd's daughter unsuccessfully sued for infringing her father's silent classic.

from the barrage of accusations of plagiarism that would continue to come from playwrights and novelists.[56]

Lloyd v. *Witwer* did not stop writers from accusing filmmakers of unintentionally taking their popular stories and plays. But the case proved to be a major legal turning point for courts and for Hollywood. It confirmed the position that had been developing since *Biograph* v. *Edison* in 1904: that film plot ideas would be borrowed from literature, vaudeville, and everywhere else and reused again and again by filmmakers. *Lloyd* v. *Witwer* gave Hollywood studios both the confidence and the latitude to pursue the cinematic exploration of common narratives and to engage with the stories that make up popular culture. When Harold Lloyd's granddaughter, Suzanne Lloyd, sued the Walt Disney Company for plagiarizing *The Freshman* in the Adam Sandler vehicle *The Waterboy* (1998), almost seventy years after the *Witwer* case, courts could throw the lawsuit out without writing an opinion. The story of the college loser who becomes a football hero was a time-tested subgenre (figs. 2.8 and 2.9). No one owned the idea, and no one should have known that better than Harold Lloyd's daughter.[57]

JAMES M. CAIN VERSUS JAMES M. CAIN: *SCÈNES À FAIR* AND THE ORGANIZATION OF WRITERS

Lloyd v. *Witwer* and the many film plagiarism cases that preceded it pointed to the similar structure that films shared with works of literature, plays, and other films. But judges were still left without any real tools for separating unprotectable genre conventions and themes from the original material in each new film. A decade after the Harold Lloyd trial, another case, this one involving the hard-boiled detective novelist James M. Cain and Universal Studios, introduced one of the most powerful tools that courts have developed for separating common genre elements (ideas) from original contributions (expression): the *scènes à fair* doctrine.[58]

The case between Cain and Universal began in 1938. In the mid-1930s, James M. Cain wrote several novels that would eventually become Hollywood films, including *The Postman Always Rings Twice* (adapted to film six times to date) and *Serenade*. But he was having trouble establishing himself as a Hollywood writer. In 1938, however, Cain had some mild success in the film business. First, independent producer Walter Wanger hired him to work on the dialogue for a few scripts, and then Cain sold an unpublished story, titled "Modern Cinderella," to Universal to be adapted to film.

FIGURE 2.10 The "church scene" from *When Tomorrow Comes* (1939). Infringing or just typical?

Cain's story sat in a drawer for months, which is not unusual in Hollywood. But when another Universal film, *Love Affair* (1939), found box office success by pairing Charles Boyer and Irene Dunne in a sweeping romance, the studio seized on Cain's story as a chance to quickly reprise its hit formula. Universal's director John Stahl turned the Cain story into another Boyer-Dunne vehicle called *When Tomorrow Comes* (1939) (fig. 2.10).

Film critics immediately recognized the studio's attempt to repeat a successful formula. One reviewer wrote that, "It is the kind of tale made possible, but not excused, by Charles Boyer and Irene Dunne's attempt to repeat, for the matinee trade, the type of star-crossed romance more happily expressed a few months back in *Love Affair*." The same reviewer went on to call Hollywood studios "mental laggard[s]" for consistently repeating any formula that seems to work at the box office. *New York Times* critic Bosley Crowther was less kind. He noted in his roundup of the year's worst films that *When Tomorrow Comes* attempted "to recapture the beautiful heartbreak of *Love Affair*, but only succeeded in being silly. Everyone felt most embarrassed for [Boyer and Dunne]." Indeed, *When Tomorrow Comes* gained the highest honor for an overblown Hollywood weepy when the great auteur of melodramatic camp, Douglas Sirk, remade the film in 1957, the first of two remakes of *When Tomorrow Comes*.[59]

While the critics recognized *When Tomorrow Comes* as a new incarnation of the *Love Affair* formula, Cain thought a different work had been plagiarized. He had the audacity to claim that one scene in this adaptation of his own story infringed a scene in his novel *Serenade*, which Universal had not paid for the right to adapt to the screen. Cain's attack on his own work grew out of his and other writers' frustration with Hollywood's dismissive treatment of writers, who were paid for their labor but generally cut out of both the creative process and financial rewards of the film industry.

The issue in this case was not access. Many writers, both credited and uncredited, had worked on the film, and at least one of them admitted to having read *Serenade* when it first appeared. The question that remained was whether the so-called "church scene" in *When Tomorrow Comes* copied the original expression in the church scene in the novel *Serenade*. There was of course a paradox that would have complicated the case for an average viewer: the screenwriters of *When Tomorrow Comes* were creating a Cain-like script based on an original Cain story. The creative genius behind the plaintiff's novel and the defendant's film were one and the same. But Judge Leon Yankwich ignored this paradox, and he treated the novel and film as if they were by different James M. Cains.

Judge Yankwich was an influential legal scholar, and he published several widely cited articles on intellectual property law. He knew the difficulties other courts had wrestled with when deciding film adaptation cases. In the *Cain* case, Yankwich compared the scene in the book and film, which both entailed lovers taking refuge in a church while a storm brewed around them. Yankwich found the two scenes so dissimilar that he could not understand "how anyone could persuade himself that the one was borrowed from the other." Why did he have this impression? He searched for both an explanation and a broader tool that other courts could use. The details shared by the two scenes—playing a piano, praying, hunger— Yankwich reasoned, were all inevitable outcomes of putting two characters in the same situation. Once two lovers sought refuge from the inclement weather in a church, they were likely to engage in some of the same activities and experience some of the same emotions. Yankwich borrowed a dramaturgical term to explain the phenomenon: *scènes à fair*.[60]

Judge Yankwich cited the long list of cases that had considered film plots that resembled books, stories, or other films. Courts had consistently concluded that the shared plots and even shared details were not original to any story; they were so old that no one could own them. Yet no decision had yet articulated how judges and juries could separate the age-old elements and inescapable formulas from the original contributions. Drawing on the *scènes à fair* concept allowed Yankwich to explain the reasons for the similarities: storytelling logic dictated that some genres inevitably contain the same plots, characters, circumstances, and themes. Certain circumstances necessitate specific follow-up scenes. Some scenes demanded that characters experience specific emotions or perform specific actions. Yankwich continued to develop the *scènes à fair* doctrine in subsequent film cases, and eventually every federal court district adopted *scènes à fair* as an important test of similarity. Yankwich had helped to define the bottomless terms of genre storytelling for courts and for Hollywood filmmakers, who now had a logical tool for determining if a film took too much from another story.[61]

The outcome of the case, however, did not satisfy James M. Cain. Cain and many of his fellow writers continued to feel that they had been treated poorly by both Hollywood and the court system. The relationship between novelists, playwrights, and Hollywood was symbiotic. Hollywood had relied on book and play rights for source material since the *Ben-Hur* case made the studios liable for infringing the rights of authors. The studios' demand for pretested stories in the form of popular books and plays to help predict films' successes only grew larger in the decades between the *Ben-Hur* and *Cain* cases. Writers, in turn, had also come to rely on the studios' largess for support. By 1925, motion picture rights averaged $5,000 for books and $20,000 for plays. Moreover, one third of Broadway financing came from Hollywood, and in most instances, Hollywood deals added up to more than initial book sales and theater returns. Although Hollywood money invigorated Broadway and some sectors of the publishing industry, writers felt that their contributions were undervalued, and in the 1920s and 1930s, authors began to fight for their share of the new Hollywood pot of gold. Writers objected to the standard practice of studios buying film rights outright for one lump sum. The authors lost all of their creative control, and they were unable to cash in if they wrote a hit. Throughout the 1920s and 1930s, playwrights and novelists fought to license their work under terms that would allow them to share in the profits, though very few actually had that chance. Writer-director Preston Sturges was one of the handful of screenwriters to be given a share of the gross profits when he struck such a deal for *The Power and the Glory* (1933).[62]

Novelists, playwrights, and screenwriters tried to wrest some control from Hollywood under the auspices of the general writers' union, the Authors' League. In 1914, writers formed the Photoplay Authors' League, which began registering script ideas and publishing screenplays in order to secure copyright protection before the works were sold to the studios.

The league also sought to handle grievances without the intervention of the law. In 1926, playwrights struck a large victory when they successfully established a collective licensing agency in what was called the Minimum Basic Agreement. The agreement designated a law firm to negotiate dramatic and motion picture rights, and it even gave playwrights some creative control over casting, direction, and set design. The newly formed Screen Writers Guild (later the Writers Guild of America) took its cue from the Authors' League and from New York playwrights. The Screen Writers Guild began to set general terms for film rights and screen credit, and allowed writers to register titles, ideas, and scripts in order to preempt the copyright registration system. The Screen Writers Guild also used its registration system and collective power to negotiate disputes between writers or between writers and producers. Like the Production Code Administration, which regulated film content in order to avoid censorship, the Screen Writers Guild regulated disputes about originality in order to avoid the uncertainties and expense of the court system. Today, the Writers Guild of America has an elaborate method for policing writers' disputes over credit or compensation.[63]

Despite the steps taken by writers toward collective assertion of their rights, Cain feared that writers were still not receiving their due. After losing his case against Universal, Cain continued to brood about Hollywood's unjust treatment of writers. His frustration only grew when he witnessed the unauthorized adaptation of his novel *The Postman Always Rings Twice* by Italian director Luchino Visconti in 1943. Cain also wrangled with studios over the adaptation of several of his novels into a string of films noir, including *Double Indemnity* (1944), *Mildred Pierce* (1945), and *The Postman Always Rings Twice* (1946). As Cain told the *Los Angeles Times*, his "adversaries are magazine editors, book publishers, radio sponsors, movie producers, the United States Government, the Superior Court of Los Angeles and Judge Leon Yankwich." As the list suggests, Cain mixed a personal vendetta against Yankwich with an attack on everyone he perceived to be preventing authors from receiving their proper compensation from movie production.[64]

In 1946, Cain began a large-scale lobbying effort to reorganize American writers. He proposed a new organization, the American Authors' Authority, which would have subsumed the many U.S. writers' associations and guilds in order to control all publishing and ancillary rights, "DURING THE WHOLE LIFE OF THE COPYRIGHT!" Cain emphasized. He envisioned a central authority like the American Society of Composers, Authors, and Publishers (ASCAP) that would not only control all rights and licenses but would also be able to aggressively protect authors in court. When explaining the motivation for the plan, Cain openly reflected on his days sitting in court before Judge Yankwich and the lack of support he had from other writers. The Writers Guild enthusiastically endorsed the Cain plan, and it seemed poised to reorganize literary copyright and film rights.[65]

In response to Cain's proposal, the movie studios, publishing houses, and play producers—everyone Cain thought was out to get writers—founded their own organization, the American Writers Association. The group effectively labeled the Cain plan "dictatorial and monopolistic and the brainchild of Communists and their fellow travelers." Byron Price, a former vice president of the Motion Picture Association of America and an assistant secretary general of the United Nations, called the plan "a dictatorship of copyright" that would require writers to act "precisely as writers did under Hitler." The red-baiting and fascist-baiting proved successful, and the Cain plan died after months of intense public debate.[66]

This story is familiar in copyright history: two groups with very official-sounding names argue for changes to the system of rights handling, both claiming to speak for authors. But the definition of authorship was precisely the issue at stake, even more than money, credit, and control. Movie producers treated writers as technicians. Until the adoption of a 1932 Code of Practice, screenwriters were regularly listed in the credits with the set decorators and electricians.[67] The producers bought novels, plays, and screenplays as the raw material on which to build a film. They often hired a dozen credited and uncredited writers to rework the story and dialogue, as Universal did with *When Tomorrow Comes*. According to this model, writers deserved to be paid once for the labor they put into crafting their initial ideas, which were then turned into something else entirely.

From Cain's perspective—a perspective shared by many writers—novelists, playwrights, and screenwriters create new and original work; they deserve fidelity to their vision and continued compensation for any creations built on top of their work. From this theory of authorship, a royalty system is preferable to one-time payments. Under this theory of authorship, writers deserve to be compensated for the work built upon their writing, not just the labor that went into producing the initial product.

In the 1930s and indeed even today, the answer arrived at by studios, agents, and writers falls somewhere between the two poles. Most literary works are licensed to producers or studios for a one-time fee. But some authors and their works, if they have enough market value or brand recognition, are able to ask for a share in the success of films based upon their writing. Hollywood authorship exists as a spectrum—one that is constantly in flux and always under siege—rather than as a single, unchanging entity. Significantly, it is a model of authorship that is internally regulated by talent guilds and studios and through collective agreements and union arbitration rather than through the court system. Cain's specific plan for an all-encompassing and all-powerful writers union may have been squashed by Hollywood, but screenwriters and Hollywood studios did manage to bring the regulation of credit and compensation in-house, as it were, preempting much of the intervention of courts and legislation.

EAST COAST JUDGES AND THE LIMITS OF GENRE

While California courts used cases like Lloyd's and Cain's to open the door for film studios to build on familiar plotlines as freely as possible, East Coast courts pushed that door closed with equal force. On the two coasts, we can trace a simultaneous though divergent development of judicial thinking about how to apply the idea/expression dichotomy to film. The Second Circuit Court of Appeals had traditionally been the home of copyright cases that involved New York writers, publishing houses, Broadway, and the early film industry. The judges who sat on the Second Circuit were suspicious of the abundance of film plagiarism suits. On one hand, writers were clearly attempting to capitalize on the Hollywood boom by launching questionable lawsuits. One Second Circuit judge who was tired of hearing weak copyright cases, John Woolsey, liked to boast that he had initiated the practice of making plaintiffs pay the defendant's legal fees in specious plagiarism cases.[68] On the other hand, the East Coast judges were concerned that Hollywood was getting away with too much, and it was another judge on the Second Circuit, the storied Judge Learned Hand (fig. 2.11), who continually worked to correct Hollywood's profligate recycling of literature and drama. As copyright scholar Siva Vaidhyanathan assesses Hand's influence, "No jurist or legal scholar has had a greater effect on the business and content of American culture than Judge Learned Hand."[69] In a series of important copyright cases, Hand and his fellow judges forced film studios to be weary of the use of familiar plots and characters.

In a 1917 case, Learned Hand took his first swipe at other judges' growing penchant for letting film studios off the hook in plagiarism cases. The Mutual Company attempted to purchase the rights to adapt New York reporter Robert Stodart's play *The Woodsman* (1911) to the screen, which two

FIGURE 2.11 Judge Learned Hand, whose aesthetic sensibilities helped to introduce more subtlety into film copyright opinions.

Mutual actors-turned-directors made into the film *The Strength of Donald MacKenzie* (1916). The only problem with the deal was that Mutual inadvertently bought the rights from someone who had not properly secured them from Stodart. When Stodart sued Mutual, the film company decided that although it had initially sought permission, it did not really need it.

Attempting to build on the success of film companies in other plagiarism cases, Mutual's lawyers argued that the Stodart play and the Mutual film both drew from the same public domain plot elements. Although the play and film were similar, Mutual's lawyers argued, one was not an adaptation of the other.[70]

Learned Hand seemed to agree that the play's plot was "trite and conventional in the extreme." Hand, however, made it a point throughout his career on the bench to defend even the mild originality of the least artistic works. In this case, he found originality added to the plot through "the setting of the scenes, all of which are out of doors and in the supposed local color." After reading the play and viewing the film, Hand had no doubt that, "the moving picture play is without question a direct copy from this plot almost in its entirety."[71]

In a formula that Hand would rework in other cases, he wrote: "A man may take an old story and work it over, and if another copies, not only what is old, but what the author has added to it when he worked it up, the copyright is infringed." In this case, Mutual had taken more than the basic plot, which might have been too generic to be protected by copyright. Mutual had also taken Stodart's minor additions, and the law protected those additions.

In an effort to protect writers from the rapidly growing Hollywood story mill, Hand set the bar of originality much lower than judges who heard similar cases on the West Coast. But when Hand reheard *Stodart v. Mutual*, he decided to temper his initial decision and reduce the award he had granted Stodart the first time from $900 to $500 with $300 in court fees. Hand wanted to protect writers in this new environment, but he also wanted to accurately gauge the contribution of literature to the films that adapted it.

Now *Stodart* v. *Mutual* might seem like an unusual case; it was based on Mutual being swindled into thinking it had acquired the rights to the original play. A malicious deception lay at the bottom of the story. But the case was no aberration in the Second Circuit's development of its approach to Hollywood storytelling.

In a widely publicized 1930 case, Hand reformulated his position on plots and plagiarism at the same time that California courts were considering the Charlie Chaplin and Harold Lloyd cases. In the case before Hand and the Second Circuit Court of Appeals, playwright Anne Nichols claimed that Universal's film *The Cohens and the Kellys* (1926) (fig. 2.12) had plagiarized her successful play *Abie's Irish Rose* (1922). Nichols's play told a story about Jewish and Irish intermarriage, and Hand ultimately took the position that Universal, though possibly encouraged by Nichols's success with the theme of ethnic intermarriage, merely took the stock characters and situations. Fifteen years later, with Judge Yankwich's help, Hand might have referred to the characters and situations as *scènes à fair*.[72]

On its face, this case reaffirmed the growing defense of Hollywood against the barrage of plagiarism suits. But Hand was careful to point out that this case was the exception not the norm. The Second Circuit, he noted, had a strong history of finding that plagiarists had taken too much from the plots of other writers. Noting a series of cases that included *Stodart* v. *Mutual*, Hand declared, "We did not . . . hold that a plagiarist was never liable for stealing a plot." "We do not doubt," he continued, "that two plays may correspond in plot closely enough for infringement. . . . Nor need we hold that the same may not be true as to the characters, quite

FIGURE 2.12 *The Cohens and Kelleys in Atlantic City* (1929).

FIGURE 2.13 Joan Crawford in *Letty Lynton* (1932), a film which has been out of distribution since 1936 when Judge Learned Hand found that it infringed the copyright of the play *Dishonored Lady*.

independently of 'plot' proper." In *Nichols* v. *Universal*, Hand was laying the groundwork for a redefinition of the courts' methods for comparing literature and film.[73]

Hand finally had a chance to demonstrate how plots could be plagiarized in another high-profile case that he decided in 1936. The case involved an MGM (Metro-Goldwyn-Mayer) film, *Letty Lynton*, starring Joan Crawford and Robert Montgomery, although the real stars of the film were Crawford's dresses (fig. 2.13). MGM costume designer Gilbert Adrian's retro-Victorian gown designs for the film sold half a million imitations in only a few months and began a new romantic Victorian revival among Parisian designers. As one commentator noted, the dresses for the film made Crawford into "the most copied girl in the world." That is, until Hand had the film withdrawn from circulation.[74]

The film *Letty Lynton* had many antecedents. It was based in part on a famous nineteenth-century murder case in which a wealthy young woman from Glasgow, Madeline Smith, was accused of murdering her lover. The story was the subject of many newspaper accounts, and later it was the subject of a play, *Dishonored Lady* (1930), and a novel, *Letty Lynton* (1931). MGM producer Irving Thalberg first attempted to acquire the rights to the play, but objections to the sexual content from Will Hays and the motion picture Production Code Administration kept MGM from finalizing the deal. Thalberg, however, successfully acquired the rights to the novel, which he then had a team of writers turn into the screenplay for the film *Letty Lynton*.

In the *Letty Lynton* case, Hollywood's model for identifying and protecting ideas was on trial. Clearly the facts of the original murder were in the public domain, and Thalberg could have instructed scriptwriters to create their own original treatment. But for both marketing and legal reasons, the studio sought to acquire the rights to the novel or play. Studio producers like to build on tested material, and studio lawyers prefer a paper trail that demonstrates the origins of the idea in order to discourage copyright lawsuits from alternate sources.

Learned Hand was a great copyright jurist because he had a keen aesthetic sense. In the *Letty Lynton* case, Hand read the play and novel, and he watched the film closely. In one of the most eloquent and intentionally humorous decisions in copyright history, Hand relished retelling the lascivious and tawdry details of the story as each work related them. He acknowledged that the story of Madeline Smith was in the public domain, but he also noted that the dramatic elements added by the playwright and novelist could be protected by their copyrights. The screenwriters had all seen the play, so access did not need to be proven. Hand found that the film's writers had taken small but significant elements from the play, elements that did not exist in either the novel or the facts of the historical case. Hand reiterated what Second Circuit decisions had been claiming for years: an author does have a right to the details of his or her plot, and those rights can be (and in this case had been) infringed.[75]

As he did in the *Stodart* case, however, Hand also made sure to temper his ruling in the *Letty Lynton* case by carefully weighing the financial penalty for infringement. The 1936 decision was not the end of *Letty Lynton*'s legal story. The case went on for another four years as courts, including the Supreme Court, weighed the damages in the case. The trial court had awarded the entire profits of the film to playwrights Edward Sheldon and Margaret Barnes, and the court appointed a special representative to take an accounting of the film's profits. Upon rehearing the case, however, Hand noted that the screenwriters may have plagiarized the play's plot, but the play was only one of the many creative elements that went into making the film. The stars and the design of the film were also important. According to Hand, they accounted for approximately 80 percent of the value of the film, leaving one-fifth for the writers' contribution. The Screen Writers Guild and the studios had been haggling over the value of a story for decades, and here they had a legally binding formula.[76] The Second Circuit had increased the power of writers to protect their works from Hollywood appropriation with one hand, and they limited that new power with the other.

The film *Letty Lynton* has never been legally distributed since Hand's 1936 decision. But the story of Madeline Smith continued to be retold. Once *Letty Lynton*, the unauthorized partial adaptation of Sheldon and Barnes's play *Dishonored Lady*, had been removed from circulation, Sheldon was free to sell the rights to another studio. A decade later, Sheldon wrote the screenplay for a 1947 screen version of *Dishonored Lady* himself. The story of Madeline Smith also remained in the public domain, and David Lean made a film of the historical incident in 1950, *Madeline*, without acquiring the rights to the play, the novel, or the earlier film. The retelling of Madeline Smith's tale went on, but Hand signaled that a new era of close textual analysis would determine how works could be adapted. And as we will see in the next section of this chapter, Hollywood took further steps to ensure that the financial stability of its industry would not rest on the aesthetic sensibilities of a few judges, regardless of which coast they resided on.

PROTECTING IDEAS IN HOLLYWOOD

New York and Los Angeles writers, lawyers, and studio executives followed the *Letty Lynton* trial closely, and every turn in the case drew newspaper headlines in both cities. While the *Letty Lynton* case wound its way through the court system, Hollywood studios continued to field an onslaught of lawsuits from novelists, playwrights, screenwriters, and anyone who had submitted movie ideas or scripts. In one high-profile case, a magazine writer, Robert Sheets, accused William Faulkner and Twentieth Century Fox of plagiarizing his magazine story when writing the film *Road to Glory* (1937). The case dragged on for five weeks before the studios demonstrated that they had produced their script before the publication of Sheets's story and thus could not have plagiarized it. Although the studios generally won similar cases, the plethora of newspaper headlines promising million-dollar rewards in plagiarism cases seemed only to increase the number of lawsuits. Whenever they could, studios intimidated writers into backing down, but in most instances studios continued to settle plagiarism suits out of court. In rare cases, like the Sheets case, the studios fought protracted court battles. Every option, however, proved expensive and unpredictable.[77]

While the studios and writers fought plagiarism lawsuits, they were also engaged in heated and divisive labor disputes. Throughout the 1930s, the Screen Writers Guild continued to build its membership and push for better terms for writers. The Hollywood moguls responded by working equally hard to break up the guild. At one point the studio heads attempted to start their own rival organization, which would have been friendlier to studio terms. Some of the moguls even spread rumors about the guild to foment fears of communist infiltration into Hollywood, going so far as to inform J. Edgar Hoover about links between members of the guild and the Communist Party. The moguls had almost succeeded in crushing the Screen Writers Guild when, in 1937, the National Labor Relations Board (NLRB) rejuvenated it by officially finding that the producers had joined in a conspiracy to suppress the guild.[78]

After *Letty Lynton* and the NLRB's report, the tides began to shift in favor of writers, and we can detect interrelated changes in courts' approaches to plagiarism, in Hollywood labor relations, and in the traffic in stories and ideas. Over the next twenty years, the loose genre system in which filmmakers could liberally build on the storytelling traditions established by writers, dramatists, and other filmmakers was replaced by an environment of extreme caution, circumscribed by a pervasive contract system. Every creative interaction became a careful legal negotiation.

Harold Lloyd—no stranger to copyright suits—launched the case that signaled that California courts would begin to follow the Second Circuit's lead and examine plot details much more carefully. The legal debates over story and idea protection had generally pitted writers against film studios. The studios functioned as an oligopoly and preferred to settle their internal disputes out of court (there are surprisingly few copyright lawsuits between studios before the 1950s). But Lloyd was an independent producer who owned his own copyrights, and in the early 1940s Lloyd broke the unspoken code and made the unusual decision to launch three lawsuits against Universal for plagiarizing sequences of his films. Like the *Letty Lynton* case, these new Harold Lloyd cases demanded that judges sift through plots with a fine comb, and in the first case to come to trial, Lloyd won his lawsuit. The three judges who heard the case viewed Lloyd's film *Movie Crazy* (1932) and Universal's film *So's Your Uncle* (1943). In a scene that took place in a restaurant, the Universal film clearly used many gags that could also be found in Lloyd's film. But was this a case of *scènes à fair*— two comedies that naturally resembled each other because they involved fake identities and restaurants—or was it a case in which the string of gags adhered so closely that one film infringed the other? Thanks to judges Yankwich and Hand, the judges in *Universal* v. *Lloyd* had powerful critical tools at their disposal. In this case, they decided that Universal not only used the same gags as Lloyd, but the Universal film used them in the same order. A gag might be difficult to protect, but a sequence of them could be protected. Like *Letty Lynton*, this was a case of the plot, or a piece of the plot, being copied wholesale. The new *Lloyd* case announced to Hollywood that the legal interpretation of plagiarism had changed; filmmakers had to be much more careful about how they adapted ideas from literature, theater, and other filmmakers.[79]

The lesson that Hollywood learned from the James M. Cain, *Letty Lynton*, and Harold Lloyd cases, however, was not aesthetic; it was not about how to read ideas and expression more closely. While the judges in these cases used their decisions to model close reading and to limit the measurement of writers' contributions, the studios responded by spending the next twenty years revising the procedures they used for accepting scripts, purchasing rights, and dealing with screenwriters. Studios wanted to prevent another *Letty Lynton* case, not win one. The idea/expression dichotomy had become too fine a legal point on which to risk a major film, and in a new series of cases, studios and writers fought over how they would use contracts to legally traffic in story ideas. These were boom years for Hollywood agents and lawyers.

The first case that signaled the new importance of contracts was really a California sequel to the *Letty Lynton* case. *Letty Lynton*'s producer Irving Thalberg died in 1936, shortly after Hand's first *Letty Lynton* decision. Thalberg's treatment of screenwriters, however, was on trial again shortly after his death. This time a California court evaluated Thalberg's handling of a script that two writers had submitted to him for the Marx Brothers' film, *A Day at the Races* (1937). Thalberg and MGM had just lost the *Letty Lynton* case, and the *Day at the Races* case was the Marx Brothers' third plagiarism lawsuit in two years. In this case, we can see the legal protection of writers emerging out of their mistreatment in the old Hollywood system.

Although Thalberg had a reputation as the most literate of Hollywood producers, he did not see screenwriters as writers. More than that, Thalberg led the moguls' push to suppress the Screen Writers Guild: he actively worked with the FBI to identify the guild's Communist Party ties; he unofficially blacklisted guild members, refusing to employ them at MGM; and he helped to start the short-lived rival screenwriters union. Thalberg treated writers as laborers mining good ideas to be incorporated into films. Writers, for Thalberg, were technicians, not artists. He had hired five teams of writers to work on the Marx Brothers' first MGM film, *A Night at the Opera* (1935), one writing gags, another working on the plot, etc. And Thalberg also hired several teams of writers to work on the Marx Brothers' next film, *A Day at the Races*. When Thalberg's secretary received a potential Marx Brothers' script from two writers, she gave the script to Thalberg, who kept it in his possession for several months before returning it to the writers. The two writers were neither credited nor compensated for their work on the film, and they sued. The judge found many similarities between the script and the final film, and with lessons learned from Learned Hand's *Letty Lynton* decision, he decided the case in favor of the screenwriters. MGM, Thalberg, and the Marx Brothers lost their case. Producers and especially studio secretaries would no longer be so careless about their receipt and handling of stories and ideas.[80]

The post–*Letty Lynton* legal environment made it especially difficult for Hollywood studios to manage the volume of idea and script submissions. Producer Dore Schary estimated that by the late 1950s a studio typically received 20,000 story ideas a year from which they made twenty films.[81] The new legal environment also complicated the creative process that called on dozens of writers to work on a single script. Studios were forced to refine their methods for receiving and reviewing scripts, and in the 1940s and 1950s Hollywood became enmeshed in a world of contracts. The proliferation of contracts clarified the exchange between writers and studios, and the reinvigorated Screen Writers Guild negotiated to gain better

FIGURE 2.14 Billy Wilder's *Ace in the Hole* (1951), which changed contract policies in Hollywood.

contract terms for writers. But the rise of contracts also brought idea protection into the equation. Although copyright law cannot protect ideas, Hollywood was soon to learn that contracts can.

The California Supreme Court worked out the contours of idea protection through contracts in the 1940s and 1950s, culminating in a dispute over the idea behind Billy Wilder's 1951 film, *Ace in the Hole* (aka *The Big Carnival*). *Ace in the Hole* (fig. 2.14) tells the story of miners caught in a cave-in and the ensuing media circus. The plot was ripped from the headlines, based on a real event that took place in the 1920s. Copyright law cannot protect the events and facts of the story or even the idea of making a film based on a real story. But can a contract—even an implied contract—protect an idea? In *Desny* v. *Wilder* the court considered the full extent of this rising jurisprudential question.

The *Desny* case began when fledgling screenwriter and actor Victor Desny called Billy Wilder's office, wanting to pitch an idea to Wilder based on a true story. Desny described his idea to the secretary, Rosella Stewart, who took it down in shorthand. Before they hung up, Stewart assured the struggling screenwriter that if Wilder used the idea, he would, of course, be compensated. She may have said these things in passing, but the California Supreme Court thought that the conversation equaled an implied contract. The court ruled that Desny had a legal basis for his case to go to trial, and if a trial jury found that Wilder made a film based on Desny's idea, then he should be compensated as promised. Wilder, Paramount, and several other studios protested in *amicus* (friend of the court) briefs that ideas were free to be used and could not be protected by a contract. But the court disagreed. Ideas could be taken freely, used, and built upon, but they could also be controlled through contracts. The contractual ownership and control of ideas did not interfere with First Amendment rights or the public interest because other filmmakers were still free to make films based on the idea. The contract did not suppress the idea or give Desny a monopoly on its use; it simply prevented Wilder from using the idea without compensating Desny as his secretary had promised. Only five days before the case would have gone to trial, Wilder and Desny settled out of court. We will never have a court's opinion about whether Wilder stole Desny's idea. But the California Supreme Court's initial ruling in the case established a precedent for film ideas to be controlled through contracts. As Eric Hoyt points out in a detailed account of the case, the *Desny* decision left an indelible mark on the studio system. The Writers Guild of America incorporated the *Desny* victory into its 1966 Memorandum of Minimum Basic Agreement, and the *Desny* case continues to be used widely as precedent in disputes between writers and studios. One popular current guide to copyright law designed for independent filmmakers, Michael Donaldson's *Copyright and Clearance*, launches into a summary of the *Desny* case in the first few pages of the book. The half century of filmmakers freely building on existing art forms and exchanging ideas with other filmmakers had come to an end.[82]

Idea protection allowed writers some added protection against the studio behemoth. But, for the most part, studio legal departments were able to draft contracts and establish procedures for receiving scripts that protected them against suits like Desny's. And, of course, studio employees learned not to promise anything over the phone. There are a handful of famous subsequent cases in which writers or studio insiders have successfully defended their rights to ideas. Producer Julian Blaustein, for example, successfully defended his claim that he should be compensated for suggesting that Franco Zeffirelli cast newlyweds Elizabeth Taylor and Richard Burton in a film adaptation of *The Taming of the Shrew* (1967). And, in 1990, humorist Art Buchwald won a very high-profile lawsuit against Paramount for violating a contract relating to his story treatment for a film idea made into the Eddie Murphy vehicle *Coming to America* (1988).[83] But these are the exceptions—cases in which creators won contract disputes. The attention paid to the few exceptions further demonstrates just how thoroughly the studio system has been able to use contracts to control the flow of ideas in Hollywood.[84]

Copyright law's hold on American popular entertainment had come full circle.[85] Before the invention of film, courts shunned vaudeville acts as beneath the law, and vaudeville performers learned to self-police their industry through mutual surveillance and professional ethics. After fifty years of fighting to define the place of film in copyright law, the film industry had similarly learned to avoid courts through a watertight system of exchange based on contracts. The Writers Guild of America also learned to regulate the disputes between its members and between studios and writers. Rather than allowing judges to exercise their aesthetic judgment in copyright cases or leave credit and compensation in the hands of the studios, the Writers Guild instituted a thorough system of peer review to settle disputes over authorship. When two or more authors disagree over the authorship of a particular film, senior members of the guild read successive drafts and determine where and when particular writers' original contributions entered the script. The reviews are governed by complicated formulae for weighing the original contributions. Dialogue, for example, is weighted more lightly than one might expect; narrative architecture is considered the real work. As Hollywood had responded to the threat of moral and political censorship by regulating itself in the 1920s and 1930s, so the industry subsequently responded to the complications and unpredictability of copyright law, internally regulating authorship and originality though contracts, talent guilds, and collective bargaining.[86]

COPYING CHARACTERS: HOLLYWOOD VERSUS TELEVISION

Media technology and copyright law, however, do not rest for long. And just as the studio system began to fix its methods of managing the flow of ideas in Hollywood, the growth of the television industry in the 1950s upset the Hollywood model of regulating authorship. Today, we think of the television industry as a part of Hollywood, which it is. But in the 1950s, the television and film businesses were distinct, and many Hollywood leaders viewed television as a threat rather than an extension of their industry. The clash between Hollywood and television took place, in part, through disputes over how to regulate the transfer of intellectual property from film to television. And after decades of fighting for the right to draw liberally on traditions of literature and drama, film studios found themselves aggrieved at television shows borrowing from their films.

A deluge of new court cases in the 1950s considered the new area of television formats: police dramas, sitcoms, westerns, etc. But in the end, courts found formats to be very similar to film genres and film ideas. The idea for a detective show or situation comedy could not be protected for the same reasons that literary and film genres could not be protected: they are the building blocks of storytelling, which cannot be owned by anyone. Formats, however, could be protected through contracts. And like the film industry, the early television industry went through a litigious period of determining how to accept and review the tens of thousands of idea and script submissions they received every year in order to insulate themselves from lawsuits.[87]

The advent of television also upset the delicate balance of labor relations in the entertainment industry. The rebroadcasting of films on television reopened the unending debate about artists' compensation. Writers, musicians, and actors were paid for a particular film, but should they be paid again when their films aired on television? Broadcast rights for new films could be settled in contracts, but what about films made before television? Radio actors had already established contracts for residual payments when their performances were rebroadcast, and Hollywood talent followed their lead. First musicians, then actors, and finally writers reached collective bargaining agreements with studios to receive residual payments when films were aired on television.[88]

Two major areas of copyright law, however, were transformed rather than reinforced by television. Both areas, surprisingly, had been broached in Charlie Chaplin's lawsuit against imitator Amador—character protection and the limits of comedic imitation. And both areas shifted the balance of plagiarism, turning film studios from defendants into copyright plaintiffs.

To some extent, fictional characters have always moved from original works to sequels and from one medium to another. Endless poets and dramatists have reworked the same gods and heroes of classical literature. Honoré de Balzac linked many of his novels into a singular fictional universe by continually reprising the same characters. The American film industry had been particularly interested in borrowing characters from popular culture and in reusing them across different films. Thomas Edison had been involved in a legal dispute over his licensing of the Buster Brown comic-strip character for a film as early as 1904, and Hollywood studios regularly used contracts to protect characters like Rin Tin Tin, Mickey Mouse, and Frankenstein, which provided the bases for ongoing series. In a typical example of industry policing in the late 1940s, MGM protected its Three Musketeers brand by using legal agreements to prevent other studios and independent producers from making films based on Alexandre Dumas's public domain story and characters.[89]

Fictional characters took on a new importance with the introduction of television. Hollywood studios were reluctant to show their films on television at first. (It took the threat of an antitrust lawsuit from the Department of Justice to finally convince some of the major studios to release their films to television.) But early on the studios saw television as an outlet for further exploiting their character-based franchises in "crossover" series—series built around characters from films. In 1954, ABC (American Broadcasting Company) began running *The Adventures of Rin Tin Tin*, featuring the popular canine character from radio and films. The same year, ABC launched Walt Disney's *Disneyland*, featuring well-known Disney characters in shorts or excerpts from feature films. The following year, Warner Bros. broke into television production with *Warner Brothers Presents*. *Warner Brothers Presents* showcased three series based on its hit films *Casablanca* (1942), *King's Row* (1942), and *Cheyenne* (1947). Did you ever wonder what happened to Rick and his Café American after Elsa left on the plane to America with Laslo? You could tune in to find out.[90]

Crossover television series flourished because Warner Bros. had laid the legal groundwork for character protection. Warner began to test the legal waters in 1948, although its case was not finally decided until 1954. The case involved a radio rather than a television program, but the case set the parameters for character protection—an area of copyright law that became extremely important for the relationship between film and television.

The Warner Bros. case involved detective novelist Dashiell Hammett and his fictional detective Sam Spade. In 1930, Hammett published *The Maltese Falcon* with Alfred A. Knopf and proceeded to sell the movie rights to Warner Bros. The studio adapted the novel to film twice, first in a pre-Code 1931 version and later in the famous 1941 version starring Humphrey Bogart as Sam Spade. Of course, Warner Bros. had Hammett and Knopf sign a detailed contract giving Warner the exclusive right to use *The Maltese Falcon* in movies, radio, and television. Hammett and Knopf, however, did not see any reason why Hammett could not continue to write about the novel's hero, Sam Spade, and sell further rights to the use of that character. So in 1946, Hammett licensed the Sam Spade character to a subsidiary of the Columbia Broadcasting System (CBS), and CBS began airing a weekly series called *The Adventures of Sam Spade*. Warner Bros.

complained that they had already purchased the radio, television, and film rights to the *Maltese Falcon*, including the Sam Spade character. Although character licensing in films had gone on since the days of Edison, this was the first case in which a defendant claimed that his or her copyright in a story also protected the characters.[91]

Judge Albert Stephens, who wrote the decision in the case, considered the contract between Hammett, Knopf, and Warner Bros. as well as literary traditions. Stephens did not have much case law to draw on. One of the few cases he cited was Learned Hand's decision in *Nichols* v. *Universal*, the *Abbie's Irish Rose* case, in which Hand had merely suggested that the possibility of character protection existed. Judge Stephens noted that in this case a major publisher and major film studio had signed a very detailed contract, one that did not mention the Sam Spade character. He noted further that "historically and presently detective fiction writers have and do carry the leading characters with their names and individualisms from one story into succeeding stories." If Warner wanted to secure the rights to the Sam Spade character, the company needed to specify that in the contract. The character existed apart from the book, and it belonged to the author unless he or she assigned that right to someone else.[92]

But the case did not end with the reading of the contract. Stephens went on to begin to delineate the scope of character protection. He wrote that in some cases "the character really constitutes the story being told." In such cases—we can imagine a character portrait like *Citizen Kane* (1941), although the decision doesn't provide an example—the right to the story and the character might be one and the same. But in other cases, like *The Maltese Falcon*, where "the character is only the chessman in the game of telling the story," the story copyright does not cover the characters as well.[93]

Thus character protection was born (or rather reborn: the precedents of both Edison and Chaplin are virtually forgotten in the case law). Subsequent cases further defined the area, and decisions about character infringement have generally hinged on the extent to which a character is sufficiently detailed and developed, and therefore embodies particular expression rather than simply evokes a generic character. In one character case, Paramount, the studio that made the Billy Wilder film *Stalag 17* (1953), sued the producers of the television show *Hogan's Heroes* (1965–1971), claiming that the television Sergeant Schultz was a plagiarism of the film Sergeant Schultz. Despite a common misconception, the television series was not a licensed crossover of the film. In the decision, surprisingly, the television producers won. The court found that the two sergeants had different dispositions and were therefore sufficiently different. They just happened to be identically named characters with similar styles of speaking and dressing who were in comedies about Second World War prisoners trying to escape from German prisoner-of-war camps. Moreover, Hogan's Heroes took place in stalag 13 not stalag 17. (Important differences, to be sure.) Paramount may have lost the case, but in a typical story of Hollywood conglomeration, the studio won in the end: Paramount ended up owning the DVD rights to Hogan's Heroes in addition to the rights to Stalag 17.[94]

Despite occasional cases like that of the two Sergeant Schultzes, Hollywood has, on the whole, effectively wielded character protection to facilitate the boom in product tie-ins, franchises, and transmedia brands. Character-protection cases have been used to protect Walt Disney characters, Star Wars characters, and Nightmare on Elm Street's Freddie Kruger, among many other characters, from imitation on television, in comic-book characters, and as figurines. Character protection has helped consolidate control of storytelling in Hollywood's hands.[95]

TELEVISION PARODY

To a certain extent, character protection has continued to close off the imitative impulse that helped comics like Stan Laurel and Harold Lloyd learn their craft by imitating Chaplin. But even as many forms of imitation have become endangered, certain types of imitation have thrived. In particular, artists have fought hard to protect imitation that allows critique and comment. In television, as in film, comedians manned the front lines of the battle.

In the early twentieth century, several vaudeville comedians had defended, with varying degrees of success, their right to parody well-known performers. But for almost forty years the parody exception in copyright law lay dormant. The hiatus ended when television shows like The Jack Benny Program (1950–1965) and Your Show of Shows (1950–1954) began to specialize in short parodic sketches, clearing the way for staple television sketch comedy shows. In the mid-1950s, film studios sued both The Jack Benny Program and Your Show of Shows for parodying popular films. The same California judge wrote both decisions; yet the two cases resulted in opposite outcomes. Jack Benny's parody of the Charles Boyer and Ingrid Bergman adaptation of the stage success Gaslight (1944) was deemed an infringement. Sid Caesar's sketch on Your Show of Shows parodying From Here to Eternity (1953) was deemed critique and comment and thus fair use. Judge James Marshall Carter, who decided both disputes, recognized these as landmark cases, helping to define the emerging relationship between film and television. What is at stake, he wrote, is "what TV may take from motion pictures for its shorter productions, and what it may not take." After decades of fighting to protect its right to borrow from literature and theater, Hollywood now aggressively pursued television programs that borrowed from films.

Why did the court come to different conclusions in each case and what was the impact on television and Hollywood?[96] In the end, both cases came down to balancing the commercial and critical impact of the new medium on the old. Film parody had emerged as a major genre of television expression, and Carter acknowledged that significant portions of original films needed to be borrowed in order to "conjure up" the work being parodied. But he qualified this claim. The parodist could not take more than he or she needed, and the parody could not replace the market for the original.

Sid Caesar's parody, titled "From Here to Obscurity," borrowed the main characters, story, and settings of *From Here to Eternity*, but it then used these elements, according to Judge Carter, as a springboard for "new, original, and different development, treatment, and expression." Jack Benny's parody of *Gaslight*, on the other hand, took too much. At first Benny's parody, titled "Autolight," seems more a part of the Hollywood system than Sid Caesar's. Benny had already established himself as a Hollywood star in such films as *Artists and Models* (1937) and *To Be or Not to Be* (1942). Moreover, Loews/MGM studio had already approved an earlier version of Benny's *Gaslight* parody. Benny originally aired a version of "Autolight" on the radio in 1945. Not only did Loews/MGM give permission, but the sketch starred *Gaslight*'s own lead, Ingrid Bergman. The studio apparently viewed the radio parody as publicity for the film. But when Benny revived his parody for television, starring Barbara Stanwyck instead of Bergman, Loews sued.[97]

What had changed in the decade between Jack Benny's two *Gaslight* parodies? The explosion of television, which Hollywood now viewed as dangerous competition, was the major shift. After viewing the original film, the radio program, and the television program, Carter found that, unlike Sid Caesar's parody, Benny's infringed Loews' copyright in the film. Where Caesar had taken just enough to conjure the original and built on it, Benny had taken too much and added too little. Carter scolded Benny for taking "the general or entire story line and development of the original with its expression, points of suspense and build up to climax." Benny, in other words, had told the whole story and made it less likely that viewers would also see the film, which, as Judge Carter noted, movie studios frequently revived every five to ten years. Moreover, and perhaps more importantly, Judge Carter did not think Benny's version was very funny. He characterized Ingrid Bergman's performance in the original radio parody as "a travesty upon her original screen role in *Gaslight*." Aesthetic judgment remained the stock in trade of judges in copyright cases—an inescapable element of comparing art and entertainment.[98]

Carter weighed the commercial value of the creative exchange between film and television against First Amendment speech protection and the importance of being able to comment on and criticize popular culture. "As for an attack on freedom," he wrote in his decision,

> we confess we have difficulty in visualizing the loss of that freedom if Benny's activities are curtailed by this decision. Instead, the decision reaffirms a principle inherent in the democratic way of life—the right to own and enjoy one's own private property without fear of appropriation by another. The concept of private ownership of literary property is equally entitled to protection and is more in danger in this proceeding than are our other freedoms.

As one legal scholar has noted, Carter viewed his job as "protect[ing] the film industry from possible destruction by television." Carter tried to strike a balance in these two parody cases between legitimate comment that built on an existing film and giving away the best of a popular film to the television audience for free, or at least for the price of watching advertisements. Carter's two decisions did not entirely clarify the legal definition of parody, but the decisions paved the way for parodic sketch shows, from the *Carol Burnett Show* to *In Living Color*.[99]

The young television industry fought to build on the success of the film industry as the young film industry had fought to build on literature and theater. Television benefited from Hollywood's decades of court battles that broadened the legal and cultural interpretation of genre, theme, and plot. Television producers and writers also benefited from Hollywood's long struggle to come to terms with writers and talent guilds over authorship and originality. With new precedents that allowed writers to separate their characters from their stories and new (though limited) latitude for parody, the American film and television industry ended a forty-year effort (one that stretched back to the *Ben-Hur* case) to expand attitudes toward copying, borrowing, and creativity.

3

AUTEURISM ON TRIAL

MORAL RIGHTS AND FILMS ON TELEVISION

THE YEAR THAT Charlie Chaplin initiated his lawsuit against the imitator Charles Amador, Chaplin's good friend and business partner, Douglas Fairbanks, launched a lawsuit of his own. Like Chaplin, Fairbanks used copyright law to increase American filmmakers' power and control over their work. The Fairbanks case involved a few films that he made at the beginning of his movie career. In a contract with the Majestic Motion Picture Company, Fairbanks had included a provision stating that the legendary D. W. Griffith was to direct all of the films in which he appeared. Griffith did indeed proceed to work on—even if he did not direct—Fairbanks's films for Majestic. After about a year, however, first Griffith and then Fairbanks left Majestic for new opportunities. Fairbanks's star rose quickly in Hollywood, and his early films began to increase in value. Majestic's owners decided to cash in on their early investment in the star. First they sold Fairbanks's early films and all of their attendant rights to the Triangle Film Corporation. Then, in 1922, Triangle attempted to sell the Leader Company the right to reedit the films into two-reel serials.

Fairbanks immediately filed for an injunction to stop the Triangle-Leader deal. He had merely been an employee of Majestic when they made the original films, and he did not hold the copyrights. Fairbanks could not stop Majestic from selling the films to Triangle. But when Triangle attempted to license the right to reedit the films, Fairbanks argued that even though he was not the copyright owner, the new versions in the less prestigious two-reel, serial format would be "detrimental to [his] standing in his profession, in that he has never appeared in a two-reel picture, but has only appeared in feature pictures of five or more reels."[1]

The panel of New York State Supreme Court justices who decided the case looked to Fairbanks's original contract with Majestic for guidance. Although the contract failed to give Fairbanks any rights in the film, it did stipulate that Griffith was to direct the films, and, moreover, the contract gave Fairbanks the right to review the final cut of his films. A few decades later, lawsuits, contracts, and industry norms determined that final cut contracts govern the initial, theatrical release of a film but not subsequent theatrical, television, or video releases. In 1922, however, Fairbanks's final cut case had virtually no judicial precedent, and there were no industry norms to invoke. Nevertheless, the court sided with Fairbanks and granted the temporary injunction. The judges decided that the contract perpetually protected Fairbanks's artistic vision; he had the right to continue to oversee the aesthetic quality of his work even after the first theatrical run of his films.[2]

The judges who heard Fairbanks's case did not offer much insight into their thought processes. They may have been responding to Fairbanks's unusual position in the film industry. His career was a contradiction, an amalgam of art and commerce. Fairbanks was a global box-office star who made prestige movies. More importantly, Fairbanks had successfully fought for creative autonomy in the studio system. After leaving Majestic, Fairbanks started his own production company, and just a few years before launching his copyright case, Fairbanks—along with Griffith, Charlie Chaplin, and Mary Pickford—cofounded United Artists, a company that gave many filmmakers control over the distribution of their films. Fairbanks was thus emerging as an independent artist in the highly collaborative, commercial and, for many, still socially suspect medium of the movie.[3]

The year 1922 also proved to be a special year for film copyright. In addition to the Fairbanks and Chaplin cases, a third case involving artistic integrity in Hollywood was launched the same year. In this case, a New York court stopped a film company from using the name of the successful writer James Oliver Curwood to advertise a film adaptation of one of his stories, agreeing with Curwood that the film so transformed his story that it no longer resembled the original at all.[4]

Whatever the reason, the court chose to protect Fairbanks from the commercial machine of the Hollywood studio system, which always finds new ways to repackage its content. The Fairbanks case is largely forgotten, but it is perhaps the first to take on what would become one of the most important, lucrative, and complicated elements of the Hollywood studio system: the licensing of residual rights. In 1922 all but a handful of avant-garde and cult films seemed destined to be forgotten after their initial theatrical runs. But with the continuous cycle of new technologies from small-gauge home film formats to television to home video to the internet, the repackaging of films for new media has continually expanded the market for Hollywood and offered new outlets for old content.

Like Fairbanks, Hollywood filmmakers have continually seen themselves as casualties of the advance of technology and commerce. They made films for one format, and then their work was changed to suit the demands of another. In the 1920s only a few filmmakers like the United Artists founders saw themselves as having enough autonomy to demand that studios remain faithful to their creative products. With the rise of the auteur theory and the attendant restructuring of the studio system in the 1960s, however, things changed. Studios gave directors increased artistic control, and they began to market directors as the sole creators behind the highly collaborative and complex process of making movies. Directors then started to view themselves as a new breed of artist whose work requires unprecedented protection against the perceived threat of new media. They launched a campaign in courts and in Congress to prevent truncated, colorized, low-resolution, or otherwise manipulated versions of their work from being distributed. And, I argue, the larger discourse of auteurism slowly began to infiltrate both the language of court decisions and the design of proposed legislation. Eventually we ended up with a regime in which film directors and even the studios themselves have been cast as victims of new media rather than, as has historically been the case, its greatest beneficiaries.

While we have many accounts of the rise of the idea of Romantic authorship and its impact on copyright law since the eighteenth century, we do not yet have a persuasive narrative about how U.S. copyright law came to treat Hollywood directors as a special category of artistic geniuses. Indeed, we still need to recognize that directors have historically been given greater protection than their counterparts in other media. It is no coincidence that the majority of U.S. cases involving the potential for moral rights (a concept and doctrine discussed below) have involved films and filmmakers. This expanded protection for Hollywood directors is a far stranger phenomenon than protections offered to novelists and playwrights. While few books or plays are written entirely in cultural and physical isolation, studio filmmaking is a highly collaborative process that requires an elaborate financial and industrial infrastructure. Moreover, the vision of a film director as an individual creator is a myth that has been perpetuated largely by the studios. American auteur cinema began as a way of competing with the popularity of European and independent films in the 1960s, and by the 1980s it had become a full-blown marketing strategy, akin to the star system. In the United States, auteurism is a phenomenon that the Hollywood studios never fully lost control over, and, as we will see below, studios have won just about every battle over film authorship. At moments in this battle for expanded rights, the studios may have briefly lost some control over auteurs like George Lucas and Steven Spielberg, but in the end the rise in protection for film directors has served largely to increase studio control over new media.[5]

WHAT ARE MORAL RIGHTS?

Before looking at film directors' campaign for expanded rights, it is necessary to describe the kinds of rights they sought. To put it simply, as the auteur theory moved from Europe to the United States, American film directors wanted the same legal rights as European directors. This is a goal that should have been impossible, because European and U.S. copyright law are built on very different foundations. Both the Continental European and Anglo-American copyright traditions emerged out of the same concern: how to protect individual creations without hampering the free flow of ideas. And until the late nineteenth century, as Jane Ginsburg has shown, Continental and Anglo-American law continued to reflect similar social and judicial ambivalence about reconciling these goals. In the end, however, the two traditions diverged sharply.[6]

Since the first U.S. Supreme Court copyright decision, *Wheaton v. Peters* (1834), American law has treated copyright as the artificial creation of governments. Copyright is an ingenious bargain devised by legislators and courts. It rewards authors and artists with a limited monopoly on their expression in order to provide an incentive for producing culture and knowledge in the first place. Once the limited time period ends, however, the work enters the public domain and becomes the property of society. From the perspective of U.S. copyright law, authors and artists do not possess any natural or inalienable connection to their work; they only have the rights bestowed on them by Congress.

A number of provisions of U.S. law serve to dissociate the creator and the copyright, reinforcing both the artificiality and fleetingness of copyright.

Under the "work for hire" doctrine, for example, companies often hold the copyrights to their employees' creations.[7] Under this doctrine, employers are legally the "authors" of their employees' work. Most film copyrights, for example, are held by studios or production companies, which become the corporate authors. Fairbanks's films were works for hire made for the Majestic Company, the copyright owner and author.

Not only can employers rather than the creators hold copyrights, but, in addition, a copyright holder may sell the copyright in his or her work to someone else, making a copyright merely another transferable commodity. The Majestic Film Company, for example, sold all of the rights in Fairbanks's films to Triangle. Triangle then attempted to license some rights to the Leader Company.

In the United States, an author may also forgo copyright's protection and rewards entirely by dedicating a work to the public domain. Before the 1909 Copyright Act, U.S. authors had to actively seek a copyright by registering their work with the U.S. Copyright Office. The default status of all works, in other words, was as part of the public domain. After the passage of the 1909 Act, creators still needed to affix a copyright notice to their work, and since the 1976 Act, all work is automatically protected by copyright if it meets the basic criteria. But creators may still use licenses to give away some or all of their rights in the work.[8]

These facets of the law reinforce the fact that U.S. copyright exists as a legal construction that can be bought, sold, traded, or dissolved. There is nothing natural, inevitable, or obvious about copyright—at least not in the Anglo-American tradition. It is based on the market-driven and culture-driven theory that rewarding authors and artists is valuable because it benefits society. In the end, however, all work is made for and eventually belongs to society at large.

French copyright law, in particular, and Continental copyright law more generally have been built on a different philosophical foundation. French law assumes that creative work flows from the personality of its creator. As a result, creators of copyrighted work retain some control over their work even after the economic rights have been given away. French law separates the economic rights from natural or moral rights (*droit moral*). Moral rights have nothing to do with morality. Instead, in this context, the term *moral rights* refers to a bundle of additional rights given to the creator of a work. Moral rights include "(1) the right of paternity, i.e. the right to be identified as the author of the work; (2) the right of integrity, i.e. the right to object to derogatory treatments of a work; (3) the right of divulgation or of dissemination, i.e. the right to decide when and how a work should be made public (including the right not to make it public); and (4) the right . . . to withdraw a work from commerce."[9] In the moral rights tradition, commerce and social benefit are ultimately secondary to the author's or artist's sacrosanct right to protect his or her creation and reputation. (A cynic might note that reputations often hold economic value as well, and it is difficult to separate moral from pecuniary rights.) When Douglas Fairbanks argued that the reediting of his films would damage his reputation, for example, he invoked the equivalent of the right of integrity. The reediting of his films, he insisted, would have damaged his reputation and gone against his intentions in making the films. The judge in the case effectively created the right of integrity for Fairbanks by finding it hidden or implied in Fairbanks's contract.

As the Fairbanks case suggests, the United States has not entirely eschewed moral rights or denigrated the status of authors and artists. U.S. law protects many of the rights contained in the moral rights bundle through related legal doctrines like libel, slander, privacy, unfair competition, and misrepresentation (known as passing off). Contracts can also be used to protect authors' rights, and in 1990 the United States adopted limited moral rights in the Visual Artists Rights Act, which excludes motion pictures. It would be too easy to oppose moral rights and U.S. copyright. What we find when we look at the legislative history and case law surrounding moral rights for filmmakers is that policymakers and judges have consistently been swayed by filmmakers' pleas for moral rights. Over and over again, courts and Congress have come to the brink of adopting moral rights for filmmakers. But, in the end, the interests of the studios have always prevailed.

CONGRESS AND HOLLYWOOD'S ROCKY RELATIONSHIP WITH MORAL RIGHTS IN THE 1930S

The Fairbanks decision came at a time when Congress was divided about moral rights and about the role of copyright in fostering international trade, two issues that have been integrally linked. Copyright and international trade policies have remained in tension largely because of the irreconcilable foundations of Anglo-American and Continental copyright law.

U.S. copyright law has always—perhaps not surprisingly—been geared toward the protection of national interests. The first U.S. Copyright Act of 1790 limited its benefits to American citizens or residents, and the law was not updated to allow foreign authors to copyright their works until 1891.

What many European authors saw as state-sanctioned piracy prevented the United States from entering the international copyright agreement, the Berne Convention for the Protection of Literary and Artistic Works, when it was first ratified in 1886. After a later revision in 1928, the member states placed pressure on the United States to join the Convention. The 1928 agreement, however, contained a significant impediment for the United States: at the suggestion of the French delegation, it included a moral rights provision.[10]

Throughout the 1930s, Congress wavered about whether or not to join the Berne Convention. Two U.S. presidents and the Register of Copyrights, Thorvald Solberg, pushed for Berne membership, and between 1930 and 1941 at least seven separate bills proposed that the United States enter into the agreement. Hollywood's leaders paid close attention to Congress's deliberations, and both the studios and the talent guilds took part in the debates over Berne membership and the adoption of moral rights in the United States.

When the issue of joining the 1928 convention came before the Senate Foreign Relations Committee, President Herbert Hoover enthusiastically expressed his support for joining. Although the bill under consideration never made it past the committee stage, a few years later the House of Representatives passed another piece of legislation, the Vestal Bill, that again called for the United States to join the Berne Convention. The Vestal Bill contained a number of provisions that would have harmonized U.S. copyright law and Continental law. The bill would have required the United States to eliminate its registration requirement, making all eligible works automatically protected by copyright at the time of their creation. The bill would also have extended the term of copyright to fifty years after the author's death.[11]

The Hollywood studios were integrally involved in the drafting of the Vestal Bill, and they supported both joining Berne and introducing moral rights into U.S. copyright law. The Vestal Bill, however, lost support in the Senate after a Democratic senator from Washington State, Clarence Dill, denounced it as un-American. Harmonization with the Berne Convention, after all, would have dramatically transformed U.S. copyright law and brought it much closer to European law. It would not be the last time that moral rights would be accused of being un-American.[12]

Congress's interest in moral rights did not end with the Vestal Bill, however. In 1934, President Franklin Roosevelt initiated a new move to join the Berne Convention when he sent the text of the agreement to the Senate, asking that they consider ratifying it. Over the next few years, the Senate

ordered studies of the issue and considered a number of drafts of a bill proposed by Senator F. Ryan Duffy, a Democrat from Wisconsin. Just a few
years after the Vestal Bill, Hollywood now opposed the Duffy Bill, Berne
membership, and moral rights.

Why did the studios change their position on Berne and moral rights?
During the brief period between the two bills, many European countries
had adopted strict tariffs and quotas on U.S. film imports, and Hollywood
moguls argued that they had little to gain by entering into an agreement
with European regulators who had grown increasingly hostile to the American film industry. The Duffy Bill also contained a number of exemptions
for charitable organizations, broadcasters, and others, which all corporate
copyright holders seemed to oppose uniformly. The biggest controversy in
Hollywood, however, surrounded the congressional testimony of screenwriter John Howard Larson, future member of the Hollywood Ten. Tes-
tifying on behalf of the Screen Writers Guild, Larson delivered a stirring
indictment of the treatment of writers in Hollywood. Larson garnered a
lot of press, and his picture of the plight of writers seemed to suggest that
screenwriters supported the adoption of moral rights. In theory at least,
moral rights legislation might have proven to be a boon to screenwriters if it allowed them to control their work after it fell into the hands of
producers, who were only interested in the bottom line. But Larson had
not been briefed on all of the details: the Duffy Bill contained a specific
exemption that would have permitted studios to alter scripts without violating the moral rights of writers. Only a few days after Larson appeared
before Congress, the Screen Writers Guild sent a follow-up letter to the
Senate clarifying that it was now opposed to the Duffy Bill.[13] Without the
support of Hollywood studios, screenwriters, and rights holders from other
industries, the Senate indefinitely deferred the Duffy Bill.

The legislative skirmishes of the 1930s proved the incompatibility of
moral rights and the Anglo-American tradition. American copyright law is
based on statutory compromise and the idea that copyright is a negotiable
commodity. Moral rights emerge from a fundamental belief in the inalienable rights of artists. Once those natural rights become subject to negotiation and compromise, they necessarily dissipate.

The Hollywood studios have supported harmonization with international copyright law when they successfully negotiated exceptions that
benefited their industry. In 1939, just for example, the studios reconsidered the advantages of moral rights on their own terms, and they sent a
delegation to a meeting of Berne members. The Hollywood representatives argued that film producers and not directors should be considered

the rightful film authors, and producers should hold moral rights in film. In the collaborative and industrial medium of film, after all, it is far from obvious who authors a film. But Hollywood's occasional support for moral rights legislation is the exception. More often, the studios have opposed harmonization, seeing it as a potential threat to their reliance on corporate ownership. [14]

SCREEN CREDIT AND THE COLD WAR

John Howard Larson's turn toward moral rights as a panacea for the mistreatment of writers in Hollywood portended the desperate situation for writers and other artists during the Cold War. During the era of the blacklist, in particular, credit for work on films became a highly contentious subject. Many blacklisted film writers, actors, and directors found their names removed from films they had worked on and were proud of. On occasion, debates about film credit were taken to court, but writers and the leaders of the talent guilds soon learned that suspected communists had trouble winning the sympathies of U.S. courts.[15]

One significant dispute about screen credit during the early years of the Cold War involved a court battle over moral rights. The case involved four of the most famous and accomplished Soviet composers, Dmitry Shostakovich, Sergey Prokofiev, Aram Khachaturian, and Nikolai Myaskovsky. Where blacklisted writers wanted credit for their work, the Soviet composers feared that having their names on a film would suggest that they were also responsible for, or at least sympathetic to, the film's ideological messages. With a blacklist in force in Hollywood and an active Stalinist culture ministry in the Soviet Union, such fears were more than justified.

In particular, the Soviet composers opposed the use of their names and music in the William Wellman–directed defection drama *Iron Curtain* (1948). Head of the Twentieth Century-Fox music department, Alfred Newman, used public domain compositions of Soviet composers throughout the film, both as incidental music on the score and within the story. The credit sequence also listed the names of the four Soviet composers. Fox released *Iron Curtain* just one year after the Hollywood Ten appeared as hostile witnesses before the House Committee on Un-American Activities. Everyone in Hollywood was fearful of being involved in a film sympathetic to communism or the Soviet Union. But Newman does not seem to have known the stakes of his musical choices in this explicitly *anti*communist picture. Although none of the four Soviet composers were working in

Hollywood, their careers were all on the line back in the Soviet Union, and one can understand their desire to protect their reputations. Shortly before the release of *Iron Curtain*, Communist Party official Andrei Zhdanov led a purge of antirealist, formal experimentation in Soviet music. The four composers Newman had selected for the soundtrack were all condemned for their allegedly anti-Soviet compositions, and the appearance of their compositions in *Iron Curtain* added fuel to the fire.[16]

The composers are unlikely to have seen the film, and it is not known if the composers initiated the case themselves or if Stalin's government launched the case in their names; the latter is more likely. Either way, the complaint claimed that the use of the composers' names and music in the film suggested that they endorsed *Iron Curtain*'s clear anticommunist message.[17]

When New York State Supreme Court Justice Edward R. Koch, who wrote the decision, came to the moral rights claims of the composers, he relied almost entirely on a speculative law review article, since moral rights case law in the United States was so thin. Koch conceded that the existence of moral rights in U.S. copyright law was unclear. If moral rights did exist, he wondered, what kind of test would be used to measure when they had been violated: "good taste, artistic worth, political beliefs, moral concepts . . . ?" Koch entertained the idea that works in the public domain might still be subject to the terms of moral rights, although other aspects of copyright law no longer pertained. The problem in this case, Koch explained, is that the Soviet composers had not invoked moral rights properly. They did not claim, for example, that Newman's score for *Iron Curtain* distorted their work; a significantly altered composition might have been a violation of the composers' rights of integrity. And they did not claim that the work had been incorrectly attributed to them, which might have been a violation of the right of paternity. Instead, the composers feared that audiences would connect them with the film's message. Justice Koch, however, believed that audiences would not assume a line in the musical credits amounted to an endorsement of the political or ideological bent of a film, and he could not see how the use of the composers' music interfered with their moral rights, whether or not those rights existed in the United States. Koch escaped having to decide how to apply the doctrine of moral rights although, significantly, he acknowledged that such rights might be applicable to U.S. copyright law.[18]

The Soviet composers also sued Fox in French court, and there they won their moral rights claim, successfully preventing the continued distribution of the film in France. In the high-stakes political climate of the Cold War,

French courts were willing to allow artists to use moral rights to control the public perception of their political sympathies. The Soviet composers' case further suggests some of the potential power of moral rights arguments and why they have been invoked so frequently in film cases. In the politically suspicious and intolerant climates of Cold War America and Stalinist Russia, reputation was too important to leave in others' hands. Moral rights promised to give individual artists some control over their names and works when the copyrights belonged to corporations or the work had entered the public domain. Even when the political stakes have been less dramatic, artists have looked to moral rights for some foothold in the collaborative and commercial world of Hollywood.[19]

SPONSORSHIP AND THE TELEVISION FRONTIER

Although moral rights did not emerge as a weapon in the reputation battles of the Cold War, they did become important in the commercial sphere, especially after the advent of television. The repackaging of films for television (and later home video) proved to be the flash point for the conflict between filmmakers who wanted to preserve the integrity of their films, and Hollywood studios, which wanted to make money by reediting films for the small screen. But Hollywood did not embrace television all at once, and it took time for actors, directors, and studio heads to negotiate the new territory of television exhibition. Moral rights surfaced as a key term in the negotiations.

As Marshall McLuhan famously noted, "the content of any medium is always another medium."[20] And so the enormous backlog of films in studio vaults should have been the natural content pool for early television. A number of factors, however, held the major studios back from releasing their films to television. At first, the studios treated television as competition rather than as a new outlet for films. Theater owners exacerbated the sense of competition by exerting enormous pressure on Hollywood not to upset their long-standing distribution contracts. Another reason that studios held off on releasing films to television is that many film industry leaders hoped that another financial model, such as subscription television, might win out over sponsored advertising. Studios also resisted the lure of television, because the networks were not in a position, at least at first, to offer sufficiently enticing sums for film broadcast rights. A final block in the road to releasing films to television were the negotiations with "talent"— the actors, directors, writers, and musicians—who all wanted and deserved compensation for the rerelease of their work. The talent had, of course, been paid for their contributions to the initial films, but how should they be compensated for the broadcast of their work in this new medium?[21]

One by one, all of the barriers preventing Hollywood from embracing television began to fall, and studios started to produce material for the small screen. Network prices for films shot up. And through collective bargaining agreements, all of the talent guilds and licensing societies eventually arranged for residual rights to be paid to their members for television exhibition of their work. But compensation was not the only labor issue that stood in the way of Hollywood's releasing its films to television. Many film stars and directors shared Douglas Fairbanks's concerns about the impact of reedited or otherwise manipulated versions of their work being prepared for display in a new medium or format. In the case of television, the medium came with a new economic model as well: sponsored advertising. And film talent worried about the interspersing of product pitches during their films.

Since the invention of television, film writers, actors, and directors have used the copyright doctrine of moral rights to assert—or at least attempt to assert—control over the use of their work on television. Screen cowboys Roy Rogers and Gene Autry blazed the trail. Rogers and Autry were the reigning cowboy film stars in the 1930s, 1940s, and 1950s, and they both made their careers at the independent Republic Studios, which specialized in B-grade westerns, action films, and serials. While the major studios held on to their films, the small Republic studio began releasing films to television as early as 1948. But when Republic announced that it was releasing Roy Rogers's film to television, "the King of the Cowboys," as Rogers was known, protested. He was not motivated entirely by a reverence for his original big screen masterpieces; the future of his career was at stake as well. In 1951, *The Roy Rogers Show* premiered on television, and Rogers viewed the Republic films as potential competition. Rogers's lawyers drew on contract law, advertising law, and the emerging legal field of publicity rights to stop Republic from selling the television rights. The lawyers argued that showing the films with sponsored advertising amounted to Roy Rogers's endorsement of the products advertised, and Republic needed Rogers's permission for that kind of promotion.[22]

Television was still relatively new, and the models for translating one medium, film, to another, television, were just being worked out. Taking a first stab at the issue, California trial and appeals courts sided with Rogers. The courts awarded Rogers a permanent injunction, halting the sale of his films to television. The courts decided that Republic needed Rogers's permission to license his films for airing on television with commercials. As the *New York Times* reported, after the Roy Rogers cases sponsors began to back away from supporting old films released to television, fearing that other actors would join Rogers's crusade.[23]

In October of 1951, Gene Autry (fig. 3.1) realized the sponsors' fears, and he filed his own suit against Republic. Like Rogers, Autry had a television show, and he reiterated Rogers's successful complaints about sponsorship. Autry added some new claims as well. Autry invoked moral rights, claiming that the pruning of his feature films to fifty-three minutes for airing with commercials in a one-hour television slot violated the integrity of his work.[24]

The judge who first heard Autry's case saw the issue differently from the judges who decided the Roy Rogers case. Judge Benjamin Harrison took Autry's suit very seriously, as one of those special cases that had the potential to determine the future of a new medium. "This case," he wrote, "presents one of the many questions constantly arising as a result of the impact of television upon the entertainment world." On the question of whether or not showing a film on television with advertisements required additional permission from the stars, Judge Harrison disagreed with the Rogers decision. Showing advertisements during a film, Harrison observed, was no different than displaying advertisements in a theater in which a film was shown. No one asked the actors' permission to display a candy ad in the theater lobby while their film was shown inside. Why should stars be allowed to control the advertising that interrupted their films on television?[25]

The conflicting Rogers and Autry decisions led to confusion in Hollywood, and negotiations between television networks and studio heads over the release of films to television stagnated.[26] The Ninth Circuit heard both the Rogers and Autry cases on appeal. On the same day in 1954, the Ninth Circuit decided both cases, and in its decisions the court paved the way for Hollywood to release films for television. Writing for the court, Judge Homer T. Bone cemented the Autry decision: Republic did not need the actors' permission either to edit their films for television or to release the films to be shown with advertising. But Judge Bone was both a former Socialist Party member and a former senator with a reputation as a corporate watchdog. In his decision, Bone left the door open for future artists to use moral rights claims in order to assert their rights in the face of corporate abuse. Republic had merely cut the films down to fifty-three minutes to be shown with seven minutes of commercials. In this instance, according to the court, Republic had not gone too far. But, Bone warned, "cutting and editing could result in *emasculating* the motion pictures so that

FIGURE 3.1 Gene Autry fought Republic Pictures for control over the integrity of his films after they were edited for television.

they would no longer contain substantially the same motion and dynamic and dramatic qualities which it was the purpose of the artist's employment to make." He warned further that "we can conceive that some such exhibitions could be so *'doctored'* as to make it appear that the artist actually endorses the products of the programs' sponsors."[27]

Bone's choice of words is telling. Both his fear of an "emasculated" work of art and of a film "doctored" to change its relationship to the advertising suggest a view of intellectual property as an extension of one's body. The foundation of at least one common view of intellectual property, derived from seventeenth-century philosopher John Locke, holds that the right of personal property stems from our relationship with our bodies. We own and expect control over our bodies, and, by extension, we expect the same rights over our personal property and possessions. The expansion of this perspective to intellectual property underlies the doctrine of moral rights as well. If intellectual property is a natural extension of one's body, then it is truly brutal to separate creative work from its maker. This Lockean theory of property continually resurfaces in both American jurisprudence and American culture more broadly, despite the fact that it contradicts the legislative bargain of Anglo-American copyright. And by linking moral rights in film with Lockean property theory, Judge Bone established the judicial formula that would eventually lead to the expansion of moral rights for filmmakers.[28]

After the Ninth Circuit's decision, the Los Angeles Times joked that television viewers should not "be surprised if Roy Rogers or Gene Autry [came] up sponsored by the makers of such feminine things as perfume."[29] Like Bone, though in a different sense, the Times reporter feared that advertising might prove a threat to the masculinity of the screen cowboys. But the Ninth Circuit's decision proved to be prescient: audiences do not assume that the actors in a particular film endorse the products advertised during its televised showing any more than they assume that a composer endorses the ideological message of a film in which his or her music is used.

With moral rights temporarily in check, film studios were free to release their films to television without fear of interference from actors or directors. As a result, Republic stopped making new films and its primary business became licensing its old films for television. And just a few months after the conclusion of the Rogers and Autry cases, the major Hollywood studios joined Republic and began releasing their backlogs of films to television networks as well. Although moral rights is rarely, if ever, mentioned in the history of the Hollywood studios' release of films to television, the decision over Gene Autry's assertion of moral rights was clearly a pivotal event in that history.[30]

AUTEURISM COMES TO AMERICA

Hollywood's embrace of television was just one element of a larger trend toward conglomeration and consolidation. During the late 1960s and early 1970s, every Hollywood studio was either acquired by a large multinational conglomerate or became a diversified communications company on its own. Television distribution, and eventually cable, home video, and internet distribution, all became part of the regular life of a feature film.[31]

At the same time that Hollywood increased its profits by exploiting new media, however, the films themselves began to lose touch with American and international audiences. A series of financially successful independent films in the late 1960s like *Easy Rider* (1969), European art films like Michelangelo Antonioni's *Blow-Up* (1966), and soft-core pornography like *I Am Curious Yellow* (1969) showed Hollywood executives that they were failing to reach the growing audience for films with mature subject matter.[32]

The studios responded to their crisis by giving much more control—both creative and financial—to individual filmmakers. On the one hand, the new power given to directors emulated the model of the European cinemas, which were gaining a foothold in American and international markets. Pioneered by the French New Wave's call for an author-oriented cinema, the European art-house circuit celebrated a gallery of great directors, from François Truffaut and Jean-Luc Godard to Ingmar Bergman and Satyajit Ray.

On the other hand, the new economic power given to individual filmmakers resulted from the transformation of the studio system. Ever since the separation of exhibition from production and distribution after the 1948 Supreme Court order, aka the Paramount Decision, Hollywood studios had been moving toward a leaner, blockbuster-driven production model. Studios comprised of stables of writers, actors, directors, and editors seemed cumbersome and bloated. The studios became primarily distributors for films made by independent production companies. In the 1950s, some of the most successful Hollywood directors, like John Ford and Fritz Lang, set up their own independent production companies, and they cut deals with the studios to distribute and often fund their films. In the 1960s, the studios set up a generation of film-school graduates with similar deals. Warner Bros., for example, gave Francis Ford Coppola the seed funds to start his American Zoetrope company, which produced such director-driven films as George Lucas's *THX1138* (1971) and Coppola's own *Apocalypse Now* (1979). Universal entered into a distribution deal with BBS, the production company that made *Easy Rider*. And Paramount started the appropriately named Directors' Company to finance the films of Coppola, William Friedkin, and Peter Bogdanovich.

The new model of the autonomous director-general in charge of the creative and commercial elements of a production coincided perfectly with the Americanization and popularization of the auteur theory in the 1960s. French critics writing for the film journal *Cahiers du cinéma* first elaborated the *politique des auteur* in the post–World War II period. They described the ability of select directors—John Ford or Howard Hawks—to infuse films with an individual worldview, despite the collaborative, factory-like system of Hollywood. The French critics then turned to filmmaking and built on their understanding of auteurism, with its focus on individual expression and creative autonomy. American film critic Andrew Sarris began to translate the *politiques des auteurs* for American readers in the 1960s. After a series of articles in the journal *Film Culture*, Sarris published his book on the auteur theory in 1968, *The American Cinema: Directors and Directions, 1929–1968*. The idea rapidly penetrated both American culture and Hollywood, and both studios and critics had a name for the new model of studio production: auteurism.[33]

The two cultures of the New Hollywood—the complex commercial machine bent on repackaging films for new media and the director-driven system of semi-independent production—were on a collision course. Moral right would be at the center of coming conflicts between directors and studios.

AUTEURISM ON TRIAL

Two of the early star directors and studio-supported independents, Otto Preminger and George Stevens, were the first to test moral rights in the nascent auteur culture. Preminger and Stevens both became marquee-worthy director-producers in the 1950s. *Los Angeles Times* gossip columnist Joyce Haber once remarked about Preminger that "his name in an ad or on a marquee is more familiar to moviegoers than those of all but our giant performers."[34]

In 1965, both Preminger and Stevens decided to take a stand against the display of films on television, resuming the battle that Autry and Rogers had begun. Preminger and Stevens, however, were not worried about their films being used to endorse products. They feared that commercial interruptions and the shortening of films for television would destroy the integrity of their carefully crafted works of art. In other words, they wanted moral rights protection against Hollywood's manipulation of films to meet the demands of the new medium.

In the 1950s, Preminger made a series of critically successful films for his own independent company, Carlyle Productions. The outspoken Preminger publicly railed against the showing of films on television, referring to commercial interruptions as "scandalous, barbaric, awful." He boasted that he successfully withheld his films *The Moon Is Blue* (1953) and *The Man with the Golden Arm* (1955) from TV, although the explicit treatment of sex and drug addiction in those films made them unlikely candidates for television in the first place. When Columbia Pictures licensed Preminger's 1959 masterpiece *Anatomy of a Murder* to be aired on ABC, Preminger opposed the sale in court. Preminger had a final-cut contract, but by this point, industry norms and court decisions had made clear that final cut did not preclude editing for television. Columbia and its TV subsidiary, Screen Gems, had acquired the television rights to the film, and Preminger's claim rested on his moral rights assertion, though he did not use that phrase explicitly. Preminger argued that the editing of his film for television would "(a) detract from the artistic merit of *Anatomy of a Murder*; (b) damage Preminger's reputation; (c) cheapen and tend to destroy *Anatomy*'s commercial value; (d) injure plaintiffs [Preminger and Carlyle Productions] in the conduct of their business; and (e) falsely represent to the public that the film shown is Preminger's film." If this were a French court, Preminger could have claimed that his rights of integrity and attribution had both been violated. Borrowing the bodily language from the Autry case, Preminger described the edited version of his film as "mutilated."[35]

Working with very little time, the New York State Supreme Court issued a temporary injunction, and ABC aired *Anatomy of a Murder* without commercials in Los Angeles and Chicago. But when the court heard the case again with more time to deliberate, Preminger lost. Justice Arthur Klein reached a conclusion similar to the Ninth Circuit's decision in the Autry case. If Preminger's 161-minute film had been cut to 100 minutes, as ABC's brochure had falsely advertised, Klein decided, "such cuts would not be minor and indeed could well be described as mutilation." But ABC's cuts were less extensive, so he allowed the edited and interrupted version to be shown. Across the country, in California, George Stevens's very similar case—involving the films *A Place in the Sun* (1951), *Something to Live For* (1952), and *Shane* (1953) (fig. 3.2)—ended with a similar conclusion.[36]

It is strange that Judge Bone in the Autry case and Justice Klein in the Preminger case both considered the amount of material cut from the original film to be the single factor that determined whether or not the integrity had been compromised. A much more valuable test would have been whether the quality or impact or aesthetic importance of the original had been compromised. Quantitative measures can only go so far in assessing the "mutilation" of an original. Eliminating a few key moments can transform a work. On the other hand, more lengthy deletions might have little effect. The numbers of minutes cited in the two cases appear almost arbitrary. A 53-minute Autry movie is acceptable; a 100-minute Preminger movie is too short. The arbitrariness of these assertions suggests that these

FIGURE 3.2 *Shane* (1953)—"mutilated" by TV editing?

judges were not willing to take on the aesthetic evaluation necessary to oversee the stewardship of moral rights, although they were willing to lay the groundwork and necessary precedent for subsequent decisions to take advantage of moral rights.

Not only did courts and the press regularly discuss reediting of films for television as "mutilation" and "dismemberment," but the public, now tutored in the auteur theory, was starting to use the same language of bodily harm. Both the judge who decided the Stevens case and an allegedly random television viewer from Reseda, California, who was interviewed by the *Los Angeles Times*, used the same word to describe the editing of films for television: "emasculation." It is also the word that Judge Bone had used in the Autry case, and with its popularization and formalization in court decisions, the reediting of films for television took on violent, gendered connotations, in addition to absorbing Lockean property theory.[37]

The Preminger and Stevens cases sent ripples through the film and television industries. The National Association of Broadcasters (NAB) began to fear an uprising of auteurs, possibly supported by the public. In 1965, while both the Preminger and Stevens cases were under way, NAB executive

Howard Bell recommended to the NAB board that they "establish some standards on frequency and placement of commercial messages" for use when showing "certain types of movies."[38] The NAB waited for the cases to be resolved, however. When the courts effectively stopped the auteurs' revolt, the NAB decided not to change their methods of sponsorship.

Responding to the Stevens and Preminger cases, director Mervyn LeRoy explained the stakes of the cases for Hollywood directors. LeRoy had been directing high-profile studio movies since the 1920s, including *Little Caesar* (1931), *Gold Diggers of 1933* (1933), *The Bad Seed* (1956), *Gypsy* (1962), and an uncredited directing stint on the *Wizard of Oz* (1939). Unlike Preminger and Stevens, however, LeRoy was willing to meet the new technology halfway. For example, he helped advertise the television showing of his film *Quo Vadis* (1951), even though it had thirty-three commercial interruptions. He even expressed a willingness to help edit his films down for television if anyone asked. What was most important to LeRoy was attribution—the assurance that people saw the films and knew who directed them. "A man makes something like a Mervyn LeRoy production," he explained, "and when its television showing is advertised, they leave out the names of the producers and directors. . . . I worked for years on *Quo Vadis*, and I want people to know who made it."[39] LeRoy and many other filmmakers feared losing credit for their work as much as they feared assuming credit for lesser versions of their films. In both scenarios, moral rights would have helped the handful of concerned directors. But, as responses from the studios and television networks make clear, moral rights law would also have hampered or at least complicated the sale of films to television.

In all of the early television cases involving moral rights, the courts chose to nurture the new medium of television by protecting studios' rights to license new versions over individual directors' rights to protect their artistic vision. Of course, Hollywood directors had been on the other end of the equation for years—fending off complaints that their films destroyed great works of literature. The irony was not lost on everyone. An opinion piece in the *New York Times* pointed out that Hollywood directors generally responded to such claims by explaining that film is an entirely different medium. But the same directors who liberally adapted novels, like Preminger and Stevens, now sought to stop the new medium of television from tarnishing their work. "Suddenly," the *Times* piece accused, "[Hollywood directors] have become worshipers at the shrine of art—their own."[40]

A FILM BY ALLEN SMITHEE

From one angle, moral rights are simply a contract issue. Neither individual directors nor the Directors Guild of America were powerful enough to demand perpetual artistic control of their work, so they hoped that the law would recognize an inalienable natural right to control their art; they hoped that moral rights would make up for their lack of negotiating power. After the many reversals in the Rogers, Autry, Stevens, and Preminger cases, however, Hollywood began to solve the issue of television editing and commercial interruptions as they had solved most copyright problems: through contracts and labor guild policies. Hollywood, in other words, kept the problems in-house and out of the courts. Directors and other film talent were required to sign contracts explicitly waiving television rights, even when the contracts gave directors final say in the editing of the theatrical release, i.e., final cut. Standard industry contracts also began to reserve for the studios the right to adapt films infinitely into the future, for "devices not yet invented or imagined," as contracts started to read.[41]

The invention of the pseudonym Allen Smithee (with varying spellings) is another example of Hollywood bringing attribution and moral rights in-house. Starting in 1969, the Directors Guild of America developed a policy for those cases in which directors were so horrified by the studio's version of their films that they wanted their names removed from it. During the Golden Age of the studio system, when directors were on annual contracts to studios and were assigned films to work on, they had no expectation of having their individual vision come through. Critics developed the auteur theory to identify the moments when directors left an individual imprint on a film, despite the factory-like process of the studio system. After the transformation of the studio system in the 1960s, however, directors, critics, and the public all began to expect films to bear the individual vision of their directors. Directors, in turn, began to take steps to protect their reputations and the integrity of their work.

It was at this moment in the late 1960s that directors began to demand that their names be removed from films when they lost control of their vision. Starting with the film *Death of a Gunfighter* (1969) (fig. 3.3), the Directors Guild formed a board to arbitrate disputes over credit and anonymity. Directors could now appeal to the board, which had the power to decide that a director's work had been so distorted that he or she had the option of having his or her name removed and replaced with the pseudonym Allen Smithee (or some variation). Directors could

FIGURE 3.3 *Death of a Gunfighter* (1969), the first film to carry the Allen Smithee credit.

always have used pseudonyms. But as a shared pseudonym, the Allen Smithee designation also served as a marker of tensions between directors' and studios' intentions. The Allen Smithee pseudonym served as an extralegal compromise to the moral rights dilemma. Directors could withdraw their name from a distorted work, but the studio could still profit from the work. In some ways, the Allen Smithee solution is more effective than the legal version of moral rights. Moral rights might have allowed a director to withdraw a work from circulation. But the Smithee credit and the often well-publicized battles that surrounded its adoption publicly announced the integrity of the directors and often pointed audiences toward the inevitable release of the authentic version, the director's cut.[42]

The directors who have taken advantage of the Allen Smithee option have invariably come from the generation reared in the auteurist New Hollywood of the late 1960s and 1970s: Robert Altman, William Friedkin, Dennis Hopper, and many others. And it will be no surprise that directors have frequently petitioned for an Allen Smithee credit when they have been unhappy with the versions of their films that studios reedited for television. Friedkin (*The Guardian*, 1990), Hopper (*Backtrack*, 1990), David Lynch (*Dune*, 1984), and Martin Brest (*Scent of a Woman*, 1992; *Meet Joe Black*, 1998) are among the directors who have used the Smithee credit for television versions of their films, even when they attached their real names to theatrical versions.

"NO ONE OWNS THE GENRE"

The New Hollywood auteurs have occasionally asserted their rights by asking to have their names removed from work changed by the studios. More often, however, they have sought to prevent others from building on their names, reputations, and original creations. In general, trademark, unfair competition, and defamation law are better suited than copyright to protecting reputations, especially in a country without moral rights. And Coppola, Lucas, and their cohort have aggressively used these elements of the law. But they also discovered copyright law early in their careers, and they have frequently used copyright law to safeguard the new authorial powers that the studios granted them. Where filmmakers and studios spent the first decades of Hollywood's existence fighting to use age-old genre conventions without having to ask permission, the New Hollywood auteurs have, on occasion, fought for control of entire genres through copyright law.

In the mid-1970s, three of the most successful auteurs, William Friedkin, Steven Spielberg, and George Lucas, made blockbuster genre films — *The Exorcist* (1973), *Jaws* (1975), and *Star Wars* (1977), respectively. If they did not invent the blockbuster, they brought it to a new level, and they each reinvigorated the genres that they worked in. They did not transform the genres, as critic John Cawelti has described the function of many films from the same period, like *Chinatown* (1974); Lucas, Spielberg, and Friedkin did not criticize or subvert genre conventions. They paid homage to established genres; they amplified the genres' conventions; and they infused the genres with studio budgets, special effects, and stars. They turned B movies into blockbusters and converted formulaic genre fare into bold authorial statements. All three films also became the subject of copyright lawsuits.[43]

Star Wars, for example, is steeped in the genres of science fiction and fantasy, and it is filled with allusions to other films, including the re-creation of an iconic shot from John Ford's western, *The Searchers* (1956). Lucas borrowed most directly, however, from the science fiction serials of the 1930s and 1940s like *Flash Gordon* and *Buck Rogers*, with their outrageous villains, wipe transitions between scenes, and cliff-hanger endings. Despite his generous use of film history, Lucas has always had a low tolerance for work that he thinks takes inspiration from his films. Throughout his career, Lucas has used copyright law to control — or at least attempt to control — the influence of his films. Shortly after the release of *Star Wars*, Lucas created a licensing bureau to review fan fiction for potential copyright infringement.[44] This was an aggressive approach to fans who were simply sharing their own homemade creations with each other. It is especially aggressive considering that science fiction has a long history of stimulating creative work from fans. Lucas took an even stronger stance toward commercial work. Just a year after the release of *Star Wars*, the science fiction television series *Battlestar Galactica* (1978–79) appeared on U.S. television screens, presenting Lucas with his first opportunity to respond to a high-profile work that was clearly indebted to the science fiction craze he had started. (Just a few years later, all of the studios were feeding the demand for science fiction with films like Paramount's *Star Trek: The Motion Picture* and Disney's *Black Hole* [both 1979].)

Battlestar Galactica clearly owed a lot to *Star Wars*. Television critic Tom Shales dubbed *Battlestar Galactica* a "*Star Wars* superclone" (figs. 3.4 and 3.5). The similarities between the space battles of the film and television show are particularly striking and for good reason: John Dykstra headed the special-effects departments for both. According to Dykstra, Lucas had not sufficiently compensated him for his work on *Star Wars*, and when Lucas moved his special-effects company, Industrial Light and Magic (ILM), from Van Nuys to San Rafael, Dykstra took over the old building, setting up a special-effects house of his own. Dykstra urgently needed a client to pay the mortgage when the *Battlestar Galactica* job appeared. Having honed his skills at ILM, Dykstra used many of the same techniques and pieces of equipment—including his own Dykstraflex camera—that had been developed for *Star Wars*. Dykstra's contributions to both *Star Wars* and *Battlestar Galactica* raised some novel questions for studio copyright lawyers. In *Battlestar Galactica*, did Dykstra use new techniques of storytelling that were discovered while making *Star Wars* but available to all once the ideas were uncovered? Or were these techniques so closely identified with Lucas's authorial style that any use of them infringed on Lucas's monopoly on expression? Or—another possibility— was Dykstra really a coauthor of both special-effects–laden works?[45]

Lucas was not flattered by the comparisons between his movie and the television series that resembled it, nor was he willing to attribute the similarities to the genius of his special-effects guru. Lucas published a letter in *Variety* accusing *Battlestar Galactica* of selling itself as "*Star Wars* for TV," and he claimed that people were mistakenly attributing the workmanlike television series to him. "I got hundreds of letters," Lucas told biographer Dale Pollock, "from people saying, 'I think your TV show is terrible.' It was very upsetting." *Battlestar Galactica*'s producer, Glen A. Larson, defended himself in the press, protesting that he had been developing the idea for

FIGURES 3.4 AND 3.5 Did the *Battlestar Gallactica* TV series (1978–79) (*top*) take too much from *Star Wars* (1977) (*bottom*). Were both films using the same genre conventions? Or are the similarities the result of the two works having the same special-effects designer?

eleven years, before the success of *Star Wars* proved to the networks that science fiction could reach a mass audience.[46]

Lucas, however, saw deep similarities between the two works, and he insisted that Fox, the producer of *Star Wars*, sue MCA/Universal, the producer of *Battlestar Galactica*. The lawsuit made Lucas look like a sore winner, since Universal had foolishly passed on *Star Wars* even after Lucas gave them the successful *American Graffiti* (1973) just a few years earlier. Universal responded by countersuing Fox, making the even more outrageous claim that *Star Wars* infringed on Douglas Trumbull's 1972 environmental-themed science fiction film *Silent Running*, which also featured cute, small robots who beeped. The whole row sounds like internal Hollywood politics, but Lucas's investment in redefining authorship and ownership was serious, and he pursued the case for years.

In the district court, Universal asked Judge Irving Hill to decide whether or not the case had enough merit to be heard by a jury. A relatively new legal standard held that only the "total concept and feel" needed to be similar for Judge Hill to allow the case to proceed. This new standard, as Siva Vaidhyanathan explains, made film copyright law much "more unpredictable" in the 1970s, as California courts worked out the contours of the new jurisprudential concept. After viewing the film and television show, however, Judge Hill thought that all of the similarities that Lucas saw between his film and the television show were merely similar uses of well-worn science fiction conventions. As an example of the similarities, Fox noted that at one point in the Canadian theatrical release of *Battlestar Galactica* the word *android* is abbreviated as "droid," as it is abbreviated throughout *Star Wars*. But Hill was not convinced. He "doubt[ed] very much that the plaintiffs own that word," and he found most of the other examples of similarities to be so general that no one could own them either. Fox's claims amounted to a purchase on the entire science fiction genre, and "no one," Hill concluded, "owns the genre of space fantasy and of warfare in space." Fox continued to push the case, and after three years of delays, the Ninth Circuit Court of Appeals—the court that initially introduced the "total concept and feel" standard—issued a decision reversing Hill's ruling and finding sufficient merit to let the case proceed to a trial. Before a jury could hear the case, however, Fox and Universal settled out of court. According to one account, Lucas only agreed to the settlement after he received a personal apology from Universal's president, Hollywood's "last mogul," Lew Wasserman. An apology from Wasserman was no small gesture, and Lucas had successfully proven the power of the auteur in the New Hollywood.[47]

Fox v. Universal was only the beginning of George Lucas's lifelong crusade to control both commercial and fan creations that built on *Star Wars*. Fox's case against Universal, however, stemmed from a systemic change in the studio system, and not simply from George Lucas's personal feelings about authorship and intellectual property. At the same time that Lucas tried to change the dynamics of film authorship, similar lawsuits involving films directed by Lucas's fellow New Hollywood auteurs William Friedkin and Steven Spielberg were also under way.

Like *Star Wars*, both *The Exorcist* and *Jaws* borrowed heavily from genre conventions, which they then polished and marketed with studio support. In *Jaws*, Spielberg took the low-budget, teen exploitation films that filled drive-in screens, and he added the taut pacing, natural acting, and crisp cinematography of a major studio release. Despite the studio veneer, however, *Jaws* was true to its roots, and the film announced itself as a classic teen/shark movie from its opening credit sequence. Under the credits we see teenagers drinking around a beach bonfire before the eponymous shark eats a skinny-dipping coed. *The Exorcist* similarly took the conventions of the low-budget horror film and dressed them up with expensive special effects, Academy Award–nominated performances, and haunting imagery.

In contrast, Film Ventures International (FVI) was exactly the kind of company that produced the low-budget horror films and shark-attack movies *The Exorcist* and *Jaws* drew on. Starting in the 1970s, FVI's president, Edward Montoro, realized that the studios were moving into his territory, and he relocated his company to Los Angeles and developed a new business plan. Montoro began to wait for studios to renew interest in a time-tested genre before he would release a similar film. Montoro very clearly imitated the 1970s blockbusters, and he often announced as much in advertisements. But, in a sense, this is exactly what B-movie producers had always done. When one sea creature or alien invasion film found a large audience, independent producers responded by churning out lookalike films for midnight screenings and drive-ins. Even Hollywood studios made a practice of cycling though genre films after one struck a nerve with audiences. But were the genre pictures of the New Hollywood auteurs different? Did they contain so much personal vision and so many innovations that they demanded more protection than other genre films?

Montoro discovered the answer when he released exorcism and animal-attack films on the heels of Friedkin's and Spielberg's hits. In 1974, FVI distributed the exorcism film, *Behind the Door*, one year after *The Exorcist*. Two years later, and one year after *Jaws*, FVI made the *Jaws*-like bear attack film *Grizzly*, which by some accounts grossed over $30 million that year. Throughout the 1970s, FVI continued to release low-budget exploitation films, including *Beyond the Door II* (1977) and *Day of the Animals* (1977) with Leslie Nielson. Then, in 1981, FVI picked up the U.S. distribution for an Italian film called *L'ultimo squalo*, which was released in some countries as *The Last Jaws*, though FVI distributed it in the United States as *Great White*. One year earlier, Universal had released *Jaws 2* (1978), and the studio was preparing *Jaws 3-D* (1983). Montoro's run as a B-movie copycat was coming to an end.[48]

The studios behind both Friedkin's and Spielberg's films took FVI to court. They had paid for singular cinematic statements by rising auteurs, and they were not going to share their investment with others. Ironically, Universal Studios, the studio that made *Battlestar Galactica*, also made *Jaws*, and in the case against FVI, they were protecting the same broad claim to Spielberg's authorship that they fought against in the case against Lucas. Of course, intellectual property always looks different when it belongs to you.

There may have been contradictions in Universal's positions, but Montoro was not the most sympathetic defendant. In fact, he resembles a B-movie antihero himself. While fighting multiple copyright lawsuits against the studios, Montoro also ended up in court for failing to pay actors and directors, and he clearly made a living by capitalizing on the success of others' films. He may also have ended his career abruptly after absconding with $1 million in company funds. But did Montoro really take Friedkin's and Spielberg's original ideas, or was he simply using the genre conventions that they used, too?[49]

The same court heard both the *Exorcist* and *Jaws* cases, although it came down on different sides in each. In *The Exorcist* case, Warner Bros. did not claim that the story of FVI's *Behind the Door* was substantially similar to Friedkin's. Instead, they used the "total concept and feel" standard in a novel way, arguing that FVI's film copied *The Exorcist*'s style of special effects. They claimed that FVI had copied the character of the possessed child Regan as well. The court denied a preliminary injunction, which would have halted exhibition of *Behind the Door*. Like the *Star Wars* decision, this court found that both FVI and Friedkin had drawn from the same well of "haunted-house type" effects, and they had not used the effects in a substantially similar sequence. As for the character of Regan, the court explained that no one could own the idea of demonic possession, which the court imbued with some pseudoscientific validity by calling it a "phenomenon." Moreover, the judges opined, the inner turmoil experienced by the children in both films was the logical response of a person struggling with demonic possession. In other words, these films were both using the same genre elements and similar, logical plot lines.[50]

In the *Jaws* case, however, the same court found that *Great White* resembled Spielberg's shark film too much to simply be two instances of the same genre or even subgenre. I have not seen *Great White*, which the court enjoined from further distribution. But reading the court's comparison, the similarities sound simply like the recipe for a shark movie. "The opening scene in both films," the decision tells us, for example, "depicts teenagers playing on the beach." Moreover, "the salty skippers, both . . . have English-type accents and are experienced shark hunters." In other instances, the court seemed to stretch very far to find connections. "The local shark expert in *Great White* . . . ," the decision explained, "is a combination of two characters in *Jaws*." All of the characters that the court describes sound like stock characters from a shark-attack movie: the politician concerned only with the image of the town, reckless teenagers, "salty" skippers. If *Great White*'s creators combined two characters from *Jaws*, that is a significant difference, not a similarity. Further, most of the action that the court describes also sounds like predictable genre storytelling: a shark attacking a dingy, a girl who falls into the water only to be saved from a lurking shark at the last minute, a finale in which the skipper is eaten but the shark is ultimately killed. The one persuasive comparison described in the court decision is that the shark in *Great White* is accompanied by bass tones on the soundtrack, clearly a reference to the signature of John Williams' unforgettable theme. The two films may have been substantially similar, but the decision does not do a convincing job of outlining the similarities. The originality of a genre film comes from the subtleties, not from the use of stock characters and predictable plots. Nevertheless, the court thought that enough similarity existed for an "ordinary observer" to notice the shared "total concept and feel" of the two works—the standard introduced by the Ninth Circuit.[51]

It may very well be true that *Great White* took too many elements from *Jaws*, and the other FVI films borrowed less from the blockbusters they resembled. But clearly two larger structural elements had collided to reopen debates over the ownership of film ideas. The Ninth Circuit had introduced a vague standard for determining similarity, and Hollywood had redefined film authorship in such a way that rising auteurs felt entitled to new levels of protection for their contributions to genre categories. These were not moral rights cases, although they all used copyright to police the reputation and integrity of filmmakers. This spate of cases, however, revealed that the New Hollywood auteurs were prepared to defend their authorial claims. And it would not be long before Lucas, Spielberg, and others turned to the legal doctrine of moral rights to protect their vision of the auteur.

MONTY PYTHON'S "NAUGHTY BITS"

Contemporaneously with the rise of the New Hollywood auteurs, another group of fiercely independent artists were making their way into British living rooms, challenging social mores and pushing accepted standards of representation. *Monty Python's Flying Circus* first aired in Britain on October 5, 1969, but it would take another five years before the show premiered in the United States. When *The Flying Circus* appeared on New York City's PBS station, Channel 13, it quickly became the most popular and profitable series in the station's history, and other PBS stations across the country picked up the show as well. On public television, however, the Pythons only reached a limited market. Then, in 1975, ABC offered to syndicate the show for a national audience. At the time, the Pythons were about to launch a feature film, *Monty Python and the Holy Grail* (1975), and they were reaching for a wider American public. Nevertheless, they turned down the ABC offer, wary of the artistic compromises that would come with commercial television. The Pythons initially made *The Flying Circus* for the British Broadcasting Company (BBC), and they had not designed the format to be interrupted by commercials or truncated to fit new timeslots. Undeterred, ABC officials did some further investigation, and they learned that Time-Life Films held the U.S. syndication rights to the Python shows. ABC proceeded to license several of the later Python episodes for a late-night program called *The Wide World of Entertainment*. Thus began the next pivotal chapter in filmmakers' (and television makers') campaign for moral rights as protection against television editing. For the first time, however, the artists would triumph against the commercial film studios and television networks (fig. 3.6).[52]

Still suspicious of commercial television, the Pythons thought they had been assured by ABC executives that the shows would air unchanged and in their entirety, although they understood that there would be commercial interruptions. When the Pythons saw a tape of the ABC show, however, the comedy team realized that it had been misled. ABC cut approximately twenty-four minutes of each 90-minute program. ABC not only abbreviated the shows, however; they cut out more than forty clips that the network deemed offensive or indecent. Sketches lacked endings. Seemingly tame gags, like a cat being used as a doorbell or a woman wiping her feet on a loaf of bread, were excised. According to Python illustrator Terry Gilliam, who served as the lead plaintiff in the case, "all mentions of the body were cut out," including bleeping out the Pythons' signature euphemism,

FIGURE 3.6 Monty Python successfully blocked their work from being edited for U.S. television.

"naughty bits." Earlier judges had warned that television editing might result in the emasculation of films. Did the Pythons losing their naughty bits to ABC's scissors qualify?[53]

With less than two weeks to the next scheduled airdate, the Pythons asked for an injunction to stop ABC from showing the recut version of *The Flying Circus*. Like Preminger's and Stevens's claims, the Pythons sought to protect their artistic integrity. But this was also a clash of cultures. The iconoclastic Pythons built their reputation on challenging social conventions and the stodgy limitations of television representation. "The Python's form of experimentation," Marcia Landy observes,

> was at odds with the needs of commercial television to satisfy sponsors, the direct and indirect forms of censorship, and concerns about ratings. In short, the philosophy of the BBC world inhabited by the Pythons and that of the major networks of American television tended to utilize the medium differently.[54]

Editing *The Flying Circus* to conform to the very standards that it attempted to subvert robbed the show of its humor and its appeal. In the Python case, courts were asked to decide whether standards of network television nullified the essence of the Pythons' irreverent humor. Terry Gilliam and the other Pythons did not complain about the number of cuts or the amount of time deleted from the shows, as Preminger and Stevens had. They complained that the continuity, the humor, and the integrity of their shows had been lost. The case would hinge on the qualitative transformation of the shows' content, rather than an arbitrary quantification of art (minutes cut or percentages deleted).

From a contractual perspective, this case looked a bit different than the Autry, Rogers, Preminger, and Stevens cases. The Pythons had the British television equivalent of a final-cut contract, but in the world of British broadcasting the authorial rights seemed to stretch beyond the first airing of a show. The Pythons also retained the rights to their scripts, and they claimed that the ABC version was an unauthorized adaptation—a derivative work—based on their scripts. The question of who controlled the rights remained in question throughout the many permutations of this case, but judges who heard arguments in it all agreed that the Pythons retained some right to complain about the distortion of their work.[55]

The Pythons may have had a stronger claim to control their work than the American directors who had gone down the same path before them, but their complaint was couched in the same bodily (Lockean) language. Terry Gilliam called the ABC versions "amazingly bowdlerized and butchered," and the official complaint used the term that had emerged as the technical legal designation for moral rights violations through television editing: "mutilation." The Pythons hired young copyright litigator Robert Osterberg to represent them, and they asked for the headline-garnering sum of $1 million in damages. The edited versions of the Python shows, Osterberg argued, had hurt the Pythons' reputation and falsely represented their work; ABC, moreover, had failed to get the Pythons' consent before creating a derivative work.[56]

With only seven days before *The Flying Circus*'s ABC airdate, Terry Gilliam and Michael Palin flew to New York to testify before Judge Morris Lasker. In a daylong hearing, Judge Lasker heard from ABC executives, the editor who worked in ABC's Standards and Practices office, and, of course, Gilliam and Palin. The ABC employees explained that they were simply doing the business of a television network, and that canceling a show at this late date would be a significant financial burden. At one point during the day, ABC's lawyers accused the Pythons of having "unclean hands," of simply using the case for publicity, but the speciousness of that accusation was soon revealed.[57]

On behalf of the Pythons, Terry Gilliam spoke eloquently about the dangers of censoring art, and he brought the case back to the larger issues of the clash of corporate and artistic cultures and the right of integrity—the moral rights—at stake in the case. Gilliam worried that the ABC version would give the impression that "Monty Python has finally accepted the standards of commercial television, as opposed to our own standards." And he explained that "there is an element of integrity in what we have done. Good, bad, or indifferent, it doesn't really enter into it. It seems to me it is an element of integrity. I think the show that is going out compromises that integrity."[58]

The star witness in the case turned out not to be the comedians or the heavy-handed ABC editor but a color television that the court clerk wheeled in, so that Judge Lasker could compare an original BBC show with the edited ABC version. (Just one year after Sony had released its Betamax video recorder, such technical displays were themselves novel and impressive.) For the demonstration, the Pythons and their lawyers brazenly chose an episode that included a courtroom scene mocking a military judge. Luckily for the Pythons, Judge Lasker seemed to enjoy the show thoroughly, exchanging grins with his law clerk during the trial sketch. Lasker also let slip that he had seen a half-dozen episodes of the *Flying Circus* on PBS as well as *Monty Python and the Holy Grail*. The court reporter had apparently never seen the Pythons before, and he laughed heartily throughout the entire episode. When the edited ABC version was shown, it not only lacked the naughty bits, it also had long segments of black leader where commercials would have been inserted. After everyone in the courtroom had already laughed at the jokes and situations the first time, the ABC version would most likely have fallen flat even if there were no changes.[59]

At the end of the proceeding, Judge Lasker returned to his quarters for only thirty minutes before emerging with the good and bad news. Lasker was clearly sympathetic to the Pythons' claims; he described the ABC version as "an impairment of the integrity of [the Pythons'] work," which caused the material to "lose its iconoclastic verve." But he decided not to grant an injunction. ABC's lawyers had convinced Lasker that preventing the airing of the show so close to the scheduled airdate would harm the network financially more than the airing would harm the group's reputation. In an attempt to find a compromise, Lasker proposed another solution. The Pythons, he suggested, could preserve their integrity by adding a disclaimer at the beginning of the show. The ABC executives liked this idea, and a producer approached Palin and Gilliam about collaborating on a humorous disclaimer. But the ABC executives underestimated the Pythons' seriousness in this matter.

Gilliam and Palin refused to collaborate with ABC, and the disclaimer they drafted was decidedly not funny: "The members of Monty Python wish to disassociate themselves from this program, which is a compilation of their shows edited by ABC without their approval." Needless to say, the ABC team did not immediately begin printing the disclaimer. Instead, the livid ABC lawyers immediately filed a motion with the Second Circuit Court of Appeals (conveniently located upstairs in the same courthouse as the district court), and a three-judge panel heard their concerns the next day.[60]

The ABC lawyers appealed to the panel of judges with an unusually frank statement that captured the media industry's general objection to moral rights:

> To accept the conditions imposed by the Court [i.e., the Pythons' disclaimer] would only invite actions for injunctive relief by every writer, artist, cameraman, director, performer, musician, lighting engineer, set and dress designer, editor and sound-effects man and many others who contribute to making a motion picture or television program on the claim that his component part in the composite undertaking was not according to his liking or artistic sense.[61]

Film and television are, for the most part, collaborative arts, especially when practiced as part of a large, mainstream media company. Giving some or all members of the process of media production the right to control the integrity their work by removing it from the public or removing their name from the work, even after contractual obligations have been met, would threaten to disrupt the smooth functioning of mass-media industries.

Sympathetic to ABC's concerns, the appellate judges amended Lasker's solution slightly to favor the network, and they allowed ABC to draft a milder alternative to the Pythons' disclaimer. ABC's version read simply, "Edited for television by ABC." As the Pythons' good friend, Hendrik Hertzberg, pointed out in the New Yorker, this was a very strange statement. Monty Python's Flying Circus had originally been edited for television — British public television. "RE-EDITED FOR ABC TELEVISION BY ABC," Hertzberg wrote, "would have been less concise and more embarrassing, but also more exact."[62] This was not a case of editing in order to translate a film to a new medium. It was editing as cultural translation, fitting iconoclastic British public television into the box of commercial American network television.[63]

The Second Circuit Court of Appeals heard the case again the following April. Although the judges had appeared sympathetic to ABC in the first round of the case—denying an injunction and softening Judge Lasker's disclaimer solution—the court emerged as the Pythons' greatest champion. In a stunning decision—perhaps the strongest defense of moral rights in U.S. case law—the Second Circuit reversed the earlier decision, finding completely in the Pythons' favor. Writing for the majority, Judge Joseph Lumbard argued that the Pythons were likely to succeed in their claim that ABC's version violated their contract with the BBC. But he did not think copyright law, as it stood, provided enough protection for the Pythons or for other creative artists threatened by corporate misuse of their work. He quickly dismissed the idea that a disclaimer at the beginning of a show could adequately account for the harm done; what if someone tuned in after the start of the show? As a remedy to the plight of artists, Lumbard insisted on writing moral rights into U.S. case law. Fully aware of the implication of his decision, Lumbard first reminded readers that up to that point, moral rights had not been recognized by U.S. copyright law: "American copyright law," he wrote,

> as presently written, does not recognize moral rights or provide a cause of action for their violation, since the law seeks to vindicate the economic, rather than the personal, rights of authors.

But then he went on to argue that the U.S. copyright law was insufficient:

> Nevertheless, the economic incentive for artistic and intellectual creation that serves as the foundation for American copyright law cannot be reconciled with the inability of artists to obtain relief for mutilation or misrepresentation of their work to the public on which the artists are financially dependent.[64]

To meet the needs of artists, Lumbard turned to the 1946 Lanham Act, which protected consumers from misleading advertising. The Lanham Act, he argued, could also be invoked to protect the Pythons from ABC's distorted and "caricatured" version their show.[65]

The Pythons' lawyer, Robert Osterberg, warned his clients that ABC was most likely prepared to take the case to the Supreme Court to protect its business. So having won an important victory, the Pythons agreed to drop the pursuit of a monetary award in exchange for putting an end to the case.[66]

The Monty Python case has had many repercussions, both for the Pythons and for the entertainment industry. For the Pythons, this victory hardened their commitment to defending their unique artistic vision. Many critics thought that the Pythons' legal battle was vindicated when the ABC version of *The Flying Circus* lost the Emmy award to Shirley MacLaine's television special *Gypsy in My Soul*; the BBC version would surely have won.[67] As a result of the legal debacle, the BBC returned all *Flying Circus* rights to Monty Python, with the exception of United Kingdom broadcast rights. This ensured that the group would enjoy a financial cushion, and it gave them tremendous power to control the use of their material. Just a few years later, they fought a high-profile legal battle over the censorship of *The Life of Brian*, and the Pythons gained a reputation for tirelessly policing their work. Because of the Pythons reputation, other artists have exercised extra caution when invoking the group. Years after the ABC case, for example, *South Park* creators Trey Parker and Matt Stone asked the Pythons' permission to parody the classic "Dead Parrot" sketch, even though fair use probably protected their parody. *South Park* regularly relies on fair use to parody other works, but Monty Python's is different. Even in an age of ubiquitous online video clips, the Pythons have broken new ground in order to control their reputation. After low-resolution excerpts of the group's most famous sketches began to appear on YouTube, the Pythons refused to engage in the futile activity of trying to take down every infringing copy. Instead, they uploaded high-quality versions themselves and gave them away for free. They would rather give away their work than see its integrity compromised. Integrity can pay, however, and their free giveaway resulted in more purchases of their full-length television shows and films.[68]

On a broader scale, the Pythons achieved the victory that had eluded Hollywood directors for decades. They demonstrated that the line between acceptable and egregious transformations of film and media work could indeed be crossed, and rights of attribution and integrity could be protected through the related legal doctrines. Many years later, in 2003, a Supreme Court decision, *Dastar* v. *Twentieth Century Fox*, limited the precedent set by Monty Python. But at a crucial moment in film directors' campaign for moral rights, the Python decision offered a public image of artists standing up to media conglomerates. It was an image that gave hope to the New Hollywood auteurs who were engaged in similar legal battles on the West Coast, and it is a precedent that has continued to fuel the campaign for authorial rights in Hollywood.

COLORIZATION AND THE BERNE CONVENTION

Film actors and directors had been fighting for moral rights in court since the studios first began releasing films to be aired on television. But they had not returned to ask Congress for moral rights since the 1930s. An opportunity to seek a legislative solution arose again in the mid-1980s when, almost simultaneously, Congress revived discussions about joining the Berne Convention and several Hollywood studios began experimenting with new methods of computer-altered video, most notably adding color to black-and-white films, or "colorization" as the process became known.

The new move to join Berne gained momentum when Hollywood's lobbyists at the Motion Picture Association of America (MPAA) reversed its 50-year-old stance and started to push for Berne membership. The studios and the MPAA decided that the international treaty might offer a new weapon in the fight against global film and video piracy, and they thought this could be achieved without adopting moral rights in the United States. They suggested that current defamation, privacy, unfair competition, and contract law already protected the same bundle of rights as moral rights law, and there was no need to give directors or screenwriters more control over their work than they already had.[69]

MPAA head Jack Valenti chose a surprising moment to raise the issue of Berne membership. On the one hand, rising home video markets were fueling global piracy, so joining the international treaty had the potential to give the United States greater leverage in many Berne countries. That motivation is clear. But, on the other hand, several studios were already engaged in an all-out war with the New Hollywood auteurs over the colorization process. Adding the possibility of Berne membership and the statutory moral rights provisions that could potentially accompany it dramatically raised the stakes of the colorization conflict.

The colorization story began in the 1960s when engineers in the United States and Canada developed processes for using computers to add color to black-and-white films. But the technique only began to stir controversy in the mid-1980s when the Hal Roach Studios bought a majority stake in one of the colorization companies and announced that it intended to colorize many films in its library, starting with *Topper* (1937), Laurel and Hardy's *Way Out West* (1937), *The Outlaw* (1943), and Frank Capra's *It's a Wonderful Life* (1946). One year later, Ted Turner bought the MGM film library and declared his plans to colorize a virtual canon of classics, including the untouchable *Citizen Kane* (1941).[70]

Colorization provoked strong responses from every interested party. Initially, consumers seemed to love colorized versions of black-and-white films, which sold far better than black-and-white versions of the same film. Former actress and, at the time, First Lady Nancy Reagan agreed with the colorization boosters, remarking that she "didn't think *Topper* could ever be improved, but [she and the President] were most impressed with the colorization of that fun movie." An equal number of filmmakers, critics, and other purists spoke passionately about the harmful effects of the colorization process. "Colorization," explained Woody Allen, "is like elevator music: it has no soul."[71]

Frank Capra initially offered partial funding for the colorization of *It's a Wonderful Life* (fig. 3.7) in exchange for a share in the profits. He soon realized, however, that the film had entered the public domain for failure to renew the copyright (the renewal year came during a transfer of ownership and was overlooked). When Capra learned that the Hal Roach Studios didn't need his permission or his funding, he quickly became an opponent of colorization on ethical and aesthetic grounds. But the real opposition to colorization did not come from the filmmakers whose films were being colorized; it came from the New Hollywood auteurs, who were already engaged in a protracted power struggle with the studios over control of their films. George Lucas, Steven Spielberg,

FIGURE 3.7 *It's a Wonderful Life* (1946) became one of the first film classics to be colorized.

and Woody Allen emerged as some of the most outspoken voices on the issue; all three testified before Congress and published op-ed pieces on the subject.[72]

Newspapers, film journals, and law reviews from the late 1980s and early 1990s are filled with articles, opinion pieces, and essays about the specific implications of the colorization process. Today, however, the spat over colorization looks more like the inevitable culmination of Hollywood directors' engagement with moral rights that we have been tracing in this chapter. Timing more than technology made colorization a major national debate. If the colorization episode had not arisen in the 1980s, some other catalytic event would have to have been invented.

The New Hollywood auteurs—a decade after they first discovered copyright law as a means of protecting authorship—attempted to use moral rights legislation to wrest even more power from the studios. On the other side, Ted Turner summed up the studios' position in a pithy formulation: "The last time I checked, I owned those films," he said, defending his colorization of films in the MGM library. "I can do whatever I want with them." Turner's formulation had close to two hundred years of copyright policy supporting it. But could the small victories that directors had been winning in courts be translated into a new legislative victory?

In addition to the "we own it" argument, the studios saw another proprietary advantage to colorization. They successfully convinced the U.S. Copyright Office that colorized films were derivative works, entailing sufficient creativity in the colorization process to earn new copyrights for colorized versions of films. After the Copyright Office's ruling, one of the colorization companies ran an ad in *Daily Variety*, declaring: "Add 75 years to your life," touting colorization's promise of adding years of protection to commercial versions of works that had entered or were entering the public domain.[73]

The Directors Guild of America took the lead in opposing colorization and in advocating for joining the Berne Convention and adopting moral rights in the United States. During one meeting of the Senate Subcommittee on Patents, Copyrights, and Trademarks, guild members George Lucas and Steven Spielberg took time off from the set of *Indiana Jones and the Last Crusade* (1989) to explain why U.S. directors need moral rights. It was the first time any Hollywood figure had done so since John Howard Larson testified on behalf of the Duffy Bill fifty years earlier.

In their testimony, Lucas and Spielberg drew directly on the nationalistic dimension of the auteur theory to make their case for Berne membership. "In [Andrew] Sarris's hands," film theorist Robert Stam points out:

auteur theory also became a surreptitiously nationalist instrument for asserting the superiority of American cinema. Sarris declared himself ready to
"stake his reputation" on the notion that American cinema has been consistently superior to what Sarris dismissively and ethnocentrically called "the rest
of the world."[74]

Lucas and Spielberg hoped that the senators on the subcommittee were
equally convinced that Hollywood directors were necessary for preserving
American hegemony in the global market. Lucas began by emphasizing
his own power in the film industry (while at the same time denying it), and
he invoked the need for moral rights for artists (while confusing *droit moral*
with morality). "I am not here today," he told the committee, "as a writer-
director, or as a producer, or as the chairman of a corporation. I've come as
a citizen of what I believe is a great society that is in need of a moral anchor
to help define and protect its intellectual and cultural heritage. It is not
being protected." Speaking during the final days of the Cold War, Lucas
quickly moved to the accusation that there is something communistic about
not joining Berne. "For over fifty years in seventy-six nations," he explained,
"with the notable exception of the United States and Russia, the arbiter of
the artistic disposition of a work of art has been the creator or creators of
that work." (Neither the United States nor the Soviet Union were Berne
signatories at the time.) Although nationalist fervor dominated his remarks,
Lucas also used his time to defend artists against commercial tampering.
He countered Ted Turner's infamous "I own it" axiom with one of his own:
"Buying a copyright," Lucas exclaimed, "does not make one an artist."[75]

Spielberg picked up on Lucas's nationalist rhetoric, which became
a theme of the Directors Guild during this period. Spielberg referred
to motion pictures as "perhaps our nation's foremost ambassadors to
the world," and he worried that no law would protect film from being
edited for television, noting that his film *Sugarland Express* (1974) had
been cut down from 110 to 76 minutes. He called on Congress to pass
moral rights legislation to protect the singular vision of the director and
screenwriter, and in a very strange formulation, Spielberg declared that,
"The creation of art is not a democratic process and in the very tyranny
of its defined vision lies its value to the nation." This statement was, in
its way, another nod to Cold War cultural diplomacy. Throughout the
1960s, 1970s, and 1980s, the State Department, the CIA, and the National
Endowment for the Arts promoted and circulated U.S. art, from Abstract
Expressionist painting to Hollywood films, to promote the ideological
position that only American-style democracy could foster the work of

individual geniuses and, at the same time, make their work profitable. In the 1930s, senators successfully labeled Berne membership and moral rights as un-American; in the 1980s, Lucas and Spielberg tried to reverse the equation.[76]

According to one reporter who attended the hearing, the Senate panel was far from starstruck, and they appeared skeptical of the auteurs' pleas for greater power and control. (A common mistake of the film and music industries is putting forward their most successful and independent artists to cry poverty or bemoan their lack of power.) If the directors failed to woo the members of the subcommittee, they did find many other allies in the House and Senate. In the midst of an election year, presidential hopeful Richard Gephardt proposed a bill that would have given film directors the moral rights that they asked for and exempted them from the work-for-hire contracts that gave studios ownership of their films. Gephardt had won the Iowa caucuses, but he was having trouble raising money in Hollywood. The Directors Guild gained his ear on one trip out west, and they persuaded Gephardt to introduce HR 2400, "The Film Integrity Act of 1987." Gephardt, however, misjudged Hollywood. Power still lay with the studios, not with the talent. As Ronald Brownstein of the *Los Angeles Times* reported, Lew Wasserman, head of Universal Studios and the man most responsible for launching Ronald Reagan's political career, called Gephardt's top campaign staffers and said, "What is the smartest young man in Congress running around worrying about who is colorizing films? Tell him if he doesn't like colorized films to go to every television in America and take the color knob off." Wasserman may have been willing to apologize to Lucas over the *Star Wars/Battlestar Galactica* lawsuit, but he wasn't going to sit still and allow the Directors Guild to write moral rights for directors into the Copyright Act.[77]

Despite pressure from the MPAA and prominent Hollywood figures, different members of Congress proposed a half dozen additional pieces of related legislation designed to protect the rights of film directors and sometimes writers as well. But on all counts, the studios got exactly what they wanted. The United States ratified the Berne Convention, giving the studios power to enforce copyright policy in many more countries. The Visual Artists Rights Act of 1990 created limited moral rights in some artworks, but it explicitly excludes motion pictures from the category of protected works. The one small concession that the directors received came in the form of the National Film Preservation Act of 1988, which established the National Film Preservation Board and the National Film Registry.

The bill empowered the board to select twenty-five films each year, which would be placed on the film registry. Films on the registry were protected from being shown or distributed in altered form without a label announcing the changes.[78]

The creation of the board and registry were very small concessions for the studios to make, but Jack Valenti bristled even at these token gestures. To be fair, Valenti did not like the National Film Preservation Act from the start. The act had emerged out of an amendment that representatives Robert Mrazek and Sidney Yates introduced into an appropriations bill for the Department of the Interior (an unusual route for copyright legislation, to say the least). The Mrazek-Yates Amendment called for labeling of films that had been colorized or altered in other ways. In response to the bill, Valenti arranged for a meeting with representatives from the Directors Guild and other interested parties in the offices of House Majority Leader Thomas Foley. In the closed-door meeting, they hammered out an agreement that eventually became the National Film Preservation Act. When asked why he arranged for the truce, Valenti told Kara Swisher of the *Wall Street Journal* that Mrazek "had the votes to roll me. So I felt it was better to make a compromise." Even after the passage of the bill, however, Valenti continued to voice his disgust with the resolution. Throughout the first meetings of the National Film Preservation Board, Valenti made sarcastic comments under his breath, and he refused to vote on the films for inclusion. He told several reporters that he thought it was "desperately wrong for the government to get involved in the motion picture business."[79]

Valenti and the studios were able to reign in the New Hollywood auteurs, but the directors won several subsequent consolation victories. They should have been pleased with the results of a Copyright Office report on the alteration of motion pictures. Congress frequently delays or entirely sidesteps controversial issues by ordering agencies or government offices to conduct studies. In this case, Congress requested a study of the moral rights issue from the Copyright Office of the Library of Congress. Copyright Office employees Eric Schwartz and William Patry (now both distinguished copyright experts in their own right) undertook the effort with a thoroughness and energy unusual for such reports. They heard testimony from scholars and technicians, in addition to filmmakers. Rutgers University film professor John Belton, for example, explained the difficulties of teaching films when alternate versions existed. Belton also commented that colorization was a minor problem for scholars and teachers compared to panning and scanning (i.e., reframing) of widescreen films transferred to videotape. During the hearings, American University law professor Peter Jaszi drew on popular critical theory of the 1970s and 1980s and European countries' varied experience with moral rights film law to explain the complications of determining the author of a collaborative work like a motion picture. The final report took account of the much larger context in which the colorization controversy took place. And, in the end, the report recommended that the United States adopt some form of moral rights protection for filmmakers. Unfortunately, the report appeared too late to have an effect on legislation.[80]

Film directors also scored a major victory in the French court system, proving once again that Anglo-American and Continental copyright law had taken divergent paths. Along with Spielberg, Lucas, Capra, and Woody Allen, film director John Huston had spoken out against colorization shortly before his death in 1987. When Turner Entertainment colorized his 1950 film *The Asphalt Jungle* for French television, Huston's heirs, Angelica, Daniel, and Walter, sued for violation of moral rights. *Asphalt Jungle* screenwriter Ben Maddow and many of the French motion picture guilds joined them. In 1994, six years after the case was initiated and also six years after the colorization battle had ended in the United States, France's highest court, the Cour de Cassation, ruled in favor of the Huston heirs. The court held that the colorization of the film without Huston's or his estate's consent violated his moral rights, and they awarded substantial cash settlements to the heirs, Maddow, and the French guilds. It was a decisive victory, but one that came too late to have more than a symbolic impact. By 1994, even Turner had given up on colorization; that same year he started a cable channel, Turner Classic Movies (TCM), devoted to showing movies uncut and in their original form.[81]

After decades of facing off with studios on the question of moral rights, directors achieved a pyrrhic victory. Their work would be protected like historic landmarks or natural treasures. But they gave away their chance for statutory moral rights at perhaps the one moment in the history of U.S. copyright law since the 1930s when moral rights were really on the negotiating table, the moment when Congress had international pressure to adopt moral rights as part of its ratification of the Berne Convention. Once again, lawmakers proved to be sympathetic to the condition of directors when studios altered their work. But, as they had done since the 1930s, studio leaders and representatives outmaneuvered the directors.

NEW MEDIA AND NEW ALLEGIANCES

Many of the issues raised in the colorization episode resurfaced fifteen years later when several film directors learned that new companies were using home video technologies to bowdlerize their films. Some of these companies, CleanFlicks for example, bought Hollywood DVDs and sold edited versions, with violence and nudity removed or profanity muted. Other companies, like ClearPlay, developed set-top boxes that could skip scenes and mute dialogue or sound effects in real-time as a DVD played on a consumer's television. The CleanFlicks version of Steven Spielberg's *Schindler's List* (1993), for example, had forty-three audio or video cuts and ten minutes shaved off of the movie's total running time. Even Mel Gibson's passion play, *The Passion of the Christ* (2005), had three minutes of graphic violence removed. Directors had been complaining for years about studios creating shortened or distorted versions of their films; they were certainly not going to be happy about new start-up companies creating sanitized versions.

There was a twist this time, however, and the legal dispute over film sanitizing marked an important transformation in film directors' quest for moral rights. Where directors and studios had faced off over moral rights for three-quarters of a century, they now found themselves united against a common enemy. The democratization of video-editing software and the explosion of innovation in consumer video products lowered the barrier of entry for the creation of new versions of Hollywood film. Fans and amateur filmmakers had circulated their own cuts of studio films for decades, but ClearPlay, CleanFlicks, and their competitors were starting legitimate businesses based on the reediting of Hollywood films. The sanitizing companies represented a dual threat both to the artistic integrity of the directors' work and to the studios' hegemony over ancillary distribution markets. And the directors and the studios both had reasons to stop this new business model before it established itself.

This lawsuit actually came to the directors, rather than the other way around. In 2002, owners of one of the bowdlerizing companies, Trilogy Studios, grew so proud of their work that they decided to show their edited versions to a group of Hollywood directors, including Rob Reiner and Wes Craven. Trilogy's owners hoped to license its scene-skipping software to Hollywood, and they were, apparently, surprised when the directors not only failed to praise their work but also threatened a lawsuit. It isn't clear whether or not the directors really intended to follow through on their threats. But in response, Trilogy joined a number of other editing and scene-skipping companies, who jointly filed a preemptive declaratory judgment case against twelve top Hollywood directors, including Steven Soderbergh and Steven Spielberg. They asked a Colorado court to decide if their method of copying and editing films was covered under the fair use doctrine. The directors turned around and countersued, joined by the Directors Guild of America.[82]

A Directors Guild representative echoed Ted Turner's famous "I own it" defense and explained that the editing and scene-skipping companies "have decided what the vision of the movie is to be. Copyright is about ownership, and these guys don't own it." Yet directors did not own the films either; the studios did. And without the studios' support, the directors and the guild initially relied on moral rights claims, basing their arguments on the Monty Python decision. The early court documents filed by the directors and the guild explicitly invoke the Monty Python decision as precedent. "The *Gilliam* [i.e., Monty Python] decision, from one of the preeminent of the U.S. Courts of Appeal in the areas of trademark and copyright law," one Directors Guild document read, "remains good law after nearly two decades."[83]

It would have been fascinating if a court had decided this case under these circumstances, where the directors faced off against consumer technology and editing companies rather than the copyright holders. But the studios and the MPAA decided to join the directors as parties in the case. As I have already suggested, the studios' decision to join the case most likely stems from their interest in controlling the home video market, which was being taken over by a proliferation of new technologies. The studio heads, however, never made their motivations clear. In public statements, MPAA president Jack Valenti defended Hollywood's role as a moral custodian of culture. Valenti worried aloud that if the courts permitted companies to create G-rated versions of films, other companies would create X-rated versions. "To allow one," he said, "it would seem you must allow the other. That is unacceptable to parents and the public."[84] Hollywood, he seemed to be arguing, had established a reputation as a moral guardian, and this role entitles them to control film's integrity as well. Studios, in other words, were the true beneficiaries of moral rights.

Studios, of course, owned the copyrights to most of the films being edited, and they had a right to control the creation of derivative works. But there was a larger threat from new video technologies, some of which, including video-sanitizing companies, may have been permissible under the fair use exception to copyright law. As Valenti's remarks suggest, the studios were digging in for a larger battle. For decades, directors had defended the integrity of their work against the studios' efforts to repackage film for new media. Now that the studios faced a similar threat, they aligned themselves with the directors and the same quasi-moral rights defenses they had tried to thwart in the past.

In addition to the studios, Congress became involved as well. And after almost a century of dithering about the rights of filmmakers, Congress took quick and decisive action. As a longtime member and sometime chair of the Senate Judiciary Committee, Utah's Senator Orrin Hatch is frequently involved in the crafting of copyright legislation. He is also a singer-songwriter with many recorded albums and published compositions. As his legislative record shows, he is clearly sympathetic to the position of artists and the music and film industries that promote their work. In this case, Hatch had sympathies on both sides of the issues, since many of the companies and much of the audience for the edited film versions resided in his home state. In response to the CleanFlicks lawsuit, Hatch proposed a new bill that offered a compromise between the different sides, and the bill eventually became the Family Entertainment and Copyright Act of 2005.[85]

The act has three parts, and together they tell a fascinating story of legislative compromise. First, The Artists' Rights and Theft Prevention Act makes it illegal to use a camcorder in a movie theater. Even in the digital age, most pirated new releases are the result of someone taping a feature film with a camcorder. The MPAA had been pushing for this legislation at the state level for years, and a federal law was a big gift to the film industry. The second part of the act, the Family Movie Act, took something away from Hollywood and handed it to the new video technology companies. This part of the Act legalized the scene-skipping set-top boxes, like Clear-Play, although it did not mention companies that edited and resold copies of films, like CleanFlicks. This section of the act clearly defined a legitimate business model for companies and audiences that wanted bowdlerized versions of mainstream films. A final section of the act renewed the National Film Preservation Act, acknowledging continuity with the last time that such a compromise over altered versions of films had been considered by Congress.[86]

The Family Movie Act left open the question of whether the companies that sold edited versions of films were protected, and the case continued to go forward without ClearPlay and the other scene-skipping companies that Congress had sanctioned. In a decision that relied on a fair use analysis, Judge Richard P. Matsch of Colorado showed that he was swayed by the studios' and directors' moral rights claims, as many judges had been since the 1950s. Judge Matsch adopted a heavily artist-centered view of copyright, asserting that "the intrinsic value of the right to control the content of the copyrighted work . . . is the essence of the law of copyright." He decided in favor of the directors and the studios, claiming that they had "the right to control the reproduction and distribution of the protected work in their original form." With both the artists and owners—the directors and the studios—on the same side, the case for preserving films' integrity proved to be much more persuasive than it had been when the directors made it alone.[87]

They may have been victorious together, but the novel alliance between directors and studios undid decades of conflict. And the case marks an important turn in the history of moral rights for filmmakers. Although directors routinely lost their moral rights campaigns, they successfully forged a legal language for evaluating authorial rights and reputations. Moreover, they persuasively portrayed studios' exploitation of new technology as a threat to the work of American artists. By joining the directors in the fight against film-sanitizing companies, the studios were able to successfully co-opt this image of the embattled artist and use it as a front for corporate protection. As a result, the rights of filmmakers have become a familiar rallying cry in the studios' attempts to contain digital technologies, and questions of artistic integrity and ownership have been conflated.

For the filmmakers, this new alliance represents a complete capitulation. The studios clearly did not join the case because they were opposed to editing films for new markets. Creating shortened and sanitized versions of films for television and airplane showings have long been a normal part of the distribution of a film, so it is unlikely that the studios really joined the CleanFlicks case to defend the films' integrity, as the directors had. Instead, the studio heads were defending their exclusive right to make derivative works—a stance that puts the directors in a very strange position. The directors ended up defending the studios' right to be the sole entities that could mutilate their work. They settled for the very situation they had been fighting against since Douglas Fairbanks took the Triangle company to court, embracing the devil they knew rather than submitting to a dispersed new industry of editors.

4

HOLLYWOOD'S GUERRILLA WAR
FAIR USE AND HOME VIDEO

I N 1976, Congress passed the first new Copyright Act since 1909. The new act brought many changes to the law, but the biggest change may have been contained in a very small section—little more than a paragraph—that codified the doctrine of fair use. Judges in Britain and the United States had been developing the fair use doctrine in various forms since the eighteenth century, using it to explain instances when one author or artist could use the work of another without asking permission. But despite its long history in case law, the inclusion of fair use in the U.S. statute was an important milestone. Not only did it lend legislative authority to the court-made principle, but the brevity and openness of the statute's language signaled Congress's intention to keep fair use flexible, so that it could grow with society's needs.

Why did Congress design a flexible fair use standard? At least one significant factor was the explosion of consumer media technology in the 1960s and 1970s. As a report from the House of Representatives' Judiciary Committee plainly explained, "there is no disposition to freeze the doctrine [of fair use] in statute, especially during a period of rapid technological change."[1] When that passage was written in the late 1960s, photocopiers and compact audiocassettes had stirred up the publishing and music industries. And there were already indications that home video technology would further expand the scope of copyright law, forcing it to address the private, everyday activities of consumers. Just a few of the benefits of video recorders made possible by fair use include recording a television show to watch later, incorporating a video clip into a presentation, and using a popular song in a home movie. By refusing to "freeze" a fair use standard, Congress has allowed it to evolve in step with video technology, from VCRs (videocassette recorders) and camcorders to iPhones and YouTube.

Because fair use affects the daily lives of countless media consumers in addition to media producers, its legal history tells only a small part of the story. A tiny percentage of fair use disputes find their way to court or make it onto the legal radar at all. As a result, gatekeepers rather than judges resolve the vast majority of fair use conflicts and questions. Gatekeepers can be publishers, film producers, librarians, website managers, and teachers who determine whether one copyrighted object can be incorporated into another. The ranks of fair use gatekeepers also include venture capitalists and corporate executives, who decide to support or halt the development of new technologies that rely on the fair use of media. And, finally, there are the gatekeepers in our heads; uncertainty about fair use has caused many inventors and filmmakers to avoid projects and discard new ideas for fear of a copyright lawsuit.[2]

Any attempt to understand how fair use functions beyond the courtroom must take account of the ways that ideas about fair use are communicated to gatekeepers and the public. If there is a fair use war between big media companies, on one hand, and consumers, fans, critics, educators, librarians, and artists, on the other—and I believe there is—then it is a war that is only marginally fought in courts and Congress. Gossip, rumor, and intimidation can all be effective tools for influencing fair use practices.

Organized communication campaigns influence gatekeepers as well. The Recording Industry Association of America (RIAA), the Motion Picture Association of America (MPAA), and, more recently, library associations and internet activist groups have all run large-scale educational campaigns to shape perceptions about copyright and fair use. In 2005, for example, the Business Software Alliance, an organization that represents the interests of large software companies, published a comic book series featuring "Garret the Copyright Ferret" to discourage software piracy. The following year, the MPAA convinced a Los Angeles Boy Scout troop to award merit patches (not quite as weighty as badges) to scouts who "learn[ed] about the evils of downloading." In response, a public interest law firm, the Electronic Frontier Foundation, launched several of its own educational campaigns, including the 2009 "Teaching Copyright" campaign aimed at educating young people about fair use. Needless to say, all of these campaigns had differing positions on fair use.[3]

In many instances, however, silence is the most effective weapon copyright holders have in their fair use arsenal. Ignoring a controversial example of fair use may allow one work to survive, but it does not necessarily help the next work that relies on the same principles. In 2007, for example, a filmmaker named Eric Faden made a short movie by editing together hundreds of Disney film clips, each only a word or two in length. Strung together, these words and phrases spoken by iconic Disney characters explained the basics of copyright law and fair use. How did Disney respond? They did absolutely nothing. Was this fair use? Had Faden sufficiently changed the context? Had he taken too much? Had he entered a market that rightfully belonged to Disney? These are the questions that would have been asked in court. But because Disney did nothing, we will never know the answers, and moreover, there is no clear precedent for the next filmmaker who wants to take on a similar project. Not every bold example of fair use should end in an expensive lawsuit. Nevertheless, ignoring fair use can perpetuate uncertainty in the creative marketplace. And many gatekeepers, especially those who represent large institutions, tend to respond to legal uncertainty with timidity. As a result, it is often in the interest of large media companies to remain silent and preserve the ambiguity of the fair use doctrine.

The story of the intertwined development of fair use and home video technology encompasses both legal developments and the extralegal techniques that stakeholders have devised to manage fair use. It is really the story, we will see, of a gradual transformation in approaches to fair use. Hollywood's lawyers and lobbyists went through several stages of adjusting to fair use and home video. First they ignored the rising importance of fair use in an environment of rapid technological innovation; next they fought fair use in courts and Congress; and finally they devised strategies for managing, controlling, and even accepting fair use. Along the way, other stakeholders like librarians, amateur filmmakers, and media fans took stands as well.

FAIR USE GOES PUBLIC

In nineteenth-century U.S. cases, judges invoked fair use to protect abridgments of and quotation from published work. It allowed one author to quote from and criticize a rival's work without having to ask permission. In the 1960s and early 1970s, however, while Congress was busy drafting the new Copyright Act, fair use took on a new purpose. It began to protect average readers, listeners, and viewers in addition to authors and other creators.

In the wake of the Kennedy assassination and, later, the Watergate scandal, we will see, fair use started to become a tool for insuring public access to information. The Second Circuit Court of Appeals in New York began to decide fair use cases by weighing individual copyright holders' right to profit from their work against society's right to information and culture. Of course, copyright law has always balanced the rights of creators with the rights of society. But in these cases the so-called "passive" readers and viewers of texts were brought into the equation, not just future creators, who needed to quote from and reuse copyrighted material. When MAD magazine's writers claimed that their parodies of some Irving Berlin songs were fair use, the Second Circuit panel agreed on public interest grounds. "Courts," the decision read, " . . . must occasionally subordinate the copyright holder's interest in a maximum financial return to the greater public interest in the development of art, science and industry." Another Second Circuit decision built on the MAD magazine decision to conclude that billionaire Howard Hughes could not use the copyrights he had purchased in a few magazine profiles of him to prevent the distribution of a new biography. MAD magazine's parodies of well-known works of art and culture introduced social criticism and, often, political commentary to its readers. And the public had a right to know about an important public figure like Hughes, even if he was, at the same time, intensely private. The public interest arose again when the Time-Life Company set strict limits on the use of Abraham Zapruder's famous home movie of the Kennedy assassination, which the publishing company purchased in the days after the event. In one instance, Time-Life tried to stop the publication of a book that offered a novel theory of the assassination, and a New York trial court invoked the Second Circuit's public interest standard. "There is a public interest," the decision read, "in having the fullest information available on the murder of President Kennedy." Moreover, the book did not damage the market for the Zapruder film (fig. 4.1). "The Book," the decision explained, "is not bought because it contained the Zapruder pictures; the book is bought because of the theory." These cases began to remake fair use into a doctrine that explicitly safeguarded the public's right to information, not just a tool for allowing new creators to build on and critique the work of others.[4]

The growing idea that fair use helped to protect the public's right to information served as an important backdrop during the more than fifteen

FIGURE 4.1 Using images drawn from Abraham Zapruder's film of the Kennedy assassination was found to be a fair use, because it served the public interest.

years of congressional debate leading up to the passage of the 1976 Copyright Act. New technologies like photocopiers, cable television, and later VCRs expanded users' ability to access news and information. In congressional testimony and in court briefs, representatives from consumer technology companies regularly argued that the public's right to information necessitated the protection of photocopying and cable television. But no consensus emerged about whether fair use could carry the weight of protecting the public's right to information. The Supreme Court ended up evenly divided on the case that questioned whether photocopying scientific articles was fair use (Justice Harry Blackmun recused himself, leaving only eight Justices to deliberate—and disagree). And after the Supreme Court heard two different cases regarding the rights of cable television companies, Congress stepped in and imposed a statutory license on cable rebroadcasts of over-the-air television signals.[5]

While courts factored the public into fair use decisions, Congress considered many versions of the bill that would become the 1976 Copyright Act. Legal scholars worried that fair use had become an escape hatch for legislators who wanted to avoid making difficult decisions about regulating new technologies. In a widely cited 1970 essay, Harvard law professor (and future Supreme Court Justice) Stephen Breyer audaciously questioned the usefulness of any copyright law in a world of easy, pervasive duplication.

On the question of fair use and photocopying, Breyer feared that the ambiguity of the fair use doctrine "may breed disrespect for the copyright law" as a whole. Breyer's old teacher and Harvard colleague, Benjamin Kaplan, was similarly skeptical about the effectiveness of fair use for regulating new technology. Speaking to an audience at Columbia University, Kaplan rejected any legislative solution that employed fair use to solve the photocopying dilemma. "It seems hardly a statesmanlike result," Kaplan told his audience, "to leave a sizable fraction of the population (including, I fancy, some in this audience) thus uncertainly subject to civil and even criminal liability for acts now as habitual to them as a shave in the morning." Were photocopying and VCRs, which Kaplan mentioned in the next sentence, becoming too pervasive and too important to be left regulated by the fuzzy fair use standard?[6]

Professor Kaplan was not alone in thinking that the proposed copyright legislation hit too close to home. During committee hearings, members of Congress were repeatedly interested in one small subset of the public: their own children. The debates surrounding a 1971 amendment that incorporated sound recordings into the Copyright Act foreshadowed the legal skirmish over internet file sharing that took place three decades later. At one House Judiciary Committee hearing, there was bipartisan skepticism about the viability of new laws that could potentially turn countless children, including their own, into criminals. Pennsylvania Republican Edward Beister asked then Assistant Register of Copyrights Barbara Ringer about the legal responsibility of his son, who liked to record music off of the radio. "I can tell you," Representative Beister worried out loud, "I must have a pirate in my home." Ringer assured the congressman that the amendment under consideration at the time would not have turned his son into a pirate. Ringer then turned to speculation about home videotaping, which was still only in reach of the wealthiest Americans. (In 1971, Sony was marketing its U-Matic video recorder to institutions for $1,000, and its first consumer Betamax model was four years away.) Ringer did not bother to opine about fair use. Her response was much more pragmatic: "You simply cannot control [home videotaping] . . . ," Ringer explained. "I do not see anybody going into anybody's home and preventing this sort of thing."[7] For the first time, any copyright regulation that addressed emerging technologies would apply to activities undertaken by millions of Americans in the privacy of their own homes. The scope of copyright law had grown irrevocably, and Congress was understandably reluctant to consider new legislation that would have been unpopular with voters as well as potentially unenforceable.

When Gerald Ford signed the new Copyright Act into law in October 1976, it confirmed Professor Kaplan's fears: Congress dealt with new consumer technologies by codifying the laconic fair use standard and leaving courts and others to work out the contours of the doctrine.

A LOST OPPORTUNITY: HOLLYWOOD AND THE 1976 COPYRIGHT ACT

If Congress escaped having to craft a law that addressed home taping, it was largely because Hollywood executives failed to recognize the inevitable popularity of video recorders. The VCR is what management scholars refer to as a disruptive technology, a technology that transforms the market in unexpected ways. Disruptive technologies often prove to be the most revolutionary and, for those who bet correctly, the most lucrative. But they are also the technologies that incumbent businesses fear the most, the technologies that require the greatest adaptations and the largest risks. Although home video technology had been in development for decades, Hollywood executives were caught off guard when Sony released its consumer-targeted Betamax video recorder in May 1975.

Before the advent of the Sony Betamax, heads of film and television companies actively discouraged the development of consumer video recording technology, assuming that they could stave it off forever. Broadcasters began using commercial video recorders in the 1950s, and technology companies in Europe and Asia experimented with home video systems in the 1950s and 1960s. But CBS was the only major network or film studio to develop a home video recording device. In 1967, after a decade in development, president of CBS Laboratories Peter Goldmark demonstrated his Electronic Video Recorder or EVR to wildly optimistic press reports. Although the EVR could play only prerecorded tapes at the time, Goldmark predicted a new age of video recording. Home video, he told the *New York Times*, was "a new medium, a new dimension. . . . For the first time in video history it can free the individual set owner from complete dependence on the programmer or broadcaster." Goldmark, however, may have momentarily forgotten that the programmers and broadcasters paid his salary. CBS's president William Paley soon killed the project, which he had opposed from the start. Paley had been a pioneer in developing television's primary business model—a model that remains largely in place today—and he did not want to see it destroyed. Television executives do not strive to air high-quality or even popular television shows. They use television shows to capture specific demographics, and then they sell their audience's attention (or "eyeballs" in industry parlance) to advertisers. Shows with high ratings are regularly canceled if they do not also capture the demographics that advertisers seek. Years after the EVR had disappeared, MPAA president Jack Valenti was asked if VCRs served the public interest by allowing U.S. citizens who worked during live broadcasts of presidential addresses to record them for later viewing. Valenti conceded that if the VCR were only used in such instances, he would condone it. But, he continued to explain, advertising enables networks to make television free to viewers, and commercial time is sold by calculating when viewers watch a show, not just the size of the audience. Advertising, in a sense, underwrites the civic functions of television, and neither Paley nor Valenti could see the public or commercial good in developing a technology that would disrupt the time-bound model television viewing.[8]

Paley's counterparts at MCA, the media conglomerate that owned both Universal Studios and the television production company Revue Pictures, took another approach. MCA combated home recording by investing in a disk-based, playback-only technology. But MCA's DiscoVision, as the device was called, could not compete with the promise of freedom from the "complete dependence on the programmer or broadcaster." The first disk-based video systems also suffered because they were late to market, released after the Sony Betamax had already begun to attract consumer interest. And playback-only systems did not have an impact on the consumer market until the advent of the DVD.[9]

Despite the blinders of American media executives, few others could ignore the inevitability of home video technology. Journalists regularly reported on new technical developments, and law journals were filled with essays addressing possible solutions to the legal challenges posed by home video. In 1967 a perceptive University of Chicago law student wrote,

> As the technological and economic problems are solved, and new devices are produced to satisfy the "home viewer" market, it will become more important to provide the motion picture copyright owner with broader rights to the performance of his work, thereby permitting him to commercially exploit and receive the economic benefits of a growing "home viewer" market.[10]

As the law student observed, the late 1960s was a window of opportunity in which film and television industry representatives could have lobbied for their right to control and profit from emerging home video technology.

Instead, they looked the other way. When members of Congress debated the implications of home audiotape in 1971, Hollywood's lobbyists at the MPAA remained silent, relieved that those problems belonged to the music industry and not (yet) to Hollywood. When Congress discussed home taping during the drafting of the 1976 Copyright Act, Hollywood representatives chose not to ask for expanded rights that covered home video. In the end, because Hollywood executives did not seek a legislative solution before 1976, they were condemned to address home taping on a range of different fronts over the following decades.

WHAT WE HAVE HERE IS A FAILURE TO NEGOTIATE

Hollywood lawyers first addressed home taping in the negotiating room, not the courtroom. And they faced off against educators, who, the 1976 Copyright Act makes clear, have one of the strongest claims on fair use. The 1976 Act lists both "teaching" and "scholarship" in the nonexclusive list of activities protected by fair use, and another section creates a specific exemption for the use of copyrighted materials in the classroom. But not all educational uses are exempt nor are they necessarily fair uses. Rather than make specific determinations about what constitutes educational fair use, Congress formed committees to devise guidelines for educational fair use.

The committees were comprised of key stakeholders and gatekeepers. Publishers sat in a room with representatives from educational organizations and hammered out an extensive set of guidelines for the photocopying of books. Similarly, music recording company representatives agreed to a series of guidelines that allowed the copying of music for educational use. In many instances, these guidelines allowed for the copying of entire works to be distributed to a classroom full of students. Despite more than a century of case law, fair use remained a changing and unpredictable doctrine, and publishing and music executives preferred to allow some copying as long as they could help set the limits. Both the photocopying and music fair use guidelines were completed in 1976 and read into the *Congressional Record*. They did not have the effect of law, but they had Congress's clear endorsement.[11]

In another room, representatives from the MPAA, the Hollywood talent guilds, and several television networks met with representatives from library and educational organizations. They attempted to draft guidelines for educational uses of taped television broadcasts. But unlike their counterparts in the music and publishing industries, the group failed to agree on a set of guidelines. They tried and failed again the following year in an intense four-day marathon. The major sticking point was the MPAA's refusal to accept the position that recording an entire work could ever be fair use. MPAA lawyer James Bourous stated the film industry's position: "Quite frankly, it is the view of the motion picture companies that the taping of entire copyrighted works off the air is an infringement and not a fair use." (Ironically, Bourous later switched sides and went to work for VCR manufacturer JVC.) Undeterred by the film industry's stubbornness, Wisconsin Democrat Robert Kastenmeier led a series of congressional hearing to further advance the discussion. It took five years, but a set of guidelines for the use of taped broadcasts in educational contexts was eventually read into the *Congressional Record* in 1981. In the end, the MPAA refused to endorse the guidelines, although several of their member companies did.[12]

The "Off-Air Taping Guidelines" permitted an entire broadcast work to be used, but it set limits on the number of times a tape could be shown in class (once) and the length of time that could elapse between the taping of the broadcast and its use in class (ten school days). Tapes also had to be erased within forty-five days of the initial taping. In the first major legal treatise on fair use, William Patry reproduced and explained the "Off-Air Taping Guidelines" in detail, with the expectation that they would become a template for educational fair use. But despite a congressional endorsement, the "Off-Air Taping Guidelines" have very rarely been used. Some secondary schools and universities have distributed the guidelines to their faculty and technical staffs over the years, but there is no evidence that the guidelines have ever been systematically enforced. While the guidelines may have been too permissive to gain the MPAA's endorsement, they were too restrictive to be useful to educators. Without widespread adoption among educational institutions and with limited industry support, courts have simply (and correctly) overlooked the "Off-Air Taping Guidelines." The MPAA's hard line on taping and its refusal to negotiate with gatekeepers proved once again that they could delay the elaboration of video fair use. But they could not stop it.

NEWS, EDUCATION, RESEARCH, AND THE FOUR FACTORS

The introduction of the VCR led to the development of new companies and organizations built around the ability to tape broadcast television. And many of these companies operated in the untested margins of fair use. Schools taped television programs for use in classes; archives collected news and other TV ephemera; market research firms recorded commercials for analysis; and news programs recorded televised events for use in their broadcasts. The media company lawyers who sat out during the drafting of the 1976 Copyright Act and who stalled the negotiations over the "Off-Air Taping Guidelines" finally took notice of the impact of VCRs. They responded with a series of lawsuits, and the decisions that emerged began to concretize the boundaries of fair use of video recording.

None of the court decisions in these cases used the "Off-Air Taping Guidelines," relying instead on the four-factor test that had been developed in the first nineteenth-century U.S. fair use cases and delineated in the 1976 Copyright Act. The four factors encourage judges and juries to consider the different markets and contexts for the use of copyright work. The first factor questions the purpose of the new use. As interpretation of this factor has evolved, it has become common to reframe it, asking whether the context has been changed. Is a song intended to entertain, for example, being quoted in a work of criticism? Are publicity posters being incorporated into a historical collage? Both of these transpositions of context would add weight to a fair use decision. The second factor questions the nature of the copyrighted works being used. Judges have often interpreted this factor as giving works of art greater protection than didactic works, such as an instruction manual. The third factor asks whether the new work has taken more of the original than is appropriate, which does not necessarily preclude using the entire original. And the final factor asks courts to consider the new work's impact on the market for the original; will consumers buy the new work in place of the original? The four factors contain some overlap, and it is not always clear how to apply them to a particular example. There is surely much room for subjective interpretation when applying the factors. But they have, nevertheless, been the mainstay of fair use court decisions since the nineteenth century.[13]

The earliest cases that dealt with fair use and videotaped television pitted corporate media companies against new businesses and organizations that were built on fair use. As a result, courts relied more heavily on the fourth factor, questioning the impact of videotaping on commercial television. Was fair use allowing some businesses to be built on the backs of others? And if so, when should the line be drawn to separate the new businesses that enhanced the public's right to information from those that simply usurped the role of traditional media companies?

One of the first large-scale projects to use videotape in the context of research began before both the passage of the 1976 Act and the arrival of the Sony Betamax. Starting in the late 1960s, the Vanderbilt Television News Archive began to tape and preserve network television news. The archive quickly drew attention, and scholars, law enforcement agencies, members of Congress, and even Nixon White House staffers used its resources. In Lucas Hilderbrand's fascinating study of the archive, he shows how the debates over the use of the archive intersected with larger debates about access to information. Conservatives seized on the archive's collection to demonstrate liberal bias in network news coverage, and police studied the archive's footage of the 1968 Democratic National Convention riots as a form of training for future outbreaks.[14]

The television networks responded to the archive's activities by attempting to impose a license on the use of the material. But Vanderbilt resisted, and CBS eventually sued the archive for copyright infringement. The archive's lawyers defended their client on public interest grounds. They claimed that the value of the archive to society—its ability to make important videos available for reference—outweighed CBS's monopoly on its broadcasts. With the Watergate scandal looming in the background, reporters inevitably began to compare CBS's attempts to control tapes of its broadcasts with Nixon's contemporaneous attempts to control his White House tapes. And access to information rose to the level of a national security issue.[15]

The lawsuit dragged on for years, and the controversy surrounding the Vanderbilt Television News Archive led to several attempts to create legislation that would create a federal news archive at the Library of Congress or elsewhere. The Vanderbilt archive proved to be an important motivator for Congress when it included an exemption in the 1976 Copyright Act protecting libraries making single archival copies. The exception did not include motion pictures or musical works, but thanks to Senator Howard Baker from Vanderbilt's home state of Tennessee, the exception did apply to television news programs. Appropriately, it became known as the "Vanderbilt exception." After the passage of the 1976 Act, Vanderbilt successfully petitioned to have the CBS case dismissed from court, now that its archiving practices were clearly protected by the statute. This was a rare instance in which a dispute over the fair use of videotaped television could be addressed by legislation. After the passage of the 1976 Act, courts were left to decide whether new video ventures met the four-factor test.[16]

The Vanderbilt archive used expensive commercial taping machines at first. After the introduction of half-inch consumer VCRs, it became much more affordable for schools and businesses to develop video libraries and take advantage of off-air videotaping. In the New York State public school system, fair use ran into a conflicting legislative imperative. Since 1948, the New York State Legislature's Board of Cooperative Educational Services (known as BOCES) had helped schools pool resources and cut costs. As soon as the Betamax hit the market, the Erie County School District began to act on this mandate by recording educational television shows and distributing the tapes to the schools in its district. The multimedia office dedicated to the project, however, may have acted overzealously. During school hours, they continuously taped educational programs from television, and they made copies of the tapes to be distributed to surrounding schools. During the 1976–77 school year alone, Erie distributed 10,000 tapes. Educational video makers, including Time-Life—no stranger to fair use cases—and Encyclopedia Britannica, sued BOCES, the Erie school district, and the employees involved. The lead defendant, a school district employee, had the unfortunate last name Crooks, making the case—aptly as it turned out—"Encyclopedia Britannica v. Crooks."

The Erie tape-making office was a nonprofit organization, and the tapes were used solely for educational purposes. But the court found that the school district had gone too far in its attempt to consolidate labor and resources. The copying was not occasional and spontaneous; it was "highly organized and systematic." The taping program was designed to save the schools from purchasing videotapes from Time-Life, Encyclopedia Britannica, and other companies. These companies already made their tapes available to schools for purchase, and the Erie program robbed them of their right to compete in the educational market. The Erie program saved time and resources, but that is not a fair use justification. The schools could very easily have obtained the same tapes from the producers. This was clearly not a fair use; it was an attempt to preempt the market for educational videos.[17]

If nonprofit educational uses could be unfair uses, some commercial uses could also be fair uses. In one case, a Berkeley MBA decided to turn his market research coursework into a business. Donald Bruzzone started a research company that analyzed audience responses to television advertisements. Bruzzone taped ads off of television and then showed still images from the ads to focus groups, studying their responses to the images and his questions. Bruzzone sold his analyses to academic researchers and to advertising companies. The Miller Brewing Company executives did not like the idea of their competitors profiting from Bruzzone's analysis of the company's commercials, and they sued to stop Bruzzone from building a business based on copying their intellectual property. In this case, the court found that even though Bruzzone's business was premised on his videotaping hundreds of hours of commercials a week, his use still qualified as fair use. He was taping the advertisements for research, and he was only showing small portions of the work—no more than he needed—to his focus groups. Unlike the Erie School District case, Bruzzone was not replacing Miller's market: Miller made advertisements to be shown on television, not sold to researchers. It may be true that Bruzzone's research affected the market by leading advertising companies to create more effective ads, but valuable criticism often influences the market this way. A theater review might help to sell more (or fewer) tickets, and the review might cause the playwright to make changes to his or her play. But that kind of impact on the market is desirable. And it is very different from a review that uses so much of the dialogue and tells so much of the story that it becomes a replacement for the original. Bruzzone's research is exactly the kind of critical activity that fair use was designed to protect, even if it is undertaken for financial gain.[18]

A fourth important videotape fair use case pitted commercial media companies against each other. It began in 1979 when the then new sports cable channel ESPN launched its flagship program *SportsCenter*. In its initial incarnation, *SportsCenter* showed daily highlights from sporting events; it later became a full-fledged magazine show. When designing the show, ESPN talked to other television stations about licensing the rights to rebroadcast excerpts from sporting events. But in light of the Bruzzone case and other fair use cases, ESPN's legal team advised the channel that taping sports broadcasts and only airing excerpts from them in the context of a news program would be fair use. The executives at the local Boston television station that had paid for the exclusive right to broadcast Boston Red Sox and Bruins games, however, worried that ESPN would cut into their viewership, and they sued ESPN.

This was a great example of a use that was both highly commercial and socially valuable, since it reported newsworthy information. But there were other factors to consider. When evaluating the case, the Massachusetts court adopted the definition of fair use from the Second Circuit's Howard Hughes case, the decision that held that fair use protected the "public's interest in the dissemination of information." The Massachusetts court also drew comparisons to the Zapruder film case, and the public interest justification used to find fair use of Zapruder's film stills in a book about the Kennedy assassination. But Judge Rya Zobel, who wrote the opinion, thought the comparison ended there. The Kennedy assassination, she wrote, was a "unique and extraordinary . . . historical event." The public's right to read a theory about the assassination of a president could not be compared to their right to see sports highlights. Fair use protects news reporting and "the public's right to access such information," she decided, but it "is not a license for corporate theft." ESPN retained the right to report on the facts of a particular football game or tennis match, but it could not appropriate another channel's unique perspective on those facts. The WSBK-TV camera operators had positioned their cameras and chosen angles as well as light settings. The broadcast was a unique expression of the facts of the event, and protecting the station's monopoly on that expression did not prevent ESPN from reporting the facts, which could satisfy the public's right to information about the event.[19]

It is more difficult to see the logic behind the ESPN case than some of the others. If a theory about the assassination of a president could be illustrated with images taken from the sole film recording of the event, why couldn't a news story use clips from the only recording of a sports event? The original broadcast was aired for audiences who wanted to watch the drama of the game, whereas ESPN's program only showed the newsworthy moments, after the ending was known. Although this case highlighted the unpredictability of fair use, it also established an important precedent for the licensing of news footage, which emerged as a valuable business. The ESPN case demonstrated the risks involved in fair use litigation as much as it helped to clarify fair use.

These cases arose out of a particular gestational moment in the history of videotape. For a brief moment, media companies tested a litigious method of securing markets that had been newly created by the introduction of affordable VCRs. Cases that involve educational fair use or library archiving became very rare after the 1970s. Media company lawyers quickly learned that such cases can be unpredictable and schools and libraries are often more sympathetic than corporate conglomerates. But first, the largest object lesson in the pitfalls of fair use litigation lay ahead: the Sony Betamax case.

ANATOMY OF A MEDIA REVOLUTION

Sony v. Universal, the infamous Sony Betamax Supreme Court Case of 1984, has been called the "Magna Carta of the digital age." It has given the consumer electronics industry the freedom to develop countless new technologies, from Tivo to the iPod. But for Hollywood studio executives, the case was really an education in the many ways of influencing fair use practices and taming potentially disruptive new technologies. While the Supreme Court decision is undoubtedly a legal milestone, it is equally important for the lessons it taught Hollywood's leaders about what could be accomplished outside of the courtroom.

The VCR appeared at a pivotal moment in Hollywood's investment in television. After a very slow courtship, Hollywood studios became dependent on television revenues in the 1970s. In the late 1940s and early 1950s, studio heads viewed television as competition, and they fought back with CinemaScope and 3-D. Later, television became a windfall for the studios when they began to license their back catalogs and recent releases to be aired on television. Then, in 1970, the Federal Communications Commission's Financial Interest and Syndication (or Fin-Syn) rules turned the studios into the major feeder of television content. The Fin-Syn rules prevented the three networks—NBC, CBS, and ABC—from owning their own content, from being both producers and buyers of television programming. The rules may have prevented the networks from becoming vertically integrated, but they gave the Hollywood studios a near monopoly on the creation of primetime programming. After Fin-Syn was put in place, all of the studios increased their television production. MCA, however, with its successful television arm, Revue Productions, remained far ahead of other studios in terms of its output for the small screen.

When Sony was developing its Betamax video recorder, the president of its U.S. division, Harvey Schein, mistakenly thought television powerhouse MCA might be his closest ally. Schein hired the advertising firm Sony Doyle Dane Bernbach to sell the Betamax, and following Schein's lead, the firm targeted MCA with its first campaign. As *New Yorker* writer James Lardner tells the story, the advertisers proposed an ad that read, "Now You Don't Have to Miss *Kojak* Because You're Watching *Columbo* (or Vice Versa)." It was an appeal to the ability of the VCR to free consumers from the tyranny of the television schedule; they could finally watch two programs that aired simultaneously. But the ad was also a direct appeal to MCA, the company that made both shows. The advertising agency sent a copy of the ad to MCA for approval, but MCA president Sidney Sheinberg was deeply disturbed by the ad copy. Sheinberg's job was not to increase the size of his television audience; it was to sell shows to television networks. Anything that hurt the financial model of the networks would inevitably jeopardize MCA as well. Sony's Harvey Schein, who had been a protégé of William Paley at ABC, should have known that. Sheinberg had other reasons to resist the Betamax; MCA had been working for years to develop

DiscoVision, its own disk-based, playback-only system. When Sheinberg realized that Sony had won the race to market its home video technology, the former Revue Productions junior counsel led the charge to sue Sony for copyright infringement. Even if the lawsuit did not succeed in burying the VCR, it could at least delay Americans' adoption of the technology until after MCA released DiscoVision.[20]

Surprisingly, Sheinberg found little support in Hollywood for his lawsuit. Perhaps the lawyers at other studios were worried about the capriciousness of fair use decisions. If so, they would have been right: the Sony case was overturned twice during its journey through the U.S. court system. In subsequent interviews, and hindsight being 20/20, heads of other studios have tended to remember that they refused to join the case because they saw the future clearly: that home video would be a boon for Hollywood. It is more likely that they were wary of entering into expensive and uncertain litigation. In the end, the only other studio that agreed to join MCA's suit was the Walt Disney Company. Like MCA, Disney was a pioneer in creating television programming, and television remained an important part of its output. Walt Disney himself made one-time shows for NBC as early as 1950 and 1951, and he launched a regular series, *Disneyland*, for ABC in 1954. When the Disney Company joined the suit, the studio still regularly released television movies, and it was preparing a major revival of its 1950s television hit, *The Mickey Mouse Club*. The Disney studio also had a time-tested method of rereleasing films on TV and in theaters. As long as new generations of children came along, Disney had an endless supply of ticket buyers for its classics. But if audiences started to tape Disney shows and create their own libraries, it could potentially hurt Disney's ability to rerelease its television shows and movies. Disney is such a global force today that it is difficult to remember that, in the 1970s, Disney was still a relatively small, niche studio. It had theme parks in California and Florida and a library full of classic films and TV shows, but it was not the global conglomerate that it would become. Like so many Hollywood executives, Disney's leadership was holding on to its trusted formula and blind to the opportunities ahead. Ironically, it is the rise of home video that turned Disney into a major studio. Releasing Disney classics like *Snow White* (1937) and *Fantasia* (1940) on home video in the 1980s gave Disney the capital to fund its next wave of classic films like *The Little Mermaid* (1989) and *Beauty and the Beast* (1991).[21]

Disney may have joined the suit, but it was abundantly clear that the lawsuit divided the Hollywood studios. MCA's and Disney's combined programming only accounted for around 10 percent of television content, and as the Supreme Court would later note, they could hardly be seen as speaking for the film and television industries as a whole. In fact, other studios implicitly demonstrated their criticism of MCA's position by not joining the suit. And during the years of testimony in the case, several television producers spoke in favor of home taping.

With limited support, MCA's subsidiary, Universal Studios, and Disney filed their complaint against Sony in 1976, shortly after the Betamax went on sale in U.S. stores. From the beginning Universal and Disney filed complaints like buckshot. They not only sued Sony, they also included the Doyle Dane advertising agency, a number of VCR retailers, and a lone VCR early adopter (a volunteer from their law firm). If taping television shows was copyright infringement, it was not clear who would be held responsible: the individual at home, the technology manufacturer, or a conspiracy that included every link in the chain from inventor to viewer.

The newness of the technology also plagued the case. In 1976 it was unclear how consumers, educators, archivists, and others would use the VCR. Sony became one of the most heavily traded stocks in the 1970s, as investors predicted a bright future for home video. But consumers were very slow to buy the new machines. The notorious Betamax-VHS format war clearly contributed to the delayed success of the VCR. But despite the hype, this contest was relatively short-lived. Matsushita released the first VHS tape machines in 1977, and by the next year VHS was already the clear winner, outselling Betamax machines 2-to-1. Yet consumers still waited to buy VCRs. In 1980, when the format war was a distant memory, only 2 percent of U.S. households owned VCRs in either format. The VCR had a long infancy period, and no one knew the impact it would have on the entertainment industry or on the lives of U.S. consumers.[22]

The first incarnation of the Sony case dragged on through three years of litigation and five weeks of trial. Judge Warren J. Ferguson recognized that the case was too important to end in his court, and he accurately predicted that the Supreme Court would ultimately decide the case. Ferguson even expressed concern that home taping was an inappropriate matter for the courts in the first place. He suggested that the problem belonged more appropriately to a "government commission or legislative body exploring and evaluating all the uses and consequences of the videotape recorder." As many judges had in the past, Ferguson took the position that court decisions were blunt instruments and new technology demanded the subtlety of statute. But the task of regulating the VCR came to him, and Ferguson took his job very seriously. In his carefully researched and argued 128-page decision, Ferguson relied on legislative history, including the earlier

congressional testimony of Barbra Ringer, who was by this point Register of Copyrights, and Representative Robert Kastenmeier. Ferguson also
undertook a detailed fair use analysis. He concluded that copyright holders' monopoly on their work did not give them "power over an individual's
off-the-air copying in his home for private, non-commercial use." The
practice that had become known as "time-shifting"—recording a show for
later viewing—was fair use.[23]

Ferguson concluded further that "neither manufacturers, distributors,
retailers, nor advertisers were liable." MCA and Disney had drawn on the
1911 *Ben-Hur* decision and analogies to patent law to argue that if a technology's only uses were illegal, then the manufacturers of the technology
could be held liable for its use. In other words, if the VCR's sole or even
primary purpose was the illegal copying of television, then Sony could be
held accountable for consumers' infringing use. To take another example,
since guns have both legal and illegal uses, gun manufacturers are not
held responsible when a gun is used in a crime. On the other hand, when
Apple Computer founders Steve Wozniak and Steve Jobs teamed up in the
early 1970s to design and sell "blue boxes"—devices that emitted a sound
which tricked payphones into making free calls—they risked legal action,
because the blue boxes' only uses were illegal. (Luckily, the telephone
companies left them alone, so they could go on to invent the personal
computer.) In the case of the VCR, the evidence showed that the majority
of consumers were using the machines to tape broadcast television in their
homes, a practice that Ferguson found to be fair use. Moreover, most VCR
owners told the survey teams that they were erasing previously watched
tapes and reusing them; they were not building large libraries of videotape.
Ferguson held out the possibility that library building or "librarying" might
be held to be infringement if it became a pervasive practice, but there was
no evidence to support that conclusion in 1979.[24]

Two years later, an appeals court came to the opposite conclusion.
The market for VCR use had not changed significantly in the intervening
years. The major difference between the two decisions was their interpretation of fair use. More specifically, the appeals court had a different take
on the second fair use factor—the factor that questioned the nature of
the original work. In the first Sony decision, Judge Ferguson decided that
the type of shows VCR owners were taping was not relevant. When considering the public importance of *The Mickey Mouse Club*, for instance,
Judge Ferguson approvingly quoted an earlier Supreme Court case. "The
line between the transmission of ideas and mere entertainment," Justice
Earl Warren wrote, "is much too elusive for this Court to draw, if indeed

such a line can be drawn at all." Justice Warren and Judge Ferguson were attempting to meet Oliver Wendell Holmes Jr.'s 1903 call for judges to keep aesthetic decisions out of copyright cases. The appellate court in the Sony case, on the other hand, more readily made qualitative judgments. The appellate court thought that Disney's *Chip and Dale* did not necessitate the same exceptional status as scientific research papers or the sole film of the Kennedy assassination. Considering the fair use case law, the court had a point. The Second Circuit's public interest standard could be seen as requiring a distinction between information that was vital to the public and mere entertainment. And the ESPN decision reinforced this interpretation by holding that some video footage was more important to the public interest than others. Looking at MCA and Disney's evidence, the appellate court found that the public interest was not at stake here, just "business pure and simple," as the Supreme Court pronounced the movies in 1915.[25]

Certiorari, a Supreme Court review of the case, seemed inevitable, and many predicted that the Supreme Court would affirm the court of appeal's decision. MCA and Disney executives should have been celebrating. But instead the Hollywood studio heads reacted as if they had already lost the case. First, the studios realized that a decision that found home taping to be infringement would be impossible to police. Even MPAA president Jack Valenti told a congressional committee that librarying went on in his own home. In the same hearing in which Valenti famously quipped that "the VCR is to the American film producer and the American public as the Boston strangler is to the woman home alone," the admission about the video practices in his own home may be even more startling. Valenti told the members of Congress that despite the appellate court's decision, "I am going to continue taping because the plaintiffs [MCA and Disney] have said they aren't going to do anything to me. I am not committing any crime. They know that." When the mouthpiece for an industry flaunts his own acts of piracy, something has gone very wrong.[26]

What went wrong in this instance is that the VCR came to be seen as a revolutionary machine, one that fulfilled the promise popular leisure had held since the mid-nineteenth century, when working-class laborers clamored for "Eight hours for what we will." Consumers were finally free to enjoy their leisure time as they wanted, when they wanted, and in the privacy of their own homes. In the early 1980s, VCRs were also empowering "mom and pop" businesses, like drugstores and small TV repair shops that rented prerecorded videocassettes. It was a media boon equivalent to the rise of nickelodeons in the early 1900s. This revolution could not be kept down. Some experts even predicted that the appellate court's decision would lead to a short-term surge in VCR sales, just in case the device was later taken off the market or crippled.[27]

LOOKING FOR THE TOOTH FAIRY

By the time the appeals court handed down its decision, Hollywood studios had already begun to embrace home video in a limited way. Encouraged by the success of Twentieth Century-Fox and entrepreneur Andrew Blay, the studios slowly started releasing films to video. Prerecorded videotape sales made up less than 1 percent of Hollywood's total income when the appellate decision was released in 1981, but the studios were poised to move into the video market. Only two years later, that figure reached over 14 percent, or $625 million. The studio heads were also, we will see, beginning to recognize that home taping had become an unstoppable phenomenon, and they deployed the MPAA to find alternatives to the Sony lawsuit.[28]

The studios began with a strong public relations campaign, quieting critics and bringing their message to the press. When copyright luminary Melville Nimmer publicly expressed his admiration for Judge Ferguson's initial decision in favor of Sony, MCA and Disney quickly hired him as an adviser to their side. The MPAA also called on its silver-tongued president Jack Valenti to issue dozens of metaphors explaining the scourge of the VCR. In addition to analogizing the VCR to the Boston Strangler, Valenti referred to it as an "unleashed animal" turning the media market into a "jungle," and he imagined all of the VCRs as "millions of little tapeworms" consuming the industry. More tellingly, Valenti invoked the Tooth Fairy to paint a picture of the situation. Unlike the baby tooth economy, Valenti explained to members of Congress at one point, there is no force that gives studios something to replace what they lose to home tapers. Yet a Tooth Fairy–like solution is exactly what the studio heads were beginning to look for. Nimmer had not been hired simply to quiet him. Studio executives had also begun to embrace an idea that Nimmer had endorsed: that a royalty be imposed on the sale of blank tapes and VCRs to compensate producers for the money they lost to taping. It would indeed have created a Tooth Fairy–like economy.[29]

The MPAA and the Hollywood studios had resisted a legislative approach to home taping during the drafting of the 1976 Act, but Valenti soon realized that that had been a major strategic blunder. Shortly after Universal and Disney lost the district court case, Valenti began to explore a legislative solution. First he needed to sell the idea to Hollywood leaders. He began by bringing members of Congress to Hollywood, generally those influential in copyright legislation. Representative Kastenmeir, Senator Birch Bayh, and many others flew out to Los Angeles to speak with producers, guild representatives, and studio executives. Although most of the studio heads and lawyers had refused to join the Sony case, they appeared receptive to the possibility of legislation. But what kind of legislation was needed? Germany, Austria, and Norway had all adopted royalty systems that compensated content companies for the sale of devices and blank tapes. Could that work in the United States? A number of hearings were held on the possibility of a videotape royalty. The hearings gave Jack Valenti ample time to invent colorful metaphors and for the MPAA to parade Hollywood stars through the halls of Congress. But, in the end, none of the bills gained much support. The studios had proposed the royalty system too late.[30]

Sony and other consumer technology companies waged their own battle for a legislative solution, and they had the revolution on their side. Sony successfully lobbied for a videotape exemption in Japan, and the company actively pushed its case in the United States as well. Sony interested Senator Strom Thurmond in their cause when they bought land for a factory in his home state of South Carolina, and many other members of Congress were eager to ride the wave of public enthusiasm for the VCR. Championing a popular technology was easy, and politicians were reluctant to pass a bill that would have increased the price of an already expensive technology. The day after the announcement of the appellate decision declaring that home taping was not a fair use, bills began to appear that would have exempted home taping from copyright liability. Sony then joined with other consumer technology companies to solidify their hold on Congress. They formed the Right to Tape Coalition, with its apt suggestion that taping had taken on the patina of an inalienable right.[31]

Royalties on technology sales are not inherently at odds with U.S. copyright law or abhorrent to technology manufacturers. Sony's management had actually proposed a royalty scheme early on in its talks with Universal,[32] and just a few years later, in 1992, Congress imposed a royalty on the sale of digital audiotapes and tape decks. But the MPAA came around to the idea of royalties after consumer norms and expectations were too strong to be altered.

In a second attempt at a legislative solution, the MPAA pushed for the abolition of the first-sale doctrine for videotapes. The first-sale doctrine permits owners of books, videocassettes, and other media to resell or rent their individual copies. The first-sale doctrine makes the market for used textbooks possible, for example, and in the 1980s it created an active video rental market. Because of the first-sale doctrine, after buying copies of VHS tapes, stores can then rent individual copies of the tape as many times as they want. This system, however, prevents film producers from realizing the potential profits from successful video releases. A film studio profits from the sale of a tape to a rental store, but it does not receive additional revenue, regardless of the number of times a tape is rented. If Congress had abolished video rentals, as they would later abolish audio-tape and computer software rentals, it would have changed the video business. Video might have been converted into a sale-only (or "sell-through") business. But Congress rejected this proposal too. For the most part, we watch movies differently than we listen to music or use software. We listen to an album or song and use a piece of software many times, while, for the most part, we watch movies only once (children and media professors are notable exceptions). Rented music and software can be copied and those copies can be used repeatedly. The music and software industries successfully convinced Congress that rentals robbed them of direct sales; consumers were renting and taping instead of buying. But, since videos are generally watched only once, it makes less sense to force consumers to buy a product that they will not use repeatedly.[33]

The logic of video consumption, however, was only one part of the reason that the abolition of the first-sale doctrine for videotape did not gain traction in Congress. The more powerful reason is that Hollywood waited too long to make this proposal, as they had waited too long to propose any legislative solution. Like the proposal to add royalties to tape and VCR sales, the proposed repeal of video first sale came after consumers had already become accustomed to renting videotapes. Moreover, the legislation would have closed down thousands of independent rental businesses.

Although Hollywood's lobbying efforts all failed, they help to demonstrate that the enormous amount of publicity around the Sony case gives a false impression that Hollywood studios were engaged in an all-out battle against home video. Only two studios took that stand, MCA/Universal and Disney. There was much more support in Hollywood for a compromise that would have compensated the studios for losses to home taping. And if the studios had not delayed, the structure of the home video industry might have looked a lot different.

LAW BY OTHER MEANS

The Supreme Court reached its decision in the Sony case in 1984, eight years after Universal and Disney first filed their complaint. In one of the court's most famous decisions, the justices overturned the appellate court and found time-shifting to be fair use. Writing for the majority, Justice John Paul Stevens returned to examples that highlighted fair use's potential to increase access to knowledge and serve the public interest. He wrote enthusiastically about viewers' ability to "watch two simultaneous news broadcasts by watching one 'live' and recording the other for later viewing." He used additional examples of "televised sports events, religious broadcasts, and educational programs such as *Mister Rogers' Neighborhood.*" The public's right to information was clearly being served by the new technology, even if the appellate court had doubts about the social value of *Chip and Dale* cartoons. Moreover, Stevens observed that the ineffectiveness of the appellate decision was weakening copyright law as a whole. In a private note to his colleague, Justice Harry Blackmun, Stevens declared that the court could not adopt an unenforceable position like the appellate court's, one that would say: "Anyone who time shifts a single copy of a sportscast owes the copyright holder either $250 or $100, but fear not because this law will never be enforced." In retrospect, it is easy to see the Supreme Court's decision as inevitable, as reflecting widespread norms and public opinion; or, as film scholar Stephen Prince writes of the court, as "ratifying a decision that had already been made by popular fiat." And it may be that the decision could not have come out any other way. But the Sony decision was made by the narrowest 5-to-4 margin, and the Justices' deliberations were intense. In an unusual move, the Court heard oral arguments twice in the case, and we now know from internal correspondence that the justices agonized over the decision. Like Henry Fonda in *12 Angry Men* (1957), Stevens had to win over his colleagues one by one.[34]

Clearly a watershed legal event, the Supreme Court's decision came too late to have an impact on Hollywood's approach to the VCR. The appeals court's decision had proven that home taping could not be abolished. And by the time the Supreme Court's decision came, Hollywood was focused on alternate ways to manage home taping and exploit the home video market. Hollywood studios continued to pursue a legislative solution, though none was forthcoming. More successfully, they found ways to influence the behavior of home tapers and to work with rather than fight off video tape distributors.[35]

The studios continued to band together to aggressively pursue businesses that used the VCR to show films in a commercial context. They sent cease-and-desist letters to bars, hotels, video stores, dance clubs, and doctor's offices that showed videos to patrons. Most of these cases ended after the receipt of a letter; either the recipients stopped what they were doing or the studios did not follow up. "I didn't think we could beat the system," explained one bar owner after he received a letter from ABC warning him that showing tapes of soap operas was copyright infringement. The bar owner acknowledged that he was working in a "gray area," and he didn't want to be a test case. In a handful of instances, however, the studios pursued new businesses to trial. They successfully stopped video stores from growing into private or semipublic movie theaters. They were less successful when they tried to prevent a hotel from renting movies to its patrons. These were isolated cases, however. On the whole, the studios used litigation very selectively to limit infringement on their important commercial exhibition businesses. In general, the studios learned the power of using intimidation to control unwanted uses.[36]

The studios also teamed up with the Federal Bureau of Investigation and the State Department to pursue large-scale pirate networks in the United States and abroad. Hollywood and the law enforcement agencies had worked together to prevent piracy since the 1920s, and their efforts were never designed to catch every pirate. Instead, they worked by staging dramatic, high-profile raids on large pirate networks. The publicity that came from these raids was as important as the convictions. And the MPAA made sure that major newspapers were always informed of the busts. In one very public raid, the FBI uncovered thousands of videocassettes and film prints in the home of actor Roddy McDowell, who had recently completed his fifth *Planet of the Apes* film. The raid sent a strong antipiracy message to the Hollywood community, though no charges were ever brought against McDowell. They did not need to be: the dozens of stories written about the incident were enough to deter would-be Hollywood video library-builders and insider infringers.[37]

In addition to legal control, the studios took a more aggressive approach toward technological control of video technology through the development of copy protection (discussed in more detail in chapter 5). Polaroid, CBS, Universal, and other companies all developed methods of blocking the copying of both prerecorded videotapes and off-air broadcasts. Universal claimed to have a blocking method as early as the first Sony trial, but it was Macrovision technology that became the industry standard. Macrovision introduced "noise" into the video signal; televisions generally ignored the noise, but it interfered with VCRs when they attempted to copy video encoded with Macrovision. Starting in 1985, all of the MPAA's member studios began to include Macrovision in their video releases. Although video stabilization devices could easily bypass Macrovision, copy protection proved to be enough of a nuisance to deter many would-be copiers of prerecorded tapes. And the studios solidified what would become a long embrace of technical protections as a means of controlling consumer behavior.[38]

With the prolific forwarding of cease-and-desist letters, the high-profile pursuit of pirate networks, and widespread adoption of copy protection, the studios worked to make the video market safer for renting prerecorded videos. The efforts were largely successful, and in the 1980s, the video rental market was a windfall for both the studios and the rental stores. In 1986 video sales surpassed theatrical ticket sales for the first time, although that did not stop the continued growth of the theatrical ticket market throughout the 1980s.[39]

It was a halcyon period, but the studios' heads were not satisfied. They wanted more of the profits from video rentals, and they continued to be stymied by the first-sale doctrine, which allowed video stores to receive the lion's share of the profits from video hits. The studios began to combat the issue by focusing on direct sales to consumers, or "sell-through" as it is known in the industry. In order to maximize profit from video sales, the studios generally released films at a higher price of around $70 when a film was first released on video, forcing stores to pay the higher fee if they wanted to get new releases to their customers. After several weeks, prices would come down, making tapes affordable to consumers who wanted to own tapes. In an attempt to create a sell-through market, a few studios experimented with lower-priced initial releases, hoping to attract consumer purchases. This system worked with blockbusters like *E.T.* (1982) and cult films like *Star Trek II: The Wrath of Kahn* (1982). MCA, for example, made four times as much from the video sales of *E.T.* than they had made from theatrical ticket sales. But the sell-through market was less effective with typical mainstream releases, which fewer viewers wanted to own and watch multiple times.[40]

The practice of offering tapes at high prices for the first several weeks of their release left everyone unsatisfied. Video stores could not afford to buy the number of new releases that they needed to satisfy their customers; studios could only recoup the initial sales price regardless of the rental success of a film; and consumers could not get access to videos when they wanted them. Too few copies of blockbusters went too quickly from rental store shelves, and they were generally priced too high for consumers to buy them right away.

The American film industry finally solved its video rental problem as it had solved its piracy problem in the early 1900s and as it resolved its clashes over screen credit in the 1930s—by bringing regulation in-house. In the early 1900s, as we saw in chapter 1, Edison, Lubin, and the other pirates joined forces to form the Motion Picture Patents Company. In the 1930s, as we saw in chapter 2, talent guilds took over the regulation of originality and credit that might have been the province of courts. In the 1980s, Hollywood responded to its court and legislative losses through the creation of a video licensing regime. At first, different studios tried different licensing schemes. The plans varied, but they all required retailers to license rather than buy copies of tapes. Since there was no outright sale, they preempted the first-sale doctrine. The stores were legally obligated to follow the terms of the license, which required them to share rental profits with the studios. It was exactly the same deal that early filmmakers had struck with distributors in 1903, when they stopped selling film prints outright.[41]

The rental stores, however, fought back. Many small stores simply ignored the agreements, and it was difficult for studios to check up on them. Other stores fought back more aggressively. Small independent stores had created the video rental business despite the studios' lack of foresight. Now they did not want the studios coming in and taking away the market they had created. Storeowners felt, as James Lardner put it, "like colonists who had been through a few tough winters and were about to harvest a bumper crop only to learn that the mother country was going to raise taxes." The independent storeowners responded by forming a trade association, the Video Software Dealers Association, and collectively retaliating. Through the organization, they were able to defer the imposition of the studios' terms, but they could not hold them off forever.[42]

In the 1990s, Sumner Redstone's media conglomerate, Viacom, became the principal shareholder of both a movie studio, Paramount, and the largest video chain, Blockbuster. Redstone helped to broker a licensing deal between the studios and Blockbuster. It was the deal the studios had wanted all along; they would provide as many copies of new releases as Blockbuster could rent, and in return the studios would share in the rental profits. Hollywood had successfully learned to control the video market through licensing and corporate influence, despite their losses in Congress and court.[43]

FROM MARKETS TO TRANSFORMATIVE USES

Hollywood's executives and lawyers gradually learned to tame and exploit the VCR market. But a second phase of the video revolution proved to be more unwieldy. With the introduction of portable video cameras in the mid-1960s, existing genres of filmmaking that had always survived on the untested margins of fair use began to grow in size and prominence. Artists, media fans, and documentary filmmakers who had worked largely under the copyright radar began to have real clashes with the Hollywood studios. Different studios adopted different methods for addressing these communities of media makers. Almost without exception, however, the studios avoided litigation. Instead, they employed techniques for influencing perceptions about fair use. They alternately ignored, silenced, tolerated, and intimidated filmmakers who relied on fair use. In some instances, studios worked with film and video makers to promote some aspects of fair use while discouraging others. Filmmakers responded by making creative decisions based on their own assumptions about fair use, and a range of gatekeepers from festival organizers to insurance executives contributed to the situation by enforcing many of the perceptions of fair use created by the studios. The contested idea of fair use, we will see in the remainder of this chapter, has regulated the worlds of avant-garde, fan, and documentary film and video production since the 1980s.

Although studios rarely brought litigation against avant-garde artists, fans, or documentarians, the doctrine of fair use continued to develop through court decisions. And these cases clearly influenced the fair use decisions made by filmmakers and studio lawyers. In the early home video cases, questions about the public's right to information and copyright holders' right to exploit particular markets dominated fair use decisions. A few fair use decisions even stated that the fourth factor—the factor that asks whether a work impinges on the market for the original—is the most important factor.[44] A new range of cases, however, began to place more weight on the first factor, the factor that asks about the purpose for using the copyrighted material. Context began to trump commercial considerations.

The nature of parody, in particular, helped to prioritize this first fair use factor. As we saw in chapter 2, in the mid-1950s, MGM and Columbia Pictures sued *The Jack Benny Show* and Sid Caesar's *Your Show of Shows*, respectively, for copyright infringement. In both cases the parody fair use defenses were evaluated largely on the basis of the television shows' commercial impact and the amount used. Judge James Marshall Carter, who wrote both decisions, thought that Sid Caesar's parody had taken only the outline of *From Here to Eternity* and added significant new story elements and gags. That was fine. Jack Benny, on the other hand, had taken too much from the film *Gaslight* and added too little; Benny had little to offer other than a synopsis of and possibly a poor replacement for the original.[45]

Throughout the 1970s, 1980s, and 1990s, defending parodies based on fair use began to look different. In a 1980 case, for instance, a New York court considered whether a *Saturday Night Live* television parody constituted a fair use of the State of New York's 1977 advertising campaign and its eponymous song, "I Love New York." As Judge Gerard Goettel perfectly described the ad campaign in his decision,

> In the dark days of 1977, when the City of New York teetered on the brink of bankruptcy and its name had become synonymous with sin, there came forth upon the land a message of hope. On the television screens of America there appeared the image of a top-hatted Broadway showgirl, backed by an advancing phalanx of dancers, chanting: "I-I-I-I-I-I Love New Yo-o-o-o-o-o-rk!

Saturday Night Live responded with a sketch showing the deliberations of another town considering an advertising campaign to improve its image. The parody was called, "I Love Sodom." The company that owned the music rights to "I Love New York" claimed that *Saturday Night Live* used its entire jingle, and it had damaged the market for the original. Paraphrasing the skit itself, Judge Goettel responded with a careful assessment of the aesthetic function of the parodic song:

> The song "I Love Sodom" in the sketch was intended to symbolize a catchy, upbeat tune that would divert a potential tourist's attention from the town's reputation for gambling, gluttony, idol worshipping, and, of course, sodomy. The song was as much a parody of the song "I Love New York," a catchy, upbeat tune intended to alter a potential tourist's perceptions of New York as it was of the overall "I Love New York" advertising campaign.

Saturday Night Live had taken the entire piece of music, and its writers had only changed a single word, replacing New York with Sodom. Unlike the Jack Benny case from two decades earlier, Judge Goettel recognized that parodies often need to take large portions of the work they are lampooning. But even an entire work can be significantly different when it is transposed to a new context. No one would mistake a *Saturday Night Live* sketch for a New York State commercial. If the sketch did have a negative impact on the ad campaign, it was to remind people of the crime and vice being whitewashed by the song and dance routines in the commercials. The sketch was performing social and aesthetic critique, just by changing the context of the catchy jingle, and it was clearly a fair use.[46]

In a paradigm-shifting 1990 essay, Judge Pierre Leval gave a name and theory to the changing legal interpretation of fair use. Judge Leval sits on the Second Circuit Court of Appeals and has heard and written decisions in many important fair use cases. In his essay, Leval explained the reasoning he used to decide fair use cases, tracing the roots of his own thinking back to the earliest U.S. fair use decisions. Judge Leval explained that determinations of fair use turn

> primarily on whether, and to what extent, the challenged use is *transformative*. The use must be productive and must employ the quoted matter in a different manner or for a different purpose from the original. A quotation of copyrighted material that merely repackages or republishes the original is unlikely to pass the test. . . . If, on the other hand, the secondary use *adds value* to the original—if the quoted matter is used as raw material, transformed in the creation of new information, new aesthetics, new insights and understandings—this is the very type of activity that the fair use doctrine intends to protect for the enrichment of society.

Leval successfully shifted the focus onto the first factor–the "purpose" factor. He introduced a test that looked for ways that quoted works had been transformed in the new work, and he asked judges to consider whether the new work added value to the original.[47]

Leval's transformative-use test began to gain influence, and in 1994 the Supreme Court adopted the test when considering the hip-hop group 2 Live Crew's parodic rendition of Roy Orbison's 1964 pop classic "Oh, Pretty Woman." Both songs were popular and commercial music successes. And 2 Live Crew had taken the iconic opening chords of Orbison's song—the heart of his work. But they also added rap and hip-hop musical elements and clearly parodic new lyrics. The justices found that the 2 Live Crew version added criticism and comment to the original, and in Justice David Souter's elegant opinion, he wrote that, "The more transformative the new work, the less will be the significance of other factors, like commercialism." Leval and Souter's pronouncements signaled the end of a gradual shift in the determination of fair use. The shift in emphasis from the fourth to the first factor would embolden fair use communities, and it would help to strengthen the legal foundation of businesses based on fair use. The transformative-use test allowed new categories of books to be published, and it allowed internet businesses to flourish. (The 2 Live Crew decision appeared just a year after the introduction of the first web browser.) While that shift was taking place, however, Hollywood studios were in the process of changing their approach to fair use. Parallel to the transformation of the legal interpretation of fair use, film studios and several different communities of fair users were engaged in an elaborate negotiation to hammer out new ad hoc fair use guidelines (or norms).[48]

IGNORING THE AVANT-GARDE: FAIR USE AND INFORMATION COMMUNITIES

One strain of avant-garde art has always challenged the established artistic traditions that are celebrated in museums and taught in art schools. Pablo Picasso painted parodies of the works of the great masters, including Delacroix, Velázquez, and Manet. Marcel Duchamp used the entire work of another artist when he drew a mustache and goatee on a postcard of perhaps the greatest symbol of museum art, Leonardo da Vinci's *Mona Lisa*. In this same vein, avant-garde film has had a long tradition of using, reworking, and commenting on popular film. Avant-garde filmmakers have frequently incorporated clips, characters, and other copyrighted elements of Hollywood films. In the 1930s, Joseph Cornell pointed the way for the avant-garde with his film *Rose Hobart* (1936), made largely by cutting and splicing clips from Universal Picture's *East of Borneo* (1931). In the 1950s, "destruction artist" Raphael Montañez Ortiz used a tomahawk to chop up newsreel footage of an Anthony Mann western before randomly splicing the pieces back together. And in the 1960s and 1970s, Bruce Conner, the San Francisco artist known for his multimedia assemblages, made over a dozen "found footage" films using existing film material, sometimes with pop music soundtracks. These are just a few representative works of American avant-garde film, and many more films used copyrighted material without permission.

Throughout the 1960s and 1970s, American avant-garde films drew larger audiences and gained the attention of the mainstream press. Avant-garde films were screened at theaters, on college campuses, at museums, and at festivals around the world. Hollywood studios and other copyright holders, however, generally left the avant-garde alone. At the same time that the studios aggressively expanded character copyright protection to stop television producers from using studio-owned characters, Andy

FIGURE 4.2 Bruce Conner's assemblage film *Report* (1963–1967) generously used images of President Kennedy.

Warhol reimagined fictional characters to make *Tarzan and Jane Regained . . . Sort of* (1964) and *Batman Dracula* (1964, unfinished). At the same time that Time-Life carefully guarded the Zapruder film, Bruce Conner traveled the country showing versions of his *Report* (1963–1967) (fig. 4.2), his film about the Kennedy assassination that openly mixed newsreel clips, advertisements, and television commentary (though not the Zapruder footage itself).

Without specific case law, an unspoken fair use code structured avant-garde film and the avant-garde community. Filmmakers enjoyed almost complete freedom from claims of copyright infringement, as long as their work circulated only among the "underground" community. Even when their work reached more formal venues, filmmakers could remain confident that film studios would not bother them. But avant-garde filmmakers were neither ignorant of copyright law, nor were they completely free from the copyright permission system. They carefully guarded their own copyrights, and even though Hollywood stayed uninvolved, filmmakers used music cautiously. Animator Harry Smith and painter-turned-filmmaker Dov Lederberg experimented with Beatles scores on their underground films. But filmmakers understood that as soon as their work reached international festivals or was shown on television, they needed to secure music rights. When Christine Choy of the Third World Newsreel Collective sold

FIGURE 4.3 Kenneth Anger's *Scorpio Rising* (1964) inspired Martin Scorsese to use popular music in his films.

the television rights to her film about women in New York's Chinatown, *From Spike to Spindles* (1974), she did not realize that she could sell the exclusive television rights only once. But she knew to contact Bob Marley in order to secure music rights for the film (he generously granted the rights to "Get Up, Stand Up" for $25).[49]

When filmmaker Kenneth Anger released his avant-garde classic *Scorpio Rising* (1964) (fig. 4.3), he freely used old film clips, advertisements, and cartoons. Some viewers were shocked by the sexual situations depicted in the film. Many filmmakers were more surprised by Anger's flagrant use of popular music to create counterpoint and commentary. Anger's 30-minute film used a "wall-to-wall" string of popular hits by Ricky Nelson, Elvis Presley, Ray Charles, and other musicians. Even if there was no case law, filmmakers and audiences understood the code: you could not use popular music and certainly not entire songs if you intended to show your film at prominent venues. The gatekeepers in this community were film festival programmers, and they helped to enforce the rule. Many in the avant-garde community, however, did not know that Anger actually paid $8,000 to secure permission for every song on the soundtrack. As Anger later explained to interviewer Scott MacDonald, "Since I intended to submit *Scorpio Rising* to film festivals and to show it around, I decided I needed to get the rights." The licensing fee of $8,000 was an enormous expense for an avant-garde filmmaker at the time; it doubled Anger's budget and it was more than the total budget of all but a few avant-garde films. It is easy to see why it did not occur to other filmmakers that Anger had licensed the music.[50]

One member of the audience was particularly struck by Anger's soundtrack: then New York University film student Martin Scorsese. *Scorpio Rising*, he explained,

> had been banned, but the shocking thing about it wasn't the Hell's Angels stuff, it was the use of music. This was music I knew, and we had always been told by our professors at NYU that we couldn't use it in student films because of copyright. Now here was Kenneth Anger's film in and out of the courts on obscenity charges, but no one seemed to be complaining that he'd used all those incredible tracks of Elvis Presley, Ricky Nelson and the Rebels. That gave me the idea to use whatever music I really needed.

Scorsese's reminiscence points to a number of ways that copyright and fair use functioned in the intertwined worlds of avant-garde, student, and amateur film. His professors, the gatekeepers in his community, had set the fair use parameters for student projects. But in this instance, Scorsese learned a lesson from observing another film. It happened to be an erroneous lesson, based on the assumption that Anger had not cleared the rights to his soundtrack. But even this lesson based on too little information spurred Scorsese to use unlicensed rock music in his student films. And his student experimentation paved the way for his breakthrough use of (licensed) music in his early feature films like *Mean Streets* (1973) and *Alice Doesn't Live Here Anymore* (1974). In this information economy, the actions of gatekeepers, the spread of rumors, and the activity (or inactivity) of copyright holders created an ad hoc system of fair use. One of the designs of such a community is that misinformation can be as powerful as accurate information.[51]

Inspired by Joseph Cornell, Bruce Conner, Andy Warhol, and of course Kenneth Anger, video artists have created new kinds of remixed work, using copyrighted material. Like the avant-garde filmmakers, Hollywood has generally left video artists alone, allowing their work to circulate in galleries and museums free from any fear of copyright infringement. Since the mid-1960s, pioneering video artist Nam June Paik has made many works using copyrighted images. And in 1976, video artist Dara Birnbaum reassembled clips from the television show *Wonder Woman* (1975) to create a feminist critique called *Technology/Transformation* (1976). In a particularly daring example of fair use, artist Douglas Gordon's 1993 *24 Hour Psycho* slowed down the running time of Alfred Hitchcock's *Psycho* (1960) to twenty-four hours. Gordon used Hitchcock's entire film, yet the change in running time dramatically transformed the experience of watching the movie. The fast-cut shower sequence, for example, morphs into a meditative and disjointed experience in the video work.

Amidst all of the creative uses of copyrighted material reused in video art, there is one well-known example of a piece of experimental video that *was* suppressed by copyright holders: Todd Haynes's 1987 film *Superstar: The Karen Carpenter Story*. In the film, Haynes used Barbie dolls to tell the life story of popular singer Karen Carpenter, who had died a few years earlier from complications of an eating disorder and abuse of medication. Carpenter's family was sensitive to an exposé about her life, and her brother and collaborator, Richard, sent cease-and-desist letters to Haynes, complaining of music copyright infringement. *Superstar* used several complete Carpenter songs as well as segments of songs by Elton John, Gilbert O'Sullivan, and the Carpenters.

Soon after the film's release, toymaker Mattel sent Haynes material about its Barbie patents and trademarks, but the company never seems to have sent a formal cease-and-desist letter or brought any legal action. Haynes and his producer knew that music copyright would be stickier. They worried about the legal liability of using the songs on their soundtrack, and they initially attempted to secure permission for the use of the Carpenters' music. When permission was refused, they discussed fair use with several lawyers. None, however, thought that the use of entire songs qualified as fair use.[52] As Haynes tells the story now, he decided ultimately that he was making a film for a community in which permission was not necessary. Significantly, he learned his fair use lessons from Kenneth Anger:

> It was still in the era when . . . there was a kind of underground cinema that famously ignored issues of rights and stuff like that. I think Kenneth Anger was still working out the rights issues on many of his films—*Scorpio Rising*—for years after he made it.[53]

More than twenty years after the film was first shown, the *Scorpio Rising* myth still held sway over perceptions of fair use among avant-garde filmmakers. But *Superstar* began to change that.

Haynes eventually released the film as an "unauthorized" biopic. Richard Carpenter allowed the film to be shown at festivals for several years, and he may very well have continued to allow Haynes to screen it for a small underground community. After the video began to achieve cult status, however, Richard Carpenter and the Carpenters' music label, A&M, sent the cease-and-desist letters to Haynes, demanding that he curtail distribution of the film. Rather than go through an expensive trial, Haynes agreed. By that point, however, the film had a growing reputation and attempts to suppress it only made it more desirable and more popular as a bootleg. As censorship so often does, Richard Carpenter drew attention to the thing he wanted to conceal.[54]

In the years after its release, Superstar dislodged Scorpio Rising as the seminal narrative of avant-garde fair use, replacing a liberating story with a cautionary tale. The story circulated widely and portended the closing down of a previously unfettered fair use environment. Filmmakers became more cautious about their use of music and other copyrighted material. Accounts of avant-garde video and the art world of the time regularly cite Superstar as emblematic of the narrowing of fair use. And like the lessons learned from Kenneth Anger's experience, the fair use chapter of Haynes's career continues to be exaggerated and misreported. Magazines and newspapers regularly refer to Haynes's lawsuit, when he carefully avoided a lawsuit, and critics often blame Mattel for the suppression of the film rather than Richard Carpenter and A&M. In her widely read critique of corporate branding in the 1990s, No Logo, for example, journalist Naomi Klein cites Mattel's legal action against Superstar as a classic example of growing corporate censorship. And in interviews, Haynes has confirmed that people often think that Mattel and not A&M placed legal pressure on him. Like Klein, media scholar Kembrew McLeod highlights Superstar's legal troubles with both Mattel and A&M as typical of works whose suppression has chilled cultural production and exemplified the growing privatization of culture. Perhaps most tellingly, Superstar served as the centerpiece of Brooklyn-based Stay Free! magazine's gallery exhibit, "Illegal Art," which celebrated works that had been silenced by intellectual property law. As the curator of "Illegal Art" prefaced the show, "If the current copyright laws had been in effect back in the day, whole genres such as collage, hip hop, and Pop Art might never have existed." She might also have added avant-garde film and video.[55] Klein, McLeod, and the "Illegal Art" show all chronicle the very real rise of a permission culture in the 1990s and the early 2000s. But aside from Superstar, I have not located any avant-garde videos that received legal pressure of any kind during this period. (The mounting permission culture only seems to have discovered avant-garde film after the introduction of online video-sharing sites like YouTube in 2004 and 2005.) *Superstar* is a very rare instance from the 1980s and 1990s in which a work of experimental film and video has been suppressed by copyright law, even by a simple cease-and-desist letter. Through the circulation of a mythic story, avant-garde filmmakers internalized the permission culture growing around them.

The *Superstar* incident is also a case in which copyright was used to manage personal reputations, rather than preventing others from unfairly profiting from the use of original expression. We do not know exactly why Richard Carpenter and A&M chose to suppress the film, but it is surely significant that *Superstar* dramatized sensitive private debates between Richard and Karen Carpenter. Played by Barbie and Ken dolls, the characters in the film enact confrontations about Richard's sexuality, Karen's illness, and the siblings' artistic differences. The film also intercuts scenes featuring A&M owner Herb Alpert with Holocaust footage (comparisons to Hitler tend to provoke a response). Finally, although A&M records became involved, the dispute was largely between two artists, Richard Carpenter and Todd Haynes. This is true of most of the examples in which avant-garde, experimental, or underground film and video has been at the center of a copyright infringement dispute: artists rather than media corporations have initiated complaints.

More recently, a small body of case law has dealt with fair use and experimental visual artists, including Andy Warhol, Jeff Koons, Shepard Fairey, and Richard Prince. But the cases have rarely concerned film and video work, and fellow artists rather than large media corporations have generally brought the cases. Why have Hollywood studios allowed video artists to use studio intellectual property without permission? There are many possible reasons. One is that studio lawyers may genuinely think that the majority of video artists' work is protected by fair use. But the multiple cases against Jeff Koons, which have had wildly different outcomes, clearly show that the law is underdeveloped and highly unpredictable in this area. The studios' silence may be a business rather than a legal decision; studio executives may think that the audience for video art is relatively small and specialized, and video art satisfies a very different market than studio films. Perhaps studios worry about the bad public relations they may engender by attacking artists. Or perhaps the art world's self-policing economy with its cautionary myths and system of gatekeepers has satisfied most copyright holders. As we will see in the next two sections, Hollywood studios have not approached fair use in other genres of filmmaking with as much reserve.

STAR WARS FAN VIDDING AND FAIR USE BRINKSMANSHIP

Science fiction fans have a lot in common with avant-garde filmmakers and video artists. Their work often quotes from commercial media in order to make ideological or aesthetic statements. And fan film and video circulates in its own kind of underground: it is shown at conventions and clubs, and it is discussed online and in fan magazines (or zines). But Hollywood producers have approached fan communities much differently than they have approached the avant-garde. To be sure, different producers and studios have adopted disparate and shifting attitudes toward science fiction fans, and their approaches have not always been internally consistent. Science fiction fans and Hollywood producers have been engaged in a long negotiation over fair use—a negotiation that is probably still in its infancy.

A community of science fiction fan filmmakers began to emerge in the mid-1970s, although there are stories of fan films being made with the first small-gauge film formats in the 1920s. Fan film and video work responds to commercial film and television in a variety of ways. One early fan video (or vidding) pioneer, Kandy Fong, began assembling dual-projector slide shows in the 1970s to explore *Star Trek* characters' emotional lives with fellow fans at conventions. Media scholar Francesca Coppa has chronicled how Fong's experiments eventually developed into full-blown fan videos with a large following. The other urtext for fan films, George Lucas's *Star Wars* (1977), inspired fan films almost immediately. One young animator and a struggling documentary filmmaker, for example, raised funds to produce a short spoof trailer called *Hardware Wars* (1977). *Hardware Wars'* creators used the film as a "calling card," to gain the attention of Lucas and other producers.[56]

But fans did not only make films to be shared among a community of other fans or for entry into Hollywood. For every fan production that was shown at a convention or film festival, there were dozens of homemade movies that never circulated beyond a small circle of friends and family. In Milford, Connecticut, for example, the special effects created for *Star Wars* inspired a professor of medieval literature, Russell M. Griffin, to try his hand at a science fiction film. Griffin devoured books, magazines, and television documentaries that explained the technical wizardry behind *Star Wars's* special effects. The "making of" genre had practically invited him to try it for himself. Griffin had published several science fiction novels, and he learned the tricks of another medium, film, by enlisting *Star Wars* characters and action figures into a super-8 epic, *Return to*

Hoth (1981). Like many fan films, *Return to Hoth* began with a disclaimer, announcing its debt to the original; in this case the disclaimer came in the form of an apology to George Lucas. Griffin's film was made largely as a learning experiment, and it was shown to close friends and at his children's school, although it did end up winning a local film festival. Largely lost to history, these kinds of homemade films have always greatly outnumbered the widely circulated films and videos that made the convention circuit. By the time camcorders became more affordable and easier to use in the 1980s, fan vidding was pervasive, with skilled fans showing their creations at national conventions on one end of the spectrum and teenagers recording themselves dressing up or playing with action figures on the other. Studios had no choice but to ignore the latter category, and the homemade films always existed under the fair use radar.[57]

But *Star Trek* and *Star Wars* producers took notice of fan filmmakers and vidders who showed their work at conventions. The studios did not attempt to define fan fair use rights through lawsuits or amendments to the Copyright Act. Instead, they developed a range of legal, public relations, and technical remedies. Paramount Studios, which produces *Star Trek*, actively encouraged *Star Trek* fan creations—at least at first. Paramount representatives told fans that the studio considered fan zines to be fair use, and *Star Trek* founder Gene Rodenberry volubly endorsed and encouraged fan creations, even when community groups profited from their work. Rodenbery had direct contact with Kandy Fong, selling her husband *Star Trek* outtakes and requesting copies of Fong's videos. Decades later, in the mid-1990s, after Sumner Redstone's Viacom bought Paramount, studio lawyers became more aggressive and sent cease-and-desist letters to fan websites that served ads next to hosted videos. There were many casualties of this change in strategy. But for close to three decades, Paramount's relatively cordial relationship with fans helped to keep the franchise alive. As intellectual property scholar Rebecca Tushnet concludes, "Paramount has taken advantage of fan appropriation to strengthen its position and build loyalty." Recently, *Star Trek* writers and actors who appeared in official Paramount releases have also worked on fan videos, truly blurring the line between professionals and fans.[58]

Star Wars creator George Lucas and his company Lucasfilm have acknowledged and embraced fans of their franchise, but not always as warmly as Paramount and Rodenberry. Lucasfilm has sought to have a relationship with fans, but in exchange the company has demanded some control over fan creations. Lucasfilm's attempts to keep fans at arm's length is a bit surprising because, as Lucas biographer Dale Pollock has shown, *Star Wars* fans were part of Lucas's vision from the very beginning. One reason that Lucas felt confident taking a chance on a space opera in the first place is that he knew devotees of the genre would come out to see any new addition to the field. Lucas was also counting on the loyalty of science fiction fans when he gave up some of his directing salary in exchange for sequel and merchandising rights. After the film appeared, however, fans' passion for the film overwhelmed Lucas. Lucasfilm and the MPAA aggressively pursued video bootleggers, who made unauthorized video copies of the film. In fact, piracy almost immediately became part of the *Star Wars* mythology, with MPAA representatives referring to it (with some pride) as "the most infringed film in the history of the industry." Bootlegging became a sign of success as much as a problem to be controlled.[59]

Lucas and Lucasfilm have been skeptical but more tolerant of fan filmmakers and vidders than they have been of bootleggers. Lucas encountered an early test when the filmmakers of *Hardware Wars*, Ernie Fosselius and Michael Wiese, successfully got a copy of their film before their idol (fig. 4.4). Lucas reportedly called the parody "cute," and then he set up a meeting between the aspiring filmmakers and Alan Ladd Jr., who had produced *Star Wars* for Twentieth Century-Fox. Fosselius and Wiese prepared for the meeting by honing their high-concept pitches for new projects. They were understandably surprised to be met at the studio by Ladd and a team of lawyers, all of whom sat down together to watch the film. After the screening, the lawyers concluded that the parody was likely a fair use, and the filmmakers got their chance to pitch an idea. This early encounter says a lot about Lucas's grudging tolerance for fan films. Was he hoping that the lawyers would come to a different conclusion? Would the future of Lucasfilm and *Star Wars* fans have looked different if *Hardware Wars* had been less firmly in fair use territory? This incident clearly contributed to Lucasfilm's long-suffering attitude toward fans. It would not, however, be the last time that Lucas employed lawyers to assess and assert his control over fan work.[60]

As early as 1977, the year that *Star Wars* first appeared, Lucasfilm attempted to take some control of fan production by establishing a no-fee licensing bureau for amateur creations. Lucasfilm would give filmmakers and vidders permission to use copyrighted material as along as the company approved of the fans' work. This formalization of the company's relationship with fans threatened to usher in a kind of cultural revolution in the *Star Wars* fan world, in which Lucasfilm assumed the role of all-powerful censor. The company justified its activities by claiming that it

FIGURE 4.4 After viewing *Hardware Wars* (1977), a *Star Wars* spoof, George Lucas arranged for the filmmakers to meet with Fox lawyers.

wanted to protect and control its brand, and as Will Brooker has shown in his rich study of *Star Wars* fans, *Using the Force*, Lucasfilm used its powers primarily to enforce a version of "family values." The company insisted in one letter, for example, that all fanzines had to be rated PG. Since the 1970s, Lucasfilm has remained ambivalent about fan creations, alternating between salvos of cease-and-desist letters and periods of quiet. Some fans claim that Lucasfilm's occasional barrage attacks have led to self-censorship among fan communities, which may be the intent of the periodic clampdowns.[61]

Lucasfilm has also employed end user licensing agreements (EULAs) to expand its control over fan creations, claiming ownership of work created with official *Star Wars* material. EULAs often make grand statements that corporations never intend to follow through on. But *Star Wars* fans read their legal documents closely. Lucasfilm's Official *Star Wars* Fan Film Awards, for example, used a participation agreement to continue its "strategy of incorporation and containment," as Henry Jenkins puts it.[62] Begun in 2002, the contest ostensibly encourages and rewards fan video production, even making some *Star Wars* material available for use in entries. But the "control" is in the fine print. The agreement limited entries to documentaries and parodies, and it forbade the use of video clips or music from the films. Entrants were only permitted to use audio files provided by the company as well as action figures. Brooker calls the contest "a sting" meant to catch fans who refused to play by the rules, and the vidders themselves were vocal in their disdain for the new terms. Lucasfilm eventually retracted its demands, and the contest continued on newly negotiated terms. This kind of fair use brinksmanship has characterized Lucas's dealings with fans, and the Official *Star Wars* Fan Film Awards are a perfect demonstration of the collaborative nature of the rules that govern *Star Wars* fan creation: in the contest, Lucas chooses one award and the fans chose another.[63]

Together, Lucasfilm and *Star Wars* fans have thrashed out the terms of their engagement. Both Lucas and his corporation have tolerated the unauthorized use of their intellectual property as long as fans follow some understood rules. Even when these rules are broken, Lucasfilm has only occasionally taken action, usually rattling its sword with a large-scale effort rather than searching for every inappropriate fan video. Lucasfilm has even relented when fans threatened to rebel against its restrictions. This system of governance begs the question: should we call it fair use at all? Sometimes interpretations of fair use determined the outcome of these negotiations—when, for example, the Fox lawyers declared *Hardware Wars* to be a parody. More often, however, the codes of science fiction fan vidding are simply the result of a deliberative process, involving test cases, movement and retrenchment, and trial and error. Whether or not we want to call this system fair use, it is how communities of fair users define their rules of operation.

DOCUMENTARY FILMMAKERS AT THE GATES

Documentary filmmakers, like video artists and fans, regularly incorporate copyrighted material into their films and videos. They might, for example, use news footage of a march in Selma, Alabama, in a documentary about the civil rights movement. Or they might quote the John Lennon lyric, "imagine no religion," in a documentary about the clash between teaching the theory of evolution and the Bible. Or a cinema verité–style documentary might incidentally capture a TV showing *The Simpsons* in the background of another scene. There is a fair use case to be made in all of these examples (which have roots in real films). But like avant-garde media artists and fan vidders, community standards and gatekeepers rather than lines drawn strictly by copyright law have determined fair use practices in documentary film.

At a conference at Duke University in 2004, filmmaker Chris Hege-dus remarked on the changes in documentary fair use over the preceding four decades. She began by showing a clip from the 1967 film *Don't Look Back*, which her husband and frequent collaborator, D. A. Pennebaker, made about a Bob Dylan tour of the United Kingdom. In one scene, she recalled, singer Donovan walked in and played a song for Dylan. At the time, it never even occurred to the filmmakers to clear the rights to the song. That was the culture of fair use in 1967. By 2004, however, documentary filmmakers had been conditioned to think about getting permission as soon as they heard even a few bars of music in a film. In Hegedus's own 2001 film, *Startup.com*, one of the main subjects of the film looks into the camera and asks if the filmmakers will have to pay if he turns up the radio. Hegedus answers in the affirmative, and he turns up the music. Not just filmmakers, but the subjects of documentary films are aware of the pervasive permission culture. What had changed since 1967? The rise of an unlikely group of gatekeepers: insurance companies.[64]

In order to have a documentary film released in the United States, distributors insist that filmmakers obtain errors and omissions insurance (often shortened to E&O insurance). E&O insurance offers filmmakers at least some protection if their film is hit with a copyright infringement lawsuit. At some point—and it seems to have happened gradually—insurance companies decided that they would not accept fair use as a reason for the inclusion of copyrighted material in a film, and, as a result, every use of copyrighted material began to require permission.

Not every documentary needs to use a national distributor and obtain E&O insurance. In 1991, for example, University of Massachusetts professor Sut Jhally included 165 clips from MTV videos in a documentary about the treatment of women in music videos. Professor Jhally then sent out brochures and began to sell his video for classroom use. MTV sent a cease-and-desist letter, and Jhally responded by calling on the media to publicize the story. He thought that he was protected by fair use, and perhaps more importantly, Jhally—an advertising expert—did not think that MTV would want the negative publicity they might attract from a lawsuit. Jhally used his experience to start the Media Education Foundation (MEF), which now produces and distributes educational videos. MEF's videos are frequently critical analyses of media, and they often invoke fair use to make generous use of copyrighted material. Katherine Sender's 2006 film *Further Off the Straight and Narrow*, for example, uses clips throughout its one-hour running time to analyze the representation of gays and lesbians on television. The film's academic commentary would have been much less effective without the examples, and video clips clearly do not replace viewing of the shows. It is a film that no insurance company would have supported in 2006. Yet the MEF released it without copyright complaints. In fact, after releasing more than sixty films, the MEF has only ever received two letters accusing them of copyright violations. Both letters came from producers of adult films and pertained to the film *Price of Pleasure: Pornography, Sexuality & Relationships*. And both producers quickly retreated after Jhally responded with a note informing them that he thought the films were fair use. MEF has been ambivalent about media companies' silence, and at times Jhally has admitted that he wished for a lawsuit just to get some clarification about fair use. He even encouraged the two adult film companies who sent the cease-and-desist letters to sue him. Media companies' silence has not emboldened other organizations to make educational documentaries. Is the lack of legal action a form of tacit acceptance or are media companies simply stalking their prey before they pounce? That question is enough to prevent other organizations from taking the calculated risks of the MEF.[65]

MEF operates in a specialized market (education) and they exist outside of the traditional network of documentary film distributors. As long as they are willing to assume the risk, MEF can rely on a broad interpretation of fair use, because they have bypassed all of the gatekeepers. But documentarians who want their work screened in theaters or shown on PBS or the History Channel must go through the proper channels. They need a prominent distributor, and they need to obtain E&O insurance from one of a handful of companies in the United States. In early 2004, a number of media scholars, documentarians, and lawyers began to bring attention to the problem. As with many copyright matters, Duke legal scholar James Boyle was ahead of the field. Duke University's Center for the Study of the Public Domain hosted a conference, "Framed," the conference where Chris Hegedus made her remarks about the swelling permission system for documentary films. A few months later, American University law professor Peter Jaszi spoke at the Annenberg School for Communication at the University of Pennsylvania. Jaszi proposed that professional communities create codes of best practices to define and defend their exercise of fair use. As we saw above, most codes of best practices had failed in the past when they were negotiated between copyright holders and educators. But Professor Jaszi pointed to one successful code that had been created by the Society for Cinema Studies (now the Society for Cinema and Media Studies) in 1993. The society took the position that the use of film and television stills in academic books on media studies constituted fair use. The society published the reasoning of its committee, and many academic publishers (the gatekeepers in that community) began to adopt the statement as policy. Jaszi did not mention documentary filmmakers, but Patricia Aufderheide, a communications professor at American University, approached Jaszi about creating a code for documentary filmmakers.[66]

Professors Jaszi and Aufderheide raised funds from several foundations. Along with a team of graduate students, they produced a riveting study of the issue, and then they traveled around the United States organizing focus groups of filmmakers to hash out a code. When the code appeared in November 2005, it clearly and boldly delineated a set of fair use practices. The statement claimed that using copyrighted material in a historical sequence (like the 1965 Selma, Alabama, march example) or the incidental capture of copyrighted material (like *The Simpsons* example) were fair use in this particular context. The statement had an immediate impact. Several film festivals and television channels relied on the code to make decisions about showing documentaries. The cable television programming company and film distributor IFC employed the code to claim fair use on 134 clips from Hollywood films used in Kirby Dick's documentary about the MPAA rating system, *This Film Is Not Yet Rated*. The code, in other words, successfully influenced the decisions of gatekeepers.[67]

The larger and more surprising battle is that filmmakers were able to convince insurance companies to adopt the code. At first, the companies they approached refused to assume the new risk of insuring clips that had not been cleared. But after one company, AIG, quietly adopted the code, the other companies relented. The insurance companies now allow filmmakers to claim fair use as long as they follow the guidelines of the code and have a letter from a lawyer. The leading documentary film law firm, Donaldson Callif in Los Angeles, now handle dozens of fair use letters a day, and Stanford University's Law School has established a Fair Use law clinic that reviews fair use claims made by documentary filmmakers. Many lawyers reviewed the best-practices document, but this was another instance of a fair use community establishing its own code of conduct outside of the courtroom. And because the policies of gatekeepers have changed, fair use has become an option for documentary filmmakers.

THE END OF FAIR USE?

Many scholars and artists have become increasingly skeptical of fair use's ability to protect amateur creators from large media companies. Lawrence

Lessig has often polemically disparaged fair use as "the right to hire a lawyer," and in his book *Remix* he proposes augmenting fair use with a battery of specific exemptions to help amateur creators. Along similar lines, Henry Jenkins suggests going back to the drawing board and rewriting the fair use statute. While it would be nice to see clear statutory guidelines and exemptions for fans, artists, and others who rely on fair use, a statutory solution is unlikely. In countries like England that do rely more on specific exemptions, efforts to protect parody and remixing have ultimately failed to be enacted by law. A similar fate is very likely in the United States.[68]

Exemptions might also begin to replace the flexibility of fair use, which has allowed the doctrine to change over time and adapt to different cultural and political contexts. Fans do not need the same fair use conventions as scholars or documentary filmmakers or consumer technology companies. Fair use cannot be a one-size-fits-all solution. Fair use is perpetually in process, and it is negotiated not only through legal means but also, and primarily, as we have seen, *through the circulation of information among communities that rely on fair use*. The future of fair use belongs to groups that are best able to control information, not necessarily those with the best lawyers and lobbyists. In the digital age, however, the practice of fair use is increasingly restrained by technology. The next chapter examines the fate of fair use after the passage of the 1998 Digital Millennium Copyright Act.

5

DIGITAL HOLLYWOOD

TOO MUCH CONTROL AND TOO MUCH FREEDOM

I N THE early 1990s, Warner Home Video president Warren Lieberfarb was the first executive in Hollywood to see the full potential of
the DVD format. As he met with his counterparts at other studios and
convinced them to adopt the DVD, he also convinced them to learn
from the mistakes they had made with the VCR. This time, Hollywood
would not play catch-up to small rental stores; DVDs would be sold at
consumer-friendly prices, encouraging direct sales over rentals. Hollywood would not endure another format war either; the studios joined
a consortium of technology, media, and software companies that all
agreed to pool patents and adopt a single disk format; every approved
DVD player and computer operating system would be able to play the
same disks. With the DVD, Hollywood studios would not be slow to
employ copy protection as they had been with the VCR; all DVDs would
come equipped with a digital lock, the Content Scrambling System,
which would require a software key to be unlocked. And finally, Hollywood would not be late to the negotiating table; well before the DVD
was released in the United States, studio lobbyists were asking Congress for new copyright policies to protect their investment in the new
digital format.

Hollywood's lobbyists asked Congress to back the industry's
copy protection standard with a law making it illegal to bypass the

encryption—the digital locks—on DVDs. Their efforts were unsuccessful at first, and DVDs were released to the U.S. market in 1997 without the legal protection Hollywood sought. But the studios did not give up, and they found a receptive partner in the Clinton administration's Undersecretary of Commerce for Intellectual Property, Bruce A. Lehman. Together, they successfully pushed through an international treaty of the United Nations' World Intellectual Property Organization. In order to comply with the treaty (and go well beyond it), Congress passed the 1998 Digital Millennium Copyright Act (the DMCA), finally backing Hollywood's copy protection with law. The so-called anticircumvention provisions of the DMCA make it illegal to disable or bypass the copy protection on DVDs and other digital media or to traffic in anticircumvention tools. Since 1998, Hollywood has both made the locks and held the keys. And the studios control access to commercial digital media almost completely.[1]

But Hollywood studios were not the only group invested in the future of digital media in 1998. Network operators like Verizon and America Online and website hosts like Yahoo! also pushed to have the future of their businesses protected by the DMCA. More specifically, the online service providers, as they were called, worried about their responsibility for the content that traveled over their networks. Policing the massive amount of information on websites was a daunting task. Would they be held liable for copyright infringement if customers uploaded pirated material to one of their networks or websites? The service providers successfully petitioned for the addition of another section of the DMCA, which gave them "safe harbor" protection from claims of copyright infringement that took place on their networks. As long as the service providers and web hosts followed the correct procedures and worked quickly, individual web users and copyright holders were left to settle disputes on their own, without the involvement of the network and site owners.

Together, these two sections of the DMCA—the anticircumvention and safe harbor provisions—have created today's internet media environment. This chapter looks at the ways that the DMCA has changed the landscape of media production, distribution, and consumption. The DMCA has created mechanisms for turning over media regulation to Hollywood studios and, to a lesser extent, internet users. Throughout this book, I have chronicled Hollywood studios' attempts to regulate themselves in order to avoid regulation at the hand of courts and Congress. In the digital era, Congress has facilitated this self-regulation.

A SHORT HISTORY OF COPY PROTECTION

Technical copy protection began neither with the DVD nor with the Digital Millennium Copyright Act. Long before digital media, authors and collectors developed technical means for protecting writings. Diarists placed locks directly on their notebooks, and military strategists encrypted their communications with codes that required sophisticated keys to be deciphered. At Oxford University's Duke Humfrey's Library, rare books are still chained to the wall, much as they were in the fifteenth century (fig. 5.1). The American film industry also has a long history of using technical protection to block access to films, although these devices have generally been used to block competition rather than to prevent unwanted access altogether.

As I discussed briefly in the first chapter, technical differences kept early movie companies from using each other's films and equipment. Film gauges and sprocket holes, in particular, varied widely from company to company. Thomas Edison adopted the now standard 35mm film gauge when his lab began cutting Eastman Kodak's 70mm still photo film stock in half, doubling the amount of footage his cameramen could shoot. Other companies tended to use slightly larger film sizes, ranging from 38mm (Sivan/Dalphin, Geneva) to 70mm (Brit Acres, U.K.). Some companies, including Edison,

FIGURE 5.1 Early copy protection: books chained to the walls in the Duke Humfrey Library, Bodlean Library, University of Oxford. (Courtesy of and copyright © The Dean and Chapter of Hereford Cathedral and the Hereford Mappa Mundi Trust)

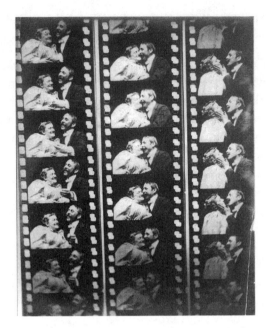

FIGURE 5.2 The placement of sprocket holes tied films to the specific projectors and cameras, much like the copy protection on digital media today. (Courtesy of the U.S. Dept. of the Interior, National Park Service, Thomas Edison National Historical Park)

tested smaller amateur gauges, usually between 13 and 21mm. The placement of sprocket holes varied as well. Edison adopted a method of using four square-shaped perforations on each side of the frame to move the celluloid through the camera and projector (fig. 5.2). But in France, the Lumière brothers placed a single sprocket hole on each side of the frame, and it was round not square. Other companies' cameras and projectors, American Mutoscope and Biograph's for instance, ran without any sprocket holes at all. They used friction to move the film through the gears.[2]

These were not simply the chance experimental differences that often accompany new inventions. The structure of the film industry depended on the design of celluloid, and Edison and Biograph fought bitter patent battles over the width of film stock and the placement of sprocket holes. Control over the technical design of film gave one company the ability to lock out its competitors. During a brief period when Edison claimed patent rights to both the 35mm film gauge and the placement of sprocket holes, he was legally (as well as technically) able to bind his films to his projectors. Unlicensed theaters were thus prevented from showing Edison films, which would not run on their projectors. And Biograph and other production companies were prevented from selling their films to theaters with Edison projectors. These legally backed technical restrictions successfully prevented legitimate competition. Edison's claims were so broad that in order to enter the market, a new company would have had to do everything from developing its own camera and projector designs to manufacturing its own film stock with a novel perforation pattern. In addition to impeding competition, technical restrictions also led to increased piracy. As we saw in chapter 1, competitors regularly copied and converted each other's films in order to use them on incompatible equipment. Things loosened up slightly in 1903 when Edison lost his claim to the 35mm film width, but he continued to control the use of his sprocket design. This was the first—but certainly not the last—time that the film industry would use a combination of legal and technical means to block competition.[3]

Film gauges and sprocket holes defined early film formats. The size and placement of perforations marked the film (the content or software) in such a way that it became compatible or incompatible with the cameras and projectors (the hardware). Seen this way, today's copy protection is simply an extension of format technology. The software encryption placed on DVDs and other digital media is really an artificial means of re-creating the real incompatibilities of physical media formats. Apple adds copy protection that only allows iTunes-purchased video to be played on Apple-manufactured or licensed products, and Microsoft does the same.

Format contests, like the one that took place over the design of early film stock, have always threatened to unsettle the film and television industries. Companies that control the patents on new technologies often have a significant advantage over their competitors. Hollywood has gone through many format overhauls, some decisive and some abortive, from the lasting adoption of 35mm film to the 3-D fad of the 1950s. Despite the format changes continually on the horizon, however, Hollywood studios have generally approached most new technologies afresh, reacting to changes as they came along rather than preparing for the inevitable format changes ahead.

There are two notable exceptions to this rule. One, as we saw above, is the adoption of the DVD. The other is the transition to sound film in the 1920s—arguably the largest format shift in the history of Hollywood. The transition to sound entailed refitting every commercial movie theater across the globe, not to mention building new sound-ready studios and labs. It is difficult to imagine the scale of that infrastructural change in an era when adopting a new format means little more than downloading some new software. Sound technology threatened to launch a major format war, but it was a war that the studios calculatedly avoided. As Douglas Gomery has shown, the large Hollywood studios did not respond haphazardly to the development of sound film technology. They worked together to make reasoned, economically motivated decisions about the adoption of new sound formats.[4]

The two studios that pioneered the use of sound, Fox and Warner Bros., were both "minor" studios at the time; they did not own large theater chains like MGM, Paramount, and the other "majors." In 1926–27, Fox and Warner began to employ different sound technologies in bids to enter the ranks of the majors. Fox used a sound-on-film system, and Warner tried a sound-on-disk method. They were incompatible technologies, although they shared some underlying patents. Any company that chose the winning format would have gained an enormous advantage in the industry, potentially blocking others from access to theaters that had adopted one or the other system. But the majors decided that the risks of losing this battle were too great. Rather than embrace either system, the five largest studios signed an agreement, collectively consenting to study the different technologies and eventually adopting a single industry standard. In the end, the majors chose a third technology, a sound-on-film system developed by a subsidiary of AT&T and Western Electric. Gradually, the new system was installed in all the major studios and movie theaters. As they would later with the DVD, film studios avoided an internal struggle over the adoption of a new format in favor of a single industry-wide standard. By adopting a single standard, the studios also avoided a clash with theater owners, who would have had to align themselves with one format or another or wait until a single format won the contest. As a result of studio executives' foresight, Hollywood enjoyed a thriving and profitable sound film business in the early 1930s, even as the Great Depression engulfed other industries.[5]

The next major format shift, the move to home video, marked an epochal change in the industry's approach to copy protection. The competing Betamax and VHS standards led to a short-lived and overhyped format war. But that was not the most important change in the film industry's approach to tying content to technology, software to hardware. When adopting a standard film stock in the 1890s and a standard sound technology in the 1920s, film companies chose between physically different formats: round or square sprocket holes, sound on disk or film. But with the VCR, the industry-wide adoption of the VHS standard was only the beginning of the effort to technically control access to films. Led by MCA/Universal, Hollywood studios pushed for the addition of artificial locks to be added to videotapes. Moreover, they asked for a new legal approach to copy protection. Earlier format wars had focused on using patent licensing to control the diffusion of technology. But new forms of copy protection were justified as a means of blocking the duplication of copyrighted material. And the studios lobbied to have their new methods of copy protection mandated by law. Perhaps for the first time, studio executives and lobbyists envisioned technical copy protection as an extension of copyright law in addition to a technology to be controlled through patents.

The first sign that a new vision of copy protection was emerging appeared during the district court's hearing of the Sony Betamax case. MCA/Universal had been searching for a legal theory that would hold Sony responsible for instances of copyright infringement involving its Betamax VCR. In addition to Universal's team of lawyers, the studio also put its engineering department to work on the problem. Universal's Academy Award–winning sound engineer, Richard J. Stumpf, was prepared to testify that Sony could install a $15 jamming device in VCRs that would stop unwanted copying. The device would have responded to signals embedded in television programs, preventing recording when copyright holders did not grant permission to have their work copied. If the device worked as promised, it is possible that Judge Warren J. Ferguson might have found that Sony had not done enough to deter its customers from using their VCRs for illegal purposes. Judge Ferguson could have found that Sony needed to employ a similar form of copy protection in order to remain free from liability when customers used their VCRs for illegal copying. (Decades later, the Ninth Circuit would reach a similar conclusion about the file-sharing software company Napster.) But instead, Judge Ferguson dismissed the argument, refusing to hear Stumpf's testimony at all. "As sure as you or I are sitting in this courtroom today," he explained to the court, "some bright young entrepreneur, unconnected with Sony, is going to come up with a device to unjam the jam. And then we have a device to jam the unjamming of the jam, and we all end up like jelly."[6]

Judge Ferguson's logic was as impeccable as his exposition was memorable. Every new form of copy protection is eventually defeated, and the copy protection arms race never ends. But the futility of the endeavor did not stop Hollywood studios from adding copy protection to VHS tapes. Even though Universal failed in its attempt to have the copy protection legally mandated, the studios continued to experiment with different technologies for blocking video copying. Macrovision emerged as the industry standard, and all of the studios eventually employed Macrovision on prerecorded tapes, despite the fact that a $200–$300 image stabilizer already on the market could easily counteract the Macrovision signal, resulting in high-quality copies.

What effect did Macrovision have? First, it did little to stop large-scale piracy. Pirates could simply purchase an image stabilizer and get on with their work. In fact, a healthy new market for image stabilizers developed, as Judge Ferguson predicted. Schools and other institutions that made clips from videotapes for fair use purposes were also largely unaffected, since many of them could also afford image stabilizers. In the end, home users felt the largest impact from Macrovision. VCR owners regularly complained that Macrovision caused interference and distortion when they played their legally purchased or rented tapes. Other home users were led to buy image stabilizers on top of their already expensive VCR purchases, or they discovered that Macrovision did not impair the copies they made when they recorded to Betamax or 8mm videocassettes. Interested readers need only open up *Popular Science* or even the *New York Times* to find articles explaining methods for getting around copy protection. In short, Macrovision was a nuisance rather than a real deterrent, and it affected home users, not pirates or organizations that might have attempted to profit from their copying.[7]

Why then did Hollywood studios continue to invest in and use copy protection? Perhaps the studio executives were content to prevent copying by VCR owners too lazy to investigate alternate means of making copies—clearly the majority of VCR owners. Perhaps they saw Macrovision as an investment in the future: they hoped that the technology would improve, or they held out hopes for legal enforcement of copy protection. Perhaps there was a psychological effect: filmmakers and the studio executives felt better knowing that their films were going out into the world with a lock, however flimsy. After all, most diary locks are easily pried open, and in World War II Allied cryptologists regularly read Germany's encrypted communications. No doubt all of these factors were important, but most practically Macrovision was important because of the message that it sent, not its effectiveness. When VCR owners encountered Macrovision, they were reminded of the limits studios wanted to place on the use of VHS tapes. In many cases, the limits studios set with Macrovision mirrored the legal limits established by copyright law. But in many other instances, Macrovision stood in the way of legitimate fair uses of video, and consumers had to decide whether or not they wanted to take the next step and get around the copy protection.

While the film industry experimented with Macrovision, music companies turned to copy protection to save them from what Recording Industry

Association of America (RIAA) president Stanley Gortikov called the "assassins" at Sony and other electronics companies. In the 1980s, Gortikov led an all-out campaign to keep digital audiotape out of the American market. Magnetic tape recorders had been available to consumers since the late 1940s, but when consumers made copies with analog media, the sound was degraded with each successive copy. The high fidelity of digital recording, Gortikov told Congress on multiple occasions, necessitated a new form of regulation. And one of the solutions that he sought was a legal mandate that copy protection systems be included in all digital audio players. Gortikov and the music industry asked further that it be made illegal to circumvent or disable the copy protection on digital audiotapes.[8]

In 1987, Senator Al Gore and Representative Henry Waxman proposed bills that would have achieved the RIAA's objectives and mandated the inclusion of anti-copying technology in digital audio players. Those bills and a subsequent Senate bill failed to win much support, but after years of negotiations the Audio Home Recording Act of 1992 finally introduced congressionally mandated copy protection to copyright law. The Audio Home Recording Act required that the Serial Copyright Management System be included in digital audiotape players. This form of copy protection allowed for the creation of backup copies, but consumers were blocked from making copies of the copies. Eliminating second-generation copies was intended to prevent the serial sharing of commercial music. Significantly, computers were specifically exempt from this legislation—a concession that the recording industry would greatly regret just a few years later. When computers and MP3 players began to replace audiotape as the major medium for music copying, the Audio Home Recording Act, which only applied to digital audiotape, became all but irrelevant.[9]

The Audio Home Recording Act's effectiveness may have been short-lived, but it gave Warren Lieberfarb and other Hollywood executives confidence to move ahead with plans to adopt the DVD format. If Congress had been receptive to the music industry's claims that the high-quality copies made possible by digital audiotape required a ban on hacking copy protection, it followed that digital video would need the same protection. The election of President Bill Clinton and Vice President Al Gore the year after the passage of the Audio Home Recording Act further indicated the ascendency of a new copyright regime for digital media—one based on locking media behind digital encryption. Shortly after taking office, Clinton and Gore formed a working group to study the growing "information superhighway." Among other findings, the group concluded that copy protection would be necessary to encourage media companies to release their content on the web. These two forces—the release of protected digital video in the DVD format and the recommendation that copy protection be legally mandated to encourage the movement of content to the web—eventually came together to create the anticircumvention provisions of the DMCA.

In 1998 the Hollywood studios finally realized Edison's dream: they were able to use a legally backed technical standard to control all uses of their digital content. As we have already seen, the DMCA made it illegal to circumvent the copy protection on digital media (including DVDs) or to traffic in circumvention tools. This mandate gave the studios the ability to block competition, as Edison once had. Since only authorized companies were licensed to use the decryption key, the studios could determine which devices would be able to play DVDs legally. Computers running the Open Source computer-operating system Linux, for example, were not authorized to play DVDs; computers running the Apple and Microsoft operating systems could play them. The studios also refused to license the decryption key for use in machines that could play DVDs from multiple geographic regions or DVD players with analog output cables that could be used for copying. Since studios' and other copyright holders' new legal powers seemed to stretch to technology as well as content, intellectual property scholars began to refer to the rights granted by the DMCA as a "paracopyright" or "pseudo copyright." The DMCA created a new layer of control on top of the traditional realm of copyright protection.[10]

In this new regime, copy protection systems do not even have to be very good. Hackers quickly cracked DVD copy protection, the Content Scrambling System (CSS), and they began to circulate the decryption key, popularly known as DeCSS. The Motion Picture Association of America, the DVD Copy Control Association (which licenses the DVD decryption key), and the studios quickly teamed up to block the distribution of DeCSS. Although the studios have consistently won cases that have sought to halt the circulation of or the unauthorized use of DeCSS, programs that use DeCSS remain widely available on the internet. Legitimate businesses are prevented from developing technologies that deploy unlicensed decryption keys, but consumers still have easy access to the tools for playing and copying DVDs and other digital media.

In this way, CSS encryption's effect is very different from that of pre-DMCA copy protection. Before the passage of the DMCA, Macrovision was an annoyance to individual home video copiers, but it did little to stop either large-scale piracy or institutions, like schools, that engaged in frequent fair use copying. CSS encryption continues to pose little threat to pirates, many of whom copy entire disks with copy protection intact. But the DMCA has dramatically raised the stakes for individuals and institutions that want to make copies of digital video files for reasons that would otherwise be protected by fair use. Neither Macrovision nor CSS discriminate between fair use and illegal copying; they hamper legal and illegal copying equally. Before the passage of the DMCA, educators, artists, and amateur video makers who believed that their copying was covered by fair use could bypass Macrovision and defend their actions in court if it came to that. The DMCA, however, made circumventing copy protection illegal, regardless of whether the copying was protected by fair use or not.

The second effect of the anticircumvention provisions is that a very large number of consumers have refused to accept the artificial limitations imposed by encryption. The DMCA has driven them to break the law, using illegal decryption programs to copy DVDs to iPods or downloading videos from file-sharing sites because no legal alternative exists. Since the Ninth Circuit Court of Appeals effectively shut down the file-sharing service Napster in 2001, the number of active peer-to-peer file sharers has almost doubled. These may be illegal activities, but they frequently result from frustration rather than malice. And as I have seen while teaching college students, year after year the use of illegal copying tools and illegal means of acquisition becomes more and more naturalized as legal alternatives remain scarce and limiting.[11]

Is this the irrevocable condition of digital media and the internet? Can these problems be solved? Former Virginia Representative Rick Boucher tried repeatedly to introduce legislation to reverse some of the most restrictive elements of the DMCA, but none of his proposed bills gained much support. It is unlikely that a legislative solution is in the offing. If there is a solution, it will have to come from the media industries themselves. Media moguls since Edison have asked for the ability to control the distribution and use of media through legally backed copy protection. Now that they have finally been granted that power, they will have to realize that it comes with much greater responsibility than they had ever imagined. An overly firm hand has alienated consumers and jeopardized the kind of technical innovation that has always increased video consumption and filled Hollywood's coffers. Hollywood studios will have to learn how to wield their power more judiciously and creatively in order win back consumers and stimulate the video market that is essential to their continued existence.

EXEMPTIONS TO THE DMCA

In a last-minute addition to the DMCA, Congress responded to the concerns of public interest groups. They empowered the Librarian of Congress to create exemptions to the anticircumvention provisions. Every three years, the Copyright Office solicits comments from anyone who can show that the DMCA has interfered with fair use and thus requires an exemption. After several rounds of written comments, a series of hearings, and a consultation with the Commerce Department, the Register of Copyrights makes a recommendation to the Librarian of Congress. The Librarian then issues the list of exemptions. Three years later, they start the process over again.[12]

Fair use advocates and legal scholars were initially excited by the rulemaking process; it promised to return the rights of consumers, educators, librarians, and the many others whose existing fair use practices had been curtailed by the DMCA. Consumer advocacy groups, legal scholars, and archivists petitioned for exemptions during the 2000 and 2003 rulemakings. By the end of the 2003 rulemaking, however, only four very narrow exemptions had been created. One exemption was designed to help blind readers turn on the Read Aloud function of ebooks even when the publisher had blocked that option. Another exemption allowed archivists to copy old video games in order to make preservation copies. All of the exemptions were very narrow, and the number of petitions for exemptions began to drop. The usually active Electronic Frontier Foundation, for example, decided to boycott the 2006 rulemaking, claiming that the process was "failing consumers completely."[13]

The biggest problem with the rulemaking was contained in the statutory language of the DMCA. It instructed the Copyright Office to create exemptions for "classes of works." But fair use is about use and context; it is not determined by the class of works being used. The exemption process and fair use were inherently incompatible. Nevertheless, more comments were submitted during the 2006 rulemaking, including one by me and two of my colleagues at the University of Pennsylvania, Katherine Sender and Michael X. Delli Carpini. We asked for an exemption for media professors who need to make clips for use in classes. At least since the 1910s, film professors have been using film clips as illustrations in classes. And the VCR made it easy for educators to put together a compilation of film and television clips for class lectures. But the DMCA's anticircumvention provisions blocked educators from updating their practice to accommodate DVDs and other digital media. Media professors were forced to either rely on low-quality analog clips or transgress the law. With the help of American University law students, we crafted an exemption that we hoped would meet the class-of-works standard, but we also made the case that use and users need to be considered in the rulemaking process.[14]

Who would oppose a few professors who wanted to make clips for use in classes? At the hearing, I was surprised to find professional lobbyists from the MPAA, Time-Warner, the DVD Copy Control Association (DVD-CCA), Pioneer Electronics, and a lawyer representing a dozen other groups opposed to any and all exemptions. Only Jonathan Band, who represented library organizations, sat on my side of the table. What were the objections? Pioneer's representative wanted to sell a DVD jukebox that the company was developing. Her argument, I guess, is that the market should be allowed to correct for lost rights. But that DVD player never appeared, and the market has not met this need. The counsel for the DVD-CCA argued that educators could develop their own DVD player — one that met their needs. The DVD-CCA licenses the keys needed to unlock DVD encryption and allow DVD players to access DVDs. After some questioning, it appeared unlikely that the DVD-CCA would authorize a DVD player to make clips in a dynamic way. Like the position of the DVD-CCA, a Time-Warner representative suggested that the tight control of the DMCA did not need to be relinquished. She noted that professors could get permission every time that they needed to use a clip. Not only would such a process be insurmountably cumbersome, but it could easily turn into a form of censorship. Documentary filmmakers, for example, are regularly turned down when they seek to license clips for use in educational films. How readily would Disney license its clips for a course on racism in the media, just for example? Finally, an MPAA executive argued that VHS tapes are good enough for educators. Professors do not need high-quality images to talk about the details of a film or television show.

While these arguments revealed the vision of total control that the mainstream film industry had been harboring since the days of Edison, they were easy to counter. And after demonstrating to the Copyright Office panel why high-quality digital clips are important to media educators, the exemption was granted. The granting of the exemption was not a foregone conclusion — just the opposite. The bar for proving harm had been set very high, and the class-of-works category seemed impossible to marry to the needs of professionals who relied on fair use. But the Librarian of Congress was able to create the exemption, because the Copyright Office staff had changed their interpretation of the statute. They decided to consider use and users in the crafting of exemptions. This was a big change.

With the new criteria for exemptions, a large and loosely aligned group of educators, filmmakers, and media professionals petitioned to have the exemption expanded in 2009. This consortium successfully broadened the exemption to include all professors, media studies students, documentary filmmakers, and noncommercial filmmakers who needed to make clips for many professional uses. The exemption process, which in 2006 appeared to be a shriveled stump no longer suitable for supporting the return of fair use rights, made good on its original promise. The exemption process became a significant venue for checking the deleterious effects of the DMCA.[15]

Why did the rulemaking process change so much? I would like to take some credit, but I think the truth is that the Copyright Office was responding to Hollywood's poor stewardship of the anticircumvention provisions of the DMCA. The rulemaking takes place every three years, and with each new rulemaking came promises from Hollywood representatives that new technologies for the flexible use of digital media were on the horizon. But in reality, each three-year period saw more uses closed off by more and more powerful copy protection. Because Hollywood studios failed to exercise their new legally backed power with restraint, and because they used the DMCA to block legitimate uses of digital media, the Copyright Office intervened.

APPLE AND THE RISE OF CLOSED SYSTEMS

One company in particular, Apple Inc., has emerged as the greatest beneficiary of the DMCA's ban on circumventing copy protection. As a direct result of the DMCA, we will see in this section, Apple moved in a few short years from having virtually no stake in the media business to being the premier legal conduit for online and mobile access to movies and television shows. Together, Apple and the DMCA brought Hollywood, often kicking and screaming, into the digital age. Under a different regulatory regime, it is clear, the online and mobile experience of media would have looked very different.

In the decade following the passage of the DMCA, Apple went from being a small, though historically important, computer manufacturer with less than 4 percent of the personal computer market to being one of the largest media retailers and device manufacturers in the world. By 2008, Apple's iPod media player controlled over 90 percent of the market, and the company's iTunes store had sold over 1 billion songs and more than 200 million TV episodes. Many changes led to Apple's success as a media giant, including new leadership, innovative products, and clever market-ing. But no factor outweighed the new media environment created by the DMCA. The same design and business strategies that led to Apple's steep decline in the 1980s, we will see, caused the company to flourish in the early twenty-first century as a direct result of the DMCA.[16]

Apple's cofounder and former CEO, Steve Jobs, had a singular vision of a closed, almost hermetically sealed, computer user experience since he was a teenager. In the days when computers were the playthings of engi-neers, hobbyists, and hackers, Jobs dreamed of turning them into discrete, user-friendly "appliances," as he liked to put it. Throughout collaborations on projects at Apple, Jobs consistently pushed for his vision of a computer experience as streamlined and simple as possible. This vision went hand in hand with increased control over user choices. When designing the Apple II, Jobs argued for the inclusion of only essential peripheral card slots on the circuit board, one for a printer and one for a monitor, making it as easy as possible for users. But Steve Wozniak, Apple's other cofounder and the principle architect of the Apple II, wanted more slots. Wozniak hoped that engineers, hobbyists, and hackers would discover new uses for the slots, and he wanted companies to be able to create new periph-eral devices to attach to the computer. Wozniak won that particular argu-ment, but Jobs's vision of a closed computer did not waiver. When Jobs led the team that designed the first Macintosh computer (fig. 5.3), memos instructed the engineers to make the technology as invisible as possible. "Seeing the guts is taboo," read one memo that went on to push engineers to hide everything except the power cord. "Ten points," it half-jokingly concluded, "if you eliminate the power cord." Improving the user experi-ence, in Jobs's vision, entailed hiding the computer's internal workings and, as a result, limiting the unintended possibilities of the machine. It also entailed blocking other companies from using Apple's platforms or interacting with Apple's hardware.[17]

A key element of Jobs's vision for Apple was that the company makes both the hardware and the software of its computers. When consumers buy an Apple, they are submersed completely in an Apple universe, and Apple has taken great pains to control the software and hardware that runs on and interacts with its devices. Like the Edison Manufacturing Company, Apple has frequently used lawsuits to prevent other companies from creat-ing interoperable devices and operating systems. The company has won many suits against potential competitors that "cloned" Apple's hardware and software. But one important case involving Microsoft proved decisive for the fate of the closed approach to computer design.

FIGURE 5.3 Steve Jobs (*left*) introduces the Macintosh computer (1984). John Sculley (*right*) introduces the Lisa. (Courtesy Getty Images)

In 1983, Apple released the first commercial operating system with a graphical user interface (or GUI). Apple's Lisa and later Macintosh operating systems had onscreen windows, mouse-controlled pointers, and the look of a virtual desktop—all of the visual elements that came to characterize the computer user experience. Apple did not invent the GUI; researchers at Xerox's experimental laboratory Xerox PARC developed the basic elements of the GUI. But in a huge strategic blunder, Xerox executives failed to see the commercial potential of their creation. After a tour of the Xerox PARC lab, Jobs set out to refine the idea of the GUI and make it a commercial product. Apple released the first mass-produced computers with GUIs, and the company licensed several elements of its design to Microsoft, where engineers began to create the GUI operating system that they would eventually call Windows. When Microsoft finally released its new operating system, however, Jobs thought it resembled the Macintosh's GUI too closely; it went beyond the narrow licensing terms, and Apple sued for copyright infringement. Microsoft's CEO, Bill Gates, responded to Jobs's claims by questioning the originality of Apple's GUI. "Well, Steve," Gates reportedly told Jobs in a private meeting, "I think there's more than one way of looking at it. I think it's more like we both had this rich neighbor named Xerox and I broke into his house to steal the TV set and found out that you had already stolen it." Copyright protects originality, and the dispute questioned not only where the ideas had come from but whether elements like virtual trash cans and folders were too obvious for anyone to own them. [18]

The case posed many novel questions for copyright law, and it dragged on for years. More important than the technical legal questions in this context, however, is how copyright law drove Apple's business strategy. As Apple's CEO at the time, John Sculley, explained, "Apple's board was absolutely convinced that we would win the suit," giving them the power to exploit their monopoly on the GUI. Apple, in other words, hoped to tie its operating system to its hardware and to be able to force consumers who wanted to use a GUI to buy an Apple computer. Apple would also have had more control over which companies could create products that worked with its closed system. Reflecting on the case years later, Sculley explained that the belief that Apple would win the case "may have lulled us into a bit of complacency." Innovation at Apple slowed down, because of their expected ability to control the desktop software environment. With control over both the hardware and software, there was no need to improve on their products.[19]

But when Apple failed to secure its monopoly, Microsoft achieved dominance in the desktop software business. Microsoft licensed its software broadly to many computer manufacturers while Apple's closed system brought the company to the brink of bankruptcy. Apple did eventually ease its grip on its products, and it licensed its operating system to several manufacturers. But it was too late. As Apple executive vice president Ian D. W. Diery told *Newsweek* in 1994, "If we had licensed earlier, we would be the Microsoft of today."[20]

Jobs left Apple during these years, and when he returned as interim CEO, one of the first things he did was heal the breach with Microsoft. In his keynote address to the 1997 Macworld conference in Boston, Jobs painfully announced a new collaboration with Microsoft. The two companies had finally ended their intellectual property dispute, and Microsoft had agreed to purchase $150 million of Apple stock. When Jobs announced that Microsoft's browser would come preinstalled on Macintosh computers, the crowd booed loudly. They did not want more Microsoft products infiltrating Apple's machines. In complete control of his audience, however, Jobs next announced that rival browsers would be preinstalled as well, "because," he said, "we believe in choice." The last line was greeted with loud and prolonged laughter from the crowd. It was a punch line that resonated on many levels. Clearly, Microsoft was the behemoth of the industry, and Apple was the much less frequently exercised choice among computer buyers. "We believe in choice" meant that Jobs believed in offering consumers an alternative to Microsoft. Jobs's line also invoked the Justice Department's ongoing investigation into Microsoft's anticompetitive decision not to preinstall the Netscape browser on computers running Windows; the DOJ would file its case against Microsoft the following year. But there was yet another uncomfortable truth embedded in Jobs's phrase—one made clear by his smirk as he delivered the line: Jobs and Apple did not believe in choice. On the contrary, at the time, the company allowed its software to be used on only one brand of computer—Apple. And its hardware ran only one operating system—Apple's. As soon as Jobs took the reigns of Apple, he canceled the short-lived licensing program, calling the Mac clone companies "leeches." And he returned to the strategy of building a seamless, user-friendly closed system of hardware and software. In another conference keynote address years later, after Apple had introduced its iPhone and iPad, Jobs defended his vision of the closed system, explaining that, "It's the complete solution."[21]

After Jobs's return to Apple, the company introduced a string of successful media products in addition to increasing its share of the desktop computer market. And it is no coincidence that the passage of the DMCA marks the turning point in Apple's history. Jobs's vision of a closed system fit perfectly with the anticircumvention provisions of the DMCA. In 2001, Apple released its first iPod music player with the slogan, "Rip, Mix, Burn." Consumers were encouraged to "space shift" their music collection, copying their CDs and transferring the tracks to their iPods. Initial iPod sales were good, but they shot up more than five times in the year after Apple introduced the iTunes Music Store. The store allowed customers to purchase music and later music videos, television shows, movies, and mobile applications. The only catch is that the majority of the material was (and remains) locked behind Apple's FairPlay copy protection software, which prevents files from being played on non-Apple products. As consumers began to build libraries of iTunes purchases, it became more and more difficult to switch to another online media store, whose content could not be played on an iPod, or to purchase a new media player, which could not play iTunes purchases. When Apple created a version of its iTunes software and store for Microsoft Windows, they promoted it with the slogan "Hell Froze Over," mocking the company's own reluctance to create products that interacted outside of the Apple universe. But iTunes for Windows was really a Trojan Horse—not a computer virus but a suspicious gift. iTunes may sit on Windows machines, but it only interacts with iPods and other Apple devices; it functions like a small Apple outpost on Windows computers. By 2004, Apple controlled more than 90 percent of the portable hard drive media market, making it very difficult for competitors, even Microsoft, to enter the field.[22]

In one sense, iTunes marks the success of the DMCA's anticircumvention provision. Surely, media companies would have been much more reluctant to release their content on the internet without copy protection. But, at the same time, iTunes' success points to the pitfalls of this approach. The DMCA gave Apple an unhealthy near-monopoly on the market. Not only has Apple's copy protection locked competitors out of the market, it has also allowed Apple to dictate the terms of online media sales. Despite repeated attempts by music companies to introduce variable pricing, Apple was able to retain its 99-cent per song price until 2007. The 99-cent price may have been good for consumers, it may even have been the right price to sustain online music sales; but Apple's ability to dictate pricing to the recording companies demonstrates the enormous power the company achieved in the media field in just a few short years. Many companies have pulled their music and videos from iTunes (or threatened to pull their content) in order to have some leverage with the primary outlet for online media. In an attempt to break free of Apple's control, one music company, EMI, began to release music free of copy protection in 2007, a move that immediately allowed a second company, Amazon.com, to launch a successful music store where so many others had failed.

Before EMI announced its decision to sell music without copy protection, Steve Jobs surprised many by publishing a public letter delineating some of the by-then-well-known problems of copy protection: it encourages piracy; eventually it will always be hacked; and it only hurts the consumers who want to use their content legally—real criminals will always find ways around it. Perhaps these were Jobs's personal feelings about copy protection. Perhaps he was showing sympathy for the many consumers who were frustrated by copy protection. Perhaps he was trying to take control of a decision that came from music companies, who all eventually followed suit and removed copy protection from their tracks. Whatever Jobs's motivation, it is difficult to avoid the conclusion that his statement did not change Apple's policy significantly. Copy protection has continued to be beneficial to Apple. All commercial video on iTunes and all of the mobile applications that it sells continue to have copy protection. And consumers who want to purchase commercial videos and applications for their iPods, iPhones, and iPads continue to find it very difficult to extricate themselves from iTunes or to use non-Apple devices.

Many former skeptics have now conceded that Apple's closed system works well in the DMCA-governed mobile media market of the early

twenty-first century. In 1998, Bill Gates told the reporter Robert X. Cringley that Steve Jobs "can't win" as CEO of Apple; the challenge was too
great. A decade later, however, Gates had to confess to another reporter
that perhaps Apple's closed system had been the best approach for the
time. In a prominent Sunday *New York Times* article that accompanied
the release of Apple's iPad, technology writer Steven Johnson announced
that the logic of computer innovation had changed. Like many others,
Johnson had promoted an open environment for innovation on the internet, what Harvard law professor Jonathan Zitrain has called the "genera-
tive" environment of the early internet. But like Gates, Johnson's view
had also come full circle. He celebrated the innovation available through
Apple's mobile application store, which he called one of "the most carefully policed software platforms in history."[23]

Apple's closed-system approach has clearly succeeded where it failed
before, and in May 2010, Apple's market capitalization surpassed Microsoft's for the first time.[24] The DMCA ensured Apple's success in several
ways. It encouraged media company executives to release content to the
iTunes store, secure in the knowledge that circumvention of copy protection was illegal. The DMCA also allowed Jobs and others in Apple's
management to sell media and portable media players, confident that
competitors could not access their platform. This has led to much innovation in the burgeoning field of mobile software applications. But a severe
price has been paid. As we have seen so many times before, the combination of copy protection and anticircumvention laws has normalized piracy.
Even iTunes users with little technical knowledge have learned how to
circumvent Apple's FairPlay copy protection. And Apple's closed mobile
application store has led thousands of users around the world to "jailbreak"
(break the encryption) on their iPhones, iPods, and iPads in order to run
third-party software.[25]

In addition, too much of the innovation has been on Apple's terms
and confined to Apple's proprietary platforms. Hundreds of thousands
of mobile applications have been created for Apple products. Speakers,
keyboards, chargers, and headphones of all kinds have been designed to
be plugged into a proprietary Apple input jack. Apple has begun to have
significant competition in the online and mobile media distribution business. It will take time to see if Google or Amazon can compete. But even
if another competitor does emerge, Apple has been allowed to domi-
nate digital media distribution for almost a decade and a half, largely
because of the DMCA. As Edison had hoped, the legal enforcement
of copy protection has allowed a single company to control the market,

and Apple has commanded this market to a degree not even Edison could have imagined.

BUILDING A "SAFE HARBOR"

When Congress passed the DMCA in 1998, online video was an extremely limited field. Only one-quarter of U.S. homes had any internet access, and most were using dial-up connections, far too slow to download or stream videos. Large companies were hurriedly creating websites to serve as their front door in cyberspace. A few companies, like Fox, even used short low-resolution video clips on their websites. In the rare instances when video was available, however, download times could be measured in minutes of video downloaded per hour, and the clips were generally very short and of poor quality. These videos suggested the potential of the medium, rather than being useful themselves. Proving the point in a widely read 1995 essay, "What Is Digital Cinema?," theorist and artist Lev Manovich likened QuickTime movies of the period to the short loops Edison presented on the kinetoscope. The video compression and formats that made instantaneous video streaming possible were still six or seven years off when legislators and studio lawyers were discussing the creation of the DMCA.[26]

By the late 1990s, another exciting development was taking place. Internet portal companies began to allow users to become their own publishers and eventually broadcasters. AOL (then America On-Line), Prodigy, and Yahoo! provided server space and tools for its customers to create "home-pages." Users posted information and photos about family activities, personal interests, or local organizations. These sites joined the user-generated sites that university faculty members and students had been posting on campus networks for decades. Online bulletin boards also allowed their members to upload and exchange information about science fiction, software development, or other topics. These were the seeds of what publisher and internet entrepreneur Tim O'Reilly would dub Web 2.0—i.e., the rise of websites that allow users to provide the content.[27]

User-generated sites were filled with copyrighted images, texts, and occasionally video that had been posted without permission. Most copyright owners waited to see how the net would develop, but a few historically protective organizations filed lawsuits to try to halt the circulation of their material. The Church of Scientology, *Playboy* magazine, and video game publisher Sega all sued bulletin board operators rather than attempt the arduous task of going after each individual uploader. In the

Church of Scientology case, the court found that Netcom, a large bulletin board host based in the San Francisco Bay area, could not be held liable for the scattered infringing uploads that occurred on some of its servers. But in both the *Playboy* and Sega cases, judges decided that the defendants could be held liable for the high-volume trading of copyrighted material that occurred among their narrowly focused communities. These bulletin boards devoted to pornographic images and video games, respectively, seemed to be made for the illicit sharing of copyrighted material. But how could the courts or Congress differentiate between services that allowed users to post material in good faith and those that were built for piracy? Should the network operators be held at all responsible for the material that users uploaded? On one hand, it would have been extremely expensive and cumbersome for copyright owners to address each instance of copyright infringement with an individual lawsuit—a lesson that the recording industry soon learned. But on the other hand, the burden of monitoring every file uploaded to a server would have stopped the web 2.0 boom before it began, crippling services like AOL and Prodigy. This was one of the dilemmas that Congress faced when crafting the DMCA.[28]

There were civil liberties issues to consider as well. In the Scientology case, the church sued a former minister who was making the organization's carefully guarded texts available online. The texts revealed some of the organization's bizarre mythology, which many thought potential converts and critics had a right to see. The court dismissed any First Amendment issues in the case, but at least some members of Congress recognized that freedom of speech could be in jeopardy if hosting companies had to share in the responsibility for every item posted on the web. The Communications Decency Act of 1996 had already provided web hosts some protection from defamation and negligence claims. But what about material that infringed copyright law? Hollywood and other large content owners pushed to make web-hosting companies directly liable for infringement that took place on their networks. But film industry leaders were so intent on passing the anticircumvention measures that they eventually capitulated. Online video also seemed to be a pipe dream in 1998, and few media moguls could have predicted the popularity of websites like YouTube. When the DMCA negotiations finally ended, the safe harbor provision resembled the Scientology decision, and it shielded online service providers from becoming entangled in copyright disputes.[29]

Congressional leaders hailed this as a perfect commercial compromise. The DMCA would be a two-pronged stimulus for the U.S. economy. The ban on circumvention would encourage Hollywood studios and other content companies to make their libraries of material available online. And, at the same time, the safe harbor provision would encourage companies to build large websites and services that encouraged the free exchange of ideas. Speaking on the floor of the House of Representatives, Congressman Barney Frank joined many others to celebrate the fair balance they had struck. "What I am most happy about in this bill," Frank said,

> is I think we have hit about the right balance. We have hit a balance which fully protects intellectual property, which is essential to the creative life of America, to the quality of our life, because if we do not protect the creators, there will be less creation. But at the same time we have done this in a way that will not give to the people in the business of running the online service entities and running Internet, it will not give them either an incentive or an excuse to censor.[30]

The safe harbor provision, however, did not come without a few conditions. Service providers like Yahoo! and YouTube must follow proper procedures and act quickly in order to be protected from copyright lawsuits brought against users. If a user uploads a video to YouTube that contains copyrighted material, the copyright holder may send a "takedown" notice to YouTube. YouTube must then remove the video from its site and notify the user who originally uploaded it. If the uploader feels that the work is protected by fair use or otherwise unfairly accused of copyright infringement, he or she may send a "counternotice" to YouTube. The copyright owner then has fourteen days in which to file a lawsuit. After the fourteen days, YouTube may repost the infringing video. If a lawsuit does ensue, it is a matter to be settled between the copyright owner and the person who uploaded the video; YouTube stays above the fray.[31]

The safe harbor provision is, in many ways, an ingenious solution to the problem caused by the scale and democratic nature of Web 2.0 sites like YouTube, Flickr, and Wikipedia. The DMCA creates a kind of self-policing and grassroots arbitration system for the web. But the notice and takedown procedures can also be abused and manipulated. Copyright owners can be too quick to send takedown notices, and large media companies have been known to send them out by the tens or even hundreds of thousands. The system also requires both copyright owners and users to have some specialized knowledge in order to take advantage of the notice and takedown system. In this way, the safe harbor provision favors corporations and wealthier copyright holders and users who have access to legal counsel. There is, for example, no way to count the number of instances in which users did not repost perfectly legal videos because they were intimidated by the receipt of a takedown notice. In other ways, however, the DMCA empowers users and places large corporations at a disadvantage. Users may take risks online that they cannot take in other media. A video artist or journalist, for example, may post a video that pushes the boundaries of fair use, knowing that they are likely to receive a takedown notice before a copyright lawsuit is filed. On the other hand, meeting the demands of the DMCA has been onerous for large copyright holders or web-hosting corporations like Google. The DMCA requires a huge investment in human labor; large offices are now entirely devoted to scouring the web for infringing material and handling DMCA takedown notices and counternotices.

Unlike the anticircumvention provisions of the DMCA, the safe harbor provision was not the realization of a hundred-plus-year dream of media moguls. The safe harbor provision is genuinely novel in the relations it establishes between copyright holders and web users. The DMCA introduces a grassroots triage and arbitration system that invites copyright owners and users to solve their own problems before courts become involved. Still in its early stages of development, the safe harbor provision has, we will see, both preserved much of the old information economy that governed fair use and changed it in significant ways.

SOWING COPYRIGHT CONFUSION

If online video was in its gestational phase in 1998, it fully matured between 2004 and 2006. The combination of Adobe Flash Player's efficient video-streaming formats and the penetration of fast broadband connections finally made video delivery over the internet feasible. Dozens of websites devoted to sharing video online began to appear, including Revver, Vimeo, Metacafe, Blip.tv, YouTube, Google Video, Veoh, and Yahoo! Video. In addition to technical advances, all of these sites depended on the safe harbor provision of the DMCA. YouTube alone was processing more than 65,000 uploads a day by the summer of 2006.[32] That volume would have been very difficult to sustain if every video was subject to a copyright analysis by companies' lawyers. This boom in video-sharing sites could not help but transform both film and television distribution and the communities that relied on fair use to make and distribute videos.

It is important to understand that YouTube did not start the culture of video sharing. This was not a case of "if you build it they will come." In fact, as Henry Jenkins has demonstrated, the opposite is true. "The emergence of participatory cultures of all kinds over the past several decades," Jenkins explains, "paved the way for the early embrace, quick adoption, and diverse use of such platforms. . . . If YouTube seems to have sprung up overnight, it is because so many groups were ready for something like YouTube."[33] Those groups include parents making home videos, documentary filmmakers, amateur comedians parodying music videos, television fans, video artists, and, apparently, anyone who happens to have recorded his or her pet looking knowingly into the camera. Other YouTube users flocked to the site to upload or view clips taken from television or commercial videos. It is not just that all of these communities preexisted YouTube, but their fair use conventions, as we saw in the previous chapter, had been worked out over decades as well. The fans, avant-garde artists, home video makers, and other fair use communities had spent decades learning when they should worry about attracting the attention of copyright holders. Fair use, after all, is built on a combination of conventions and legal precedent. Almost overnight, these long-established communities, each with their own individual relationship to mainstream media, were thrust into a completely new copyright environment. They all became subject to increased surveillance, and their cultures of fair use were homogenized as large media companies sought one-size-fits-all solutions to employing the DMCA to control copyright infringement.

The first group that Hollywood studios noticed were users who uploaded clips of *South Park*, the *Daily Show*, and other television shows and movies. A fascinating 2008 report from an American University team led by Peter Jaszi and Patricia Aufderheide outlines the many instances in which uploaded clips from commercial television and film may be protected by fair use. Brief clips might be used, for example, to start a conversation, or document a historic event.[34] It is also clear, however, that in many instances users have posted excerpts of *The Simpsons* or *The Matrix* in violation of copyright simply to replace the commercial viewing experience. Regardless of their copyright status, film and television copyright owners have retained an ambivalent position about these clips. Even when the clips are clearly infringing, they may function effectively as free marketing. And media companies have taken a haphazard approach to addressing clips on video-sharing sites.

At first, video-sharing sites looked like the inevitable extension of Hollywood's transmedia approach to storytelling and marketing. Sony bought the video-sharing site Grouper for $65 million, and media conglomerate Viacom lost frenzied bids to acquire both MySpace and YouTube.

Hollywood franchises were reaching across media, and many producers had already found that YouTube brought new viewers to their films and videos. The Monty Python group, for instance (as mentioned in chapter 3), responded to users who posted Python clips by creating their own You-Tube channel. The Pythons uploaded high-quality images and attached a plea for viewers to purchase DVDs if they liked the online videos. At least in the short term, this strategy worked. Sales of Python DVDs soared, and one of their films quickly surged to No. 2 on Amazon.com's bestseller list. When the *Saturday Night Live* sketch "Lazy Sunday" became a viral hit on YouTube, NBC sent a takedown notice and made the clip available for free on its own network site and through iTunes. After losing You-Tube to Google, Viacom became one of the largest opponents of video-sharing sites. But even as Viacom sent over 100,000 takedown notices and sued YouTube for $1 billion for copyright infringement, the company's marketers employed third parties to upload clips of Viacom content to YouTube in order to stimulate interest in its projects. According to some reports, Viacom then sent takedown notices for the removal of clips that had been uploaded at the company's own request. Legal and marketing departments have consistently clashed over the question of when to take down clips from commercial media, and they have left a wake of copyright confusion.[35]

YouTube addressed this issue by testing novel methods of partnering with media companies. NBC, CBS, Viacom, and every major music label have had on-again, off-again negotiations and agreements with YouTube to share revenue from ads displayed alongside the media companies' content, even if a YouTube user and not the company itself uploaded the video. This arrangement had the potential to revolutionize fair use: not only did YouTube introduce a method for creators to be compensated when their work was reused, but, at least for short periods, media companies were willing to test the system. Revenue sharing allowed fans, home movie makers, artists, and others to use copyrighted material for free, while the original creators of the material were compensated for the use. Whether or not the so-called "second takers," the amateur creators, should have been compensated for the revenue generated by their work is another issue. The media companies, however, have been skeptical of both the efficacy and the terms of these agreements. And negotiations over revenue sharing have resulted in very public disputes and mass take-down campaigns. It is certainly more than a coincidence that Viacom's $1 billion lawsuit against YouTube followed on the heels of failed revenue-sharing negotiations.[36]

The result of users being caught in the middle of corporate deals has been the sowing of confusion about fair use practices. There may be important legal questions to answer, but as we have seen, the norms and practices that form the culture of fair use are even more important than the legal boundaries. And the mixed signals sent out by media companies have introduced confusion into fair use communities that had long-standing traditions of using copyrighted material.

TAKEDOWN CULTURE AND THE EFF

The confusion caused by shifting corporate policies is clearly just a stage in the development of a new platform for sharing online video. Corporate policies and the practices of fair use communities will no doubt come into alignment once again, even if the process takes decades. But in the meantime, the DMCA has already changed the everyday practice of video fair use. While large media corporations search for unified approaches to managing online video, individual copyright owners and website users have attempted to use the DMCA to defend their personal claims. And one group, the nonprofit law firm and advocacy organization the Electronic Frontier Foundation (EFF), has been involved in many of the most prominent disputes. The EFF has arguably done more than any other organization to create precedents that replace the vagaries of the DMCA's safe harbor provision with concrete guidelines.

Like the internet itself, the EFF was born from the meeting of engineers and the 1960s counterculture. In 1990, pioneering software designers Mitch Kapor and John Gilmore teamed up with Grateful Dead lyricist-turned-internet-evangelist John Perry Barlow to start the EFF. In the early years, the EFF fought landmark court battles that protected civil liberties in the digital age, as the organization continues to do. Since the passage of the DMCA, EFF staff—especially attorneys Wendy Seltzer, Fred von Lohmann, and Corynne McSherry—have also taken on many of the key cases that have shaped the use of the notice and takedown system.

In 2001, Wendy Seltzer brought some transparency to takedown practices when she organized a number of law school centers to found the Chilling Effects website. Ever since Supreme Court Justice William Brenan used the term in a 1965 decision, lawyers have commonly referred to the "chilling effects" created when a policy or court decision discourages free speech or innovation. The Chilling Effects website allows users to post takedown notices and cease-and-desist letters, exposing companies that abuse the system and bringing wider attention to the DMCA more generally. The site gained notoriety in 2002 when the Church of Scientology once again attempted to use the DMCA to silence its critics. The church began to send takedown notices to internet companies that linked to a site devoted to exposing the organization's doctrines. Google acquiesced at first, removing the links. But when Google's DMCA policy was challenged, the search company formed a new DMCA policy, and its management decided to repost the links. (No form of linking has ever been found to be a copyright infringement.) After the incident, Google began to submit all of its takedown notices to Chilling Effects, making the archive an incredibly valuable resource for scholars and anyone looking for data on takedown letters.[37]

The EFF's largest impact on the use of the DMCA's safe harbor provision has come from the organization's willingness to serve as pro bono counsel to internet users who feel that they have been unfairly targeted by takedown notices. In this role, the EFF has defended home videographers, documentarians, parodists, and others who labored under the assumption that their work was protected by fair use. Although the EFF works for free, its clients still assume a significant financial risk by reposting their videos and opening themselves up to copyright infringement lawsuits. Statutory copyright damages in the United States range from $200 to $30,000 per work infringed; that number can go up to $150,000 if the infringement is willful. A simple fan mashup or a work of video art that each use ten clips from copyrighted films might lead to between $7,500 and $1.5 million in damages, plus attorney's fees. As former EFF attorney Fred von Lohmann told a group of New York University Law School students and faculty members, when he takes on a new client who wants to send YouTube a counternotice, he has to inform them of the risks: "[There is a]1 in 100 chance they [will] take your house . . . that intimidates a lot of clients." So a decision to send a DMCA counternotice is rarely undertaken casually.[38]

Copyright infringement lawsuits have been used as a form of backdoor censorship since the eighteenth century, and DMCA takedown notices are no exception. The Church of Scientology may have pioneered the use of takedown notices to silence critics, but many copyright owners followed in their footsteps. In 2007, for instance, "paranormalist" Uri Geller sent a takedown notice to YouTube. Geller rose to fame in the 1970s for his apparent ability to bend spoons and perform other psychokinetic acts. Over the years, Geller has attracted criticism from Johnny Carson and Canadian magician James Randi, who have attempted to debunk Geller's claims about his paranormal abilities. When a small Pennsylvania group posted part of a PBS *NOVA* documentary featuring both Carson and Randi criticizing Geller, Geller's lawyers had it taken down. Geller's company claimed to own eight seconds of the 13-minute video clip that had been posted. The short clip was used to establish context, and it seemed like a clear case of fair use. But that did not stop Geller from reacting quickly to protect his reputation. (I should mention at this point that I was asked by the EFF to serve as an expert witness in this case, although the case was resolved before I had a chance to make a statement on the record.) With the help of EFF, Brian Sapient, who had posted the video, filed a declaratory judgment case, asking a court to decide if Geller's takedown notice was valid. Geller's company, Explorologist Limited, filed a countersuit claiming that the video violated his copyright in the clip. It was a complicated case, with multiple complaints filed in different circuits. Geller's lawyers further muddied the waters by questioning the jurisdiction. Did the infringement occur where the file was uploaded, where the server sat, or where Geller viewed it? Was the case subject to U.S. fair use law or U.K. fair dealing law, since Geller held a U.K. copyright in the work. Increasingly, Sapient realized that it would take a long time to resolve the dispute, and Sapient and Geller settled the case out of court. Geller freely licensed the clip in question to Sapient; that way Geller did not have to concede that his copyright claims were specious. And the video could remain on YouTube. It is clear, however, that without the intervention of the EFF, Brian Sapient would not have reposted his video. The complications of the DMCA's notice and takedown provisions and the expense of launching a legal defense against a wealthy and dogged copyright holder would have taken more than Sapient's or his small organization's resources. Without the EFF, in other words, Geller would have been able to wield his takedown notice very effectively to censor criticism of his alleged abilities.[39]

The Uri Geller case is just one example of the many instances in which the EFF has helped to defend critics from large copyright holders including Viacom, the producers of (the purple dinosaur) *Barney & Friends*, and the Universal Music Group. In some instances, these were "dolphins caught in the net" (a metaphor often used by EFF attorneys) of large takedown purges. In many other instances, however, copyright holders have clearly used the DMCA to suppress unwanted criticism. The use of takedown notices to silence political speech has been particularly troubling. As Siva Vaidhyanathan pithily explains, "YouTube is where politics and culture happen online." Increasingly, politicians use YouTube to reach voters and constituents, and the notice and takedown procedures have become central to political contests. When Representative Heather Wilson of New Mexico was running for reelection in 2006, for example, reports began to surface claiming that she had illegally disposed of a police report. The report in question documented her husband's alleged inappropriate involvement with a minor. A blogger posted a clip to YouTube from a news program that showed the candidate discussing the allegations. But the television station that owned the footage quickly had it removed, and voters were denied an important political document.[40]

In the 2008 presidential race, the campaigns of candidates Barack Obama and John McCain posted dozens of videos to YouTube. Many of these videos used copyrighted news footage and other material to respond to criticism or to present a platform. But, like many other videos that incorporate copyrighted material, some of these videos disappeared soon after they were uploaded—the victims of takedown notices. CBS, NBC, Fox News, and the Christian Broadcasting Network all sent takedown notices to have Obama and McCain campaign advertisements and videos taken down. With less than one month left in the election, the McCain campaign had finally had enough. The campaign's general counsel wrote to YouTube imploring the company to ignore the notices and leave the videos up. "[O]verreaching copyright claims," the letter read, "have resulted in the removal of non-infringing campaign videos from YouTube, thus silencing political speech." The letter went on to complain that the two weeks it took to have videos reposted "can be a lifetime in a political campaign."[41]

Wired magazine and other news outlets delighted in the spectacle of Senator John McCain complaining about the law he had voted for ten years earlier.[42] But the McCain letter targeted the "overreaching copyright claims" of large media companies as well as the DMCA. The problem was the abuse of the system and not necessarily the system itself, although the safe harbor provision may just be too easily abused. YouTube could not ignore the takedown letters, as the McCain campaign suggested. To do so would be to share the liability in potential copyright infringement disputes. Fair use is too unpredictable and the financial damages are too large for YouTube or any large public company to assume that risk. And if YouTube did assume the risk for presidential campaign videos, how could the company refuse to do the same for all of the amateur video work being taken down every day?

In 2007, EFF filed another lawsuit that promises to curb some of the abuses of the notice and takedown system. When Universal Music Group (UMG) had Stephanie Lenz's video taken down from YouTube, the media conglomerate's takedown notice did not "even pass the laugh test," according to EFF attorney Corynne McSherry. Lenz's 29-second home movie showed her two children running around the family's kitchen. If you are told to listen for it very carefully, you can hear the Prince song "Let's Go Crazy" playing faintly in the background. At one point, a toddler bends his knees a few times, presumably dancing to the music. If this were a major Hollywood film, Lenz would have needed a synchronization license, even for the short excerpt of the music. But because it is a home movie, the brief, incidental recording of the music is very clearly a fair use. The use of the music had been entirely transformed, and no one would listen to the clip in place of buying the album. In fact, if it were not for Universal's takedown notice, only a handful of family members and friends would ever have seen the clip or heard the music. But like so many campaigns to censor creative works, the attempt to remove the video only brought it more attention. Lenz's clip has now been viewed well over one million times on YouTube.[43]

EFF and Lenz sued UMG for violating the safe harbor provision of the DMCA. Lenz relied on a little-used subsection of the DMCA's safe harbor provision to claim that the music company dishonestly sent the takedown notice, knowing that the video was protected by fair use. UMG, of course, claimed that they did not (and could not) know for certain if the video is protected by fair use. In most instances, UMG would be right. But the EFF chose to champion a potent example of copyright owners' overreaching, and UMG chose a poor example to defend. At the time of this writing, the case is waiting for a decision by an appeals court, but in a milestone opinion the district court that first heard the case held that UMG and other copyright owners must consider fair use before sending a DMCA takedown notice. If that decision is allowed to stand, it has the potential to put large media companies on the defensive. They will have to factor fair use more directly into their systems for sending takedown notices. If political advertisements, home videos, and amateur remixed videos are taken down in giant sweeps, UMG, Viacom, and other companies will expose themselves to thousands of lawsuits, like Lenz's, that require the companies to pay damages and possibly legal fees as well. This would clearly be a victory for filmmakers who rely on fair use. As MPAA antipiracy litigator and sometimes blogger and journalist Ben Sheffner suggests, a Lenz victory might be good for the studios too: "If copyright protection . . . becomes identified with targeting home videos of dancing babies, congressional support for the entertainment industry will inevitably suffer, and it's the real pirates who will benefit."[44]

A TECHNICAL FIX

It may be surprising that amateur creators and a few lone copyright bullies have brought most of the copyright suits involving individuals using video-sharing sites. One might be led to think that the DMCA is working effectively, that media executives are content to have infringing work taken down without prosecuting the infringers. But in fact, media company executives and legal departments have left individual cases of infringement alone, because they are going after bigger fish: the companies that own the websites and networks.

Executives at media conglomerates never fully accepted the safe harbor provisions of the DMCA. Even after the passage of the DMCA, Hollywood studios, music producers, and other content companies fought to have service providers held responsible for copyright infringement that occurs on the web. A string of lawsuits questioned companies' rights to receive safe harbor protection. In one of the first such cases, litigious science fiction writer Harlan Ellison pursued AOL for years because the company changed the e-mail address for the receipt of takedown notices without sufficient notification to users. Ellison and AOL eventually settled out of court, but the case was a warning to other web hosts to follow their DMCA obligations to the letter. A handful of subsequent cases questioned the DMCA protection afforded to video-sharing sites Grouper, Bold, Veoh, and YouTube. In all of these cases, media companies claimed that the websites promoted infringement. But all of the sites followed DMCA protocol carefully, and they all pursued legitimate paths. Veoh, for instance, banned pornography, cut deals with most major TV networks, and received venture capital funds from Hollywood insiders. Veoh also took its legal responsibilities seriously, and courts continually agreed that Veoh complied with the terms of the DMCA. But the expense of the lawsuits eventually drove Veoh to declare bankruptcy (it was later bought by an Israeli technology company). These and other cases have brought some clarification to the DMCA's safe harbor provision. As long as employees do not have specific knowledge that infringing material is being posted and the company does not profit directly from the infringing material, video-sharing sites remain free to develop their networks.[45]

Not surprisingly, YouTube has been subject to the most substantial legal attacks on its service. When Google purchased YouTube in 2006, the company wisely put aside a large legal defense fund. Even before Google's purchase, Los Angeles cameraman Robert Tur sued YouTube, and in February 2007 media giant Viacom filed a lawsuit against YouTube as well.

The lawsuits against YouTube brought out some surprising details. You-Tube cofounder Jawed Karim appears to have uploaded infringing videos himself, and another YouTube employee allegedly referred to the site as "video Grokster," comparing it to the peer-to-peer file-sharing service the Supreme Court found to "induce" its users to share illegal content. In the first round of the case, however, a New York district court handed YouTube a decisive victory, upholding their compliance with the DMCA. It is likely that the case will be heard again on appeal, but it is also clear that web 2.0 companies that act in good faith will continue to be protected from copyright infringement suits.[46]

Like the Sony Betamax case, Viacom's suit against Google appears to be the personal vendetta of a few company executives. The other major studios and conglomerates have not joined the suit. As they have done continually throughout the history of Hollywood, when media companies were unhappy with Congress's and courts' solutions, they found a third way. Viacom itself seems to be pursuing alternate solutions even as the company exerts legal pressure on YouTube. Tellingly, Viacom's complaint against YouTube covered only the period before May 2008. What happened in May 2008? Viacom signed up for YouTube's content ID system. Faced with pressure from media companies, YouTube developed a system that identifies copyrighted material and allows media companies to profit from its site. YouTube first used an audio-only identification system, designed by the company Audible Magic for Napster. The original incarnation of Napster, however, closed before the company could ever test the software. Sometime around the summer of 2007, YouTube began testing a video tool as well. When media companies sign up for YouTube's content ID system, they upload their content to YouTube's servers. YouTube then creates a digital "fingerprint" (musical excerpt or video frames) from the material. The content ID system can use these fingerprints to begin to look for matches on the website. If a match is found, copyright owners may choose from three options. They may share advertising revenue for videos that contain its copyrighted material; they may block the videos or have the audio track muted (if it is the music that is potentially infringing); or the media companies may gain access to the analytic data about the video that YouTube collects. Using YouTube's automated system, users may dispute the blocking or muting of their video if they think it is unfair. Media companies have not always been entirely happy with the terms of the content ID revenue-sharing system, and they have continued to haggle with YouTube. Viacom's lawsuit may have even begun as an attempt to gain more leverage in negotiations. But although the details are still being worked out, media companies and YouTube have found a technological fix to a dilemma they could not remedy through legal action.[47]

Fair use has been a noticeable casualty of YouTube's content ID system in the past. When the Warner Music Group changed its settings so that for nine months every video with Warner-identified music was muted, many obviously noninfringing videos were taken down without consideration. The Lenz case may make this kind of blanket policy impossible. The larger question remains, however, whether any automated system can ever factor fair use into the equation. The answer is ultimately no. Fair use is a dynamic doctrine perpetually in the process of development. No formula can ever determine fair use. But computer algorithms can be tweaked to separate out the videos most likely to fall into the fair use camp. In 2007, Disney, Fox, Sony, Microsoft, Veoh, CBS, and several other companies released a set of "Principles for User Generated Content Services." The document basically called on all web 2.0 companies to employ some form of content-identification technology or "filtering." The EFF joined with legal scholars at Harvard, American University, the American Civil Liberties Union, the pubic interest organization Public Knowledge, and others to respond with a list of "Fair Use Principles for User Generated Video Content." The latter document proposed several ingenious methods for building fair use into a computer algorithm. The fair use principles suggest that a video be removed only if "the audio track matches the audio track of that *same* copyrighted work," and "nearly the entirety (e.g., 90 percent or more) of the challenged content is comprised of a single copyrighted work." These corrections would help to accommodate a number of common genres of user-generated videos. If, for example, a user posted an entire unedited music video, the video would quickly be blocked. But if the user posted an entire music video with a parody soundtrack, the video would stay up. One popular (and hilarious) example of these videos are the so-called literal videos—videos in which creators replace the original lyrics of a song with lyrics that describe what is happening in the often nonsensical video-image track. To take another example: if a user uploaded an entire episode of the *Daily Show*, it would be taken down. But if the user simply used clips from the *Daily Show* in a compilation that included clips from Fox News and a movie or two, that video would remain up. Humans will always be more incisive fair use detectors than computers. But technical solutions can be used as a kind of triage to narrow the task of separating piracy from fair use, a task that has reached a scale beyond the reasonable ability of humans to monitor.[48]

TECHNOLOGY AND COPYRIGHT

Media copyright in the digital age has been characterized by both a fear of and faith in technology. For all of the time that Hollywood executives, lobbyists, and lawyers have spent railing against perfect digital copies and the ease of online distribution, they have also looked for technical solutions. Since the passage of the DMCA, the Motion Picture Association of America has continually lobbied to extend anticircumvention laws even further. And the studios have embraced filtering and automated content ID systems as a method of managing user-posted online videos.

These technologies have fundamentally changed the way that copyright and fair use are managed. But they also provide many continuities with the history that we have been examining throughout this book. First, technological means of managing copyright are clearly an extension of movie moguls' century-old fantasy of controlling intellectual property without the intervention of legislation or litigation. As studio leaders learned to control authorship though guilds and contracts and as they learned to control fair use through licensing and communication tactics, they now hope to preempt legal intervention by controlling digital media through technological means. Second, for all of its promise of complete control, technological management of copyright cannot upset the balance between copyright holders on the one hand and users and new creators on the other. Since the days of Edison, we have seen, overly aggressive technological controls have alienated customers and driven them to piracy. Digital locks and content filters must be used carefully in order to maintain any effective influence and authority. Technology may have altered the everyday administration of copyright, but the fundamental principles that allow the system to function remain remarkably unchanged.

CONCLUSION

THE COPYRIGHT REFORM MOVEMENT

"C OPYRIGHT LOBBYING is not a sport for amateurs," proclaimed legal scholar Jessica Litman after the passage of the 1998 Digital Millennium Copyright Act (DMCA). Litman neatly and accurately summarized the previous 300 years of copyright history.[1] But things have changed since 1998. The internet has brought amateurs into the process of policymaking in important ways. First, it has greatly expanded the range of creators and consumers who have a direct stake in copyright law. Amateur video artists who uploaded their movies to YouTube, college students who receive "settlement letters" from movie studios, and early adopters of new video technology feel the impact of copyright law every day. And many of them now regularly follow copyright policymaking as well. The web has also allowed these creators and consumers to form grassroots activist communities, and a copyright reform movement has grown up in conjunction with larger media and political reform movements. Blogs, social networks, open government initiatives, and a series of organizations have kept different constituencies informed and vocal about copyright policy. And amateurs have begun to tip the balance in the copyright wars.

The DMCA and the Copyright Term Extension Act (CTEA, also passed in 1998) were forged like all of the copyright policies that had preceded them. Representatives from powerful organizations negotiated the details largely under the radar of the mainstream press or the public. Leading up to 1998, Hollywood studios, talent guilds, telecommunications companies, and consumer technology organizations all offered congressional testimony and research reports to support their visions for new legislation. Executives from many of these companies also made strategically placed contributions to the campaigns of members of Congress.[2] Technology and content companies represented competing positions, to be sure, and there was a certain kind of balance to the system. But they all sought to expand the powers of corporate interests, and a wide range of consumers and creators were left out of the conversation.

Public interest organizations were not entirely absent from the debates, but their lobbying efforts proved to be all but ineffective. Library organizations, for example, had been active in the policy process for decades, and their staff and outside counsel participated in the hearings and debates that preceded the 1998 expansion of the Copyright Act. But with the exception of a small exemption to the DMCA that library groups neither asked for nor wanted, the libraries failed to exert any influence over the final bills. Legal scholar Peter Jaszi founded a younger organization, the Digital Future Coalition, in 1995, and it brought together an impressive list of aligned educational, nonprofit, and some commercial organizations. The coalition may have been ahead of its time, however. Underfunded and without the support of a mature blogosphere and a network for disseminating information, the Digital Future Coalition also failed to exert any significant influence over the final bills.[3] The more established Electronic Frontier Foundation and the relatively young blogs *Slashdot* and *Boing Boing* also kept their constituencies informed about developments in the major changes coming to copyright law. But their audiences were still too small and specialized, and none of these groups gained traction in the policymaking process.

Just a few years later, however, online blogs and social networking sites helped transform the web into a new engine for the organization of grassroots political movements. The 1999 Seattle protests against the World Trade Organization catalyzed a new era of liberal activism. The "Battle in Seattle" was followed quickly by the controversial election of President George W. Bush, the war in Afghanistan after the September 11th attacks, and later the war in Iraq. Organizations like Moveon.org and Meetup.com facilitated large-scale protests and letter-writing campaigns, and they have helped to raise millions of dollars for political campaigns. During the 2004 presidential election primary season, candidate Howard Dean and his campaign manager Joe Trippi proved that the internet could be used to attract the participation of significant numbers of voters, many of whom had no history of political involvement.[4]

Discussion of media reform existed on the periphery of this movement, with organizations and blogs focused on issues like media bias and the concentration of media ownership. Communications scholar Robert McChesney had been pushing for organized media reform in the United States for years in books, journal articles, and the popular press. McChesney and his frequent coauthor John Nichols railed against the "relentless lobbying from big-business interests that have won explicit government policies and subsidies permitting them to scrap public-interest obligations and increase commercialization and conglomeration."[5] Eventually, they would come to list the growing scope and length of copyright monopolies among the policies that subsidized big media companies. In 2002, McChesney, Nichols, and Josh Silver cofounded the organization Free Press with the goal of reorienting U.S. media policy to serve the public interest. The timing was perfect. Just months after the organization's website went live, the Federal Communications Commission decided to relax its media ownership rules. The commission made it easier for individual companies to own more media outlets in a local area, among other changes. With the help of Free Press, the Media Access Project, and other organizations, the news and implications of what could have been an obscure policy event spread quickly. The outcry over the FCC's new rule (which was eventually overturned in court) catapulted the one-year-old media reform organization to national prominence. Free Press recruited over 1,700 participants to its first media reform conference in Madison, Wisconsin, that year, and its membership has since swelled to over 500,000 people.[6] Free Press succeeded where many earlier organizations had faltered, because of the infrastructure provided by the network for online grassroots activism (or netroots).

A copyright reform movement evolved both independently and in conjunction with this larger netroots culture. Much of the development happened within universities. Publications by legal scholar Lawrence Lessig and media scholar Siva Vaidhyanathan in the early 2000s laid bare the cultural dimensions of copyright law for students and nonspecialists.[7] Their books were adopted for use in political science and media studies courses, and they introduced a wide variety of students and other readers to the history and impact of copyright law. With copies of Lessig's books under their arms, students followed new policy and court battles. They followed the Napster case and debated piracy and file sharing in their dorm rooms. At one high-water mark, they followed Lessig's court challenge to the extension of copyright term limits enacted by the Copyright Term Extension Act. Lessig lost the case, *Eldred* v. *Ashcroft*, when the Supreme Court decided it in 2003, but it drew new attention to the conjunction of media monopolies and copyright. The CTEA was also colloquially known as the Mickey Mouse CTEA, because copyright terms always seem to be extended just as early Disney cartoons are about to enter the public domain. The case reminded the growing reform movement of the power of large corporations like Disney to influence copyright law. Coming at the same time as challenges to the FCC's new ownership rules, the message about corporations' growing copyright monopoly brought many new converts to the copyright reform movement.

Eldred v. Ashcroft also drew attention to the plethora of new voices on campuses that joined in the debate. Scholars from across the curriculum— economists, historians, and art historians—all filed friend-of-the-court briefs in the case. And that same year, students at Swarthmore College began FreeCulture.org, picking up on a phrase Lessig used often in speeches and that would become the title of his 2004 book. The students intentionally styled themselves as sixties radicals. Within a year, they renamed the group Students for a Free Culture, with echoes of Students for a Democratic Society, and they had chapters on campuses across the county (fig. 6.1). To celebrate their one-year anniversary, the group held their first annual conference at Swarthmore. Students from across the country converged on the Swarthmore campus for a kind of policy-wonk Woodstock. Two students showed a documentary intercutting footage of copyright activists outside of a Virgin megastore in Times Square with 1960s civil rights marches. And Lessig headlined with a dazzling multimedia presentation. *Wired* magazine has called Lessig the "Elvis of cyberlaw," because of his celebrity. But he turned out to be more like the Dylan of the copyright reform movement. After providing four classic books on the subject, Lessig left copyright reform to pick up his electric guitar and pursue the issue of money's corrupting influence on the political process. Lessig took on this larger framing issue, and he joined the parent movement of copyright reform. He spoke at the Free Press's annual conference; he coauthored an op-ed column with McChesney; and he teamed up with former campaign manager Joe Trippi to found a new organization, Change Congress.

Elsewhere on campuses, law schools began to adopt a more hands-on approach to copyright. Intellectual property clinics popped up at law schools across the country. Law students supervised by faculty members at American University, Stanford, Berkeley, and many other universities began to represent a wide range of critics, artists, and educators who might otherwise not have had access to legal help. The clinics took on major cases against Warner Bros., the James Joyce estate, and the recording labels. But perhaps more important, they have worked with librarians,

FIGURE 6.1 A member of the Free Culture student organization protesting copy protection on music and movies. (*Photo:* Fred Benenson, used under a Creative Commons Attribution License)

artists, and others to help them participate in government rulemakings and requests for comments. When, for example, the Copyright Office asked for comments on the problem of orphan works—works still in copyright but for which a copyright holder cannot be located—hundreds of comments were filed, many with the help of clinic students. The public comments influenced the drafting of orphan works legislation in both the House of Representatives and the Senate, although a final bill was never passed.[8]

Both inside and outside of universities, a series of new organizations took advantage of the internet's ability to form activist communities. The copyright policymaking process had frustrated the American Library Association for a long time. But after the passage of the DMCA, they created a polished new website that allowed their members to quickly learn about policy issues affecting libraries and to reach out to their representatives with a few clicks of a mouse. In 2001 the ALA was joined by two influential organizations: the Washington, D.C.-based public interest lobbying firm Public Knowledge and the San Francisco-based Creative Commons. Public Knowledge quickly became a hub of information about copyright and telecommunications policy through its blog, podcast, newsletter, and explanatory internet videos. And its cofounder Gigi Sohn tirelessly testifies before Congress about a myriad of issues and works behind the scenes to inform congressional staffers about how new policies will affect consumers.

Creative Commons gives out free licenses that artists, bloggers, and others can attach to their work in order to give away some of the rights that the Copyright Act automatically grants them. A filmmaker, for example, may decide to attach a Creative Commons license to her work, allowing others to show it in not-for-profit settings and increasing the film's audience. Or a musician might use a Creative Commons license to allow other musicians to make their own remixes of his original compositions, facilitating a creative exchange that can be stifled by copyright law. Creative Commons licenses took off quickly. By 2003, over a million websites used the organization's licenses, and by 2009 there were more than 350 million Creative Commons licenses in over fifty countries. The Creative Commons' metrics not only measure the success of the organization, they also measure the spread of copyright awareness and, for the most part, the growth of sharing communities. In one notable exception, media scholar Bingchun Meng has shown that, in China, Creative Commons licenses are often attached to blogs and other sites to claim rather than release specific rights. Whether the licenses are used to claim or relinquish rights, however, their prevalence is a clear indication of the growing importance and prominence of copyright law to the lives of amateur creators.[9]

In addition to Public Knowledge and the Creative Commons, the Electronic Frontier Foundation has maintained its role as a leading advocate for consumer rights and the public interest. And other organizations like the Center for Social Media, the Project on Information Justice and Intellectual Property (both housed at American University), and the Organization for Transformative Works have reached out to communities that depend on fair use. These organizations have worked to educate creators, scholars, and archivists.

This netroots infrastructure has proven to be an important corrective to the backroom policymaking of the past. Every new intellectual property bill that appears on a House of Representatives or Senate committee's docket now receives an Electronic Frontier Foundation blog post or a Free Press article. The Motion Picture Association of America's statements about piracy's damage to the movie industry are countered with studies demonstrating the value of fair use to the U.S. economy. When the Federal Communications Commission adopted a rule giving movie studios more control over the devices that could play their content, Public Knowledge and other organizations led a successful charge to have the rule overturned in court. When Hollywood studios and other big content companies attempted to negotiate a new transnational agreement in secret, the copyright reform movement successfully demanded the release of the sealed documents and a more transparent negotiating process. It is not just the activists who support more generous copyright policies that have taken advantage of information networks. Many artists who want longer copyright terms and tighter restrictions have organized as well. Some of the strongest opposition to the orphan works bill, for example, came from commercial photographers, who worried that the legislation would cut into their ability to exploit their copyrighted works. Netroots has brought a wide range of new communities of creators and consumers into the debate over copyright policy.

In the short term, all of these new voices have led to a stalemate. Copyright reform activists on both sides of the issues have been successful at blocking or overturning unwanted legislation, but they have been less successful at pushing new policies through Congress. With so much public scrutiny and with one party or another invariably opposed to any new piece of legislation, the gears of copyright policymaking have slowed down.[10] But this is just one phase of a system in transition. More of the constituencies affected by copyright law are now represented at the negotiating table, and there is greater transparency in the policymaking process. In the long run, the inclusion of more stakeholders will inevitably lead to better policies and a more perfectly balanced copyright system. The future of copyright is surprisingly bright.

NOTES

INTRODUCTION: THE THEATER OF COPYRIGHT

1. An incomplete list of exceptions would include Thomas Guback, *The International Film Industry: Western Europe and America Since 1945* (Bloomington: University of Indiana Press, 1969); Ian Jarvie, *Hollywood's Overseas Campaigns: The North Atlantic Movie Trade, 1920–1950* (New York: Cambridge University Press, 1992); Richard Maltby, *Harmless Entertainment: Hollywood and the Ideology of Consensus* (New York: Scarecrow Press, 1983); Toby Miller, Nitin Govil, John McMurria, Richard Maxwell, and Ting Wang, *Global Hollywood 2* (London: British Film Institute, 2005); and Albert Moran, ed., *Film Policy: International, National, and Regional Perspectives* (London: Routledge, 1996).

2. *United States v. Paramount Pictures, Inc.*, 334 US 131 (1948).

3. Legislature of Louisiana, House of Representatives, Act No. 456, H.B. 936, 110th Cong., Regular Session, 2007. (See www.legis.state.la.us.)

4. I am adopting a formulation of fair use frequently used by legal scholar Peter Jaszi. See, for example, Patricia Aufderheide and Peter Jaszi, *Reclaiming Fair Use: How to Put Balance Back in Copyright* (Chicago: University of Chicago Press, 2011).

5. Recently, copyright lawyer and historian William Patry has denounced the rhetoric of the copyright wars as polarizing and unproductive. He wants to see the copyright wars replaced by rational economic logic. Scholars Peter Jaszi and Patricia Aufderheide have similarly attempted to free their readers "from the disempowering structure of a 'copyright wars' way of thinking." And Jaszi

and Aufderheide have successfully empowered many different communities of media makers to take advantage of fair use. These are admirable goals, and I hope that they are able to replace the copyright wars with reasoned, rational decision-making. See William Patry, *Moral Panics and the Copyright Wars* (New York: Oxford University Press, 2009), and Aufderheide and Jaszi, *Reclaiming Fair Use*, x.

6. Framing copyright as a war is particularly apt, since it has always been a highly contested area of regulation. Moreover, copyright has often served as extension of other wars, both real and metaphorical. Copyright law has been enlisted into the culture wars and used to censor heretical and scandalous texts since the eighteenth century. In chapter 1, for example, I discuss late-nineteenth-century judges' use of copyright law to dictate morality to vaudeville performers and early filmmakers. Copyright has been pressed into the service of economic wars as well. The United States, for example, regularly implores the World Trade Organization to reform trade with China and other countries by exacting stricter copyright penalties. Copyright is often just one battlefield in a larger theater of war. The idea that the creative expression contained in a work of art is itself property is, of course, another metaphor. Because copyright regulates abstract qualities like originality, authorship, and expression, it may just be inevitable that it will be thought of in terms of metaphors.

7. With all three technologies, Congress stepped in to set the terms for reusing copyrighted media rather than allowing copyright holders to have complete control over their works. These government-imposed compulsory licenses radically transformed both copyright law and the media industries. Radio DJs, for example, freely play music knowing that their stations do not have to negotiate separate licenses for every song they play. Instead, the stations pay a fee to an organization that disperses money to composers. Imagine the atrophying of music played over the air if radio stations needed to obtain separate permission for every song they played. Compulsory licenses were both a method of assimilating formerly piratical activities and, at the same time, a way of allowing media companies to profit from new technologies. Lawrence Lessig, *Free Culture: How Big Media Uses Technology and the Law to Lockdown Culture and Control Creativity* (New York: Penguin, 2004). Historian Adrian Johns reads a more metaphysical goal into piracy debates as he traces intellectual property piracy back to the eighteenth century. Johns argues that in debates about piracy, we define "the nature of the relationship we want to uphold between creativity, communication, and commerce." Johns, *Piracy: The Intellectual Property Wars from Gutenberg to Gates* (Chicago: University of Chicago Press, 2009), 5.

8. Interview with Fred von Lohmann, "Hearsay Culture," KZSU-FM, Stanford, CA (July 4, 2007).

1. PIRACY AND THE BIRTH OF FILM

1. Terry Ramsaye, *A Million and One Nights: A History of the Motion Picture Through 1925* (New York: Simon and Schuster, 1926), 309.

2. *Folsom v. Marsh*, 9 F. Cas. 342 (C.C.D. Mass. 1841). Several film theorists have noted the early theorization of film present in the *Edison v. Lubin* case. André Gaudreault has observed that the Edison cases prefigure by eighty years theorists' debates about cinematic storytelling: "The Infringement of Copyright Law and Its Effects (1900–1906)" in Thomas Elsaesser with Adam Barker, eds., *Early Cinema: Space, Frame, Narrative* (London: British Film Institute, 1990), 114–22. And Mary Ann Doane notes that early film copyright cases revolve around changing conceptions of the spectator; *The Emergence of Cinematic Time: Modernity, Contingency, Irony* (Cambridge: Harvard University Press, 2002), 156–58.

3. Lawrence Lessig discusses the move from piracy to legality in several new media in *Free Culture: How Big Media Uses Technology and the Law to Lock Down Culture and Control Creativity* (New York: Penguin, 2004).

4. For an exhaustive chronicle of the Townsend Act, see *Report of the Register of Copyrights* (Washington, D.C.: GPO, 1912), 136–38. See also William F. Patry, *Patry on Copyright* (Eagan, MN: Thomson West, 2006).

5. Interestingly, Brady was commonly considered the artist or author of all works exhibited under his name, even those shot by his assistants or commissioned by him. See Alan Trachtenberg, *Reading American Photographs: Images as History, Mathew Brady to Walker Evans* (New York: Hill and Wang, 1989), 37.

6. Pascal Kamina, *Film Copyright in the European Union* (Cambridge: Cambridge University Press, 2002), 12.

7. The phrase "spark of originality" is borrowed, anachronistically, from *Bridgeman Art Library v. Corel Corp.*, 36 F. Supp. 2d 191 (S.D.N.Y 1999).

8. See essays by Holmes, André Bazin, and Siegfried Kracauer collected in Alan Trachtenberg, ed., *Classic Essays on Photography* (New Haven: Leete's Island Books, 1980).

9. *Trade-Mark Cases*, 100 U.S. 82 (1879).

10. "The Congress shall have the power . . . To promote the progress of science and useful arts, by securing, for limited times to *authors* and inventors the exclusive right to their respective *writings* and discoveries." U.S. Constitution, art. 1, sec. 8, cl. 8 (emphasis added).

11. On *Sarony* see Paul Goldstein, *Copyright's Highway: From Guttenberg to the Celestial Jukebox*, rev. ed. (Stanford: Stanford University Press, 2003), 46–47; Jane Gaines, *Contested Culture: The Image, the Voice, and the Law* (Chapel Hill: University of North Carolina Press, 1991), ch. 2.

12. *Burrow-Giles Lithographic Co. v. Sarony*, 111 U.S. 53 (1884).

13. *Thornton v. Schreiber*, 124 U.S. 612 (1888).

14. "New Practice in the Copyright of Photographs," *Scientific American* 82.7 (Feb. 17, 1900): 102.

15. Georges Sadoul, *Lumière et Méliès* (Paris: Editions Denoel, 1985); Jay Leyda, "A Note on Progress," *Film Quarterly* 21.4 (Summer 1968): 28–33; David Bordwell, "The Art Cinema as a Mode of Film Practice," *Poetics of Cinema* (New York: Routledge, 2007); Jane M. Gaines, "Early Cinema's Heyday of Copying: Too Many Copies of *L'Arroseur arrosé (The Waterer Watered)*," *Cultural*

Studies 20.2–3 (Mar./May 2006): 227–44. For more on remakes and borrowings, see chapter 2.

16. Charles Musser, *Before the Nickelodeon: Edwin S. Porter and the Edison Manufacturing Company* (Berkeley: University of California Press, 1991), 239.

17. Charles Musser, *The Emergence of Cinema: The American Screen to 1907* (Berkeley: University of California Press, 1990), 278.

18. Musser, *Before the Nickelodeon*, 209.

19. See Lisa Gitleman, "Recording Race, Recording Sound, Recording Property," in Mark M. Smith, ed., *Hearing History: A Reader* (Athens: University of Georgia Press, 2004), 291.

20. Joseph P. Eckhardt, *The King of the Movies: Film Pioneer Siegmund Lubin* (Madison: Farleigh Dickinson University Press, 1997), 37; Musser, *The Emergence of Cinema*, 330.

21. *Edison v. American Mutoscope Co.*, 114 F. 926 (2d Cir. 1902).

22. In 1898 the Edison Company had sued Vitagraph for film duping but settled out of court. Vitagraph became a licensee of Edison and also became its surreptitious duper. See Musser, *Before the Nickelodeon*, 134.

23. Letter, James White to Howard Hayes (June 10, 1903) in *Thomas A. Edison Papers: A Microfilm Edition* (Frederick, Md.: University Publications of America, 1987–), reel 223, frames 854–856 (hereafter, *Edison Papers*).

24. Agreed Statement of Facts, *Edison v. Lubin* (*Edison Papers*, reel 223, frames 857–861).

25. Brief of Thomas A. Edison Manufacturing Company, *Edison v. Lubin* (*Edison Papers*, reel 223, frames 872–881).

26. Brief of Thomas A. Edison Manufacturing Company, *Edison v. Lubin* (*Edison Papers*, reel 223, frame 876).

27. *White-Smith Music Publishing Co. v. Apollo Co.*, 209 U.S. 1 (1908).

28. The best method for protecting computer software is still disputed, and many programs are protected by patents and licenses in addition to or instead of by copyrights.

29. Letter, William Edgar Gilmore to William Peltzer (July 29, 1902), *Edison Papers* (reel 223, frame 882).

30. Musser, *Before the Nickelodeon*, 207–208; Musser, *The Emergence of Cinema*, 207.

31. *American Mutoscope & Biograph Co. v. Edison Manufacturing Co.*, 137 F. 262 (C.C.D.N.J 1905); *Kalem Co. v. Harper Bros.*, 222 U.S. 55 (2d Cir. 1911).

32. *Edison v. Lubin*, 199 F. 993 (E.D. Pa 1903).

33. Robert Sklar, *Movie-Made America: A Cultural History of American Movies*, rev. and exp. (New York: Vintage Books, 1994), 23; Ramsaye, *A Million and One Nights*, 396; and Fred J. Balshofer and Arthur C. Miller, with the assistance of Bebe Bergsten, *One Reel a Week* (Berkeley: University of California Press, 1967), 8–9. Balshofer misidentifies Gaston as Georges.

34. *Edison Papers* (reel 188, frame 559); Kerry Segrave, *Piracy in the Motion Picture Industry* (Jefferson, NC: McFarland, 2003), 27.

35. Musser, *Before the Nickelodeon*, 208. The ad is quoted in Eckhardt, *King of the Movies*, 46.

36. Siva Vaidyanathan, *Copyrights and Copywrongs: The Rise of Intellectual Property and How It Threatens Creativity* (New York: New York University Press, 2001), 89. The economist Harold Scott Wallace also suggests that *Edison* v. *Lubin* along with other patent and copyright cases helped to stabilize the film industry. See Wallace, "Competition and the Legal Environment: Intellectual Property Rights in the Early American Film Industry," Department of Economics Working Paper Series, University of Connecticut (Oct. 1998). Film was not simply ignored by the legislators in 1909. Edison lawyer Frank Dyer lobbied to have film kept out of the 1909 Act because the existing case law was beneficial to the film industry.

37. *Bleistein* v. *Donaldson Lithographic Co.*, 188 U.S. 239 (1903).

38. *Edison* v. *Lubin*, 122 F. 240 (3rd Cir. 1903).

39. *Edison* v. *Lubin* (1903). Letter, Howard Hayes to Edison, *Edison Papers* (reel 223, frame 892).

40. Letter, William Gilmore to Howard Hayes, *Edison Papers* (reel 223, frame 884).

41. All of the correspondence and documentation about this incident can be found in a folder labeled "Correspondence: Foreign Films (1904)," *Edison Papers* (reel 223, frames 463–477). Dyer is quoted in Musser, *Before the Nickelodeon*, 277.

42. Ramsaye, *A Million and One Nights*, 321. On the Biograph cases, see Eckhardt, *King of the Movies*, 46, 54. For the correspondence between Edison and Lubin regarding the 1904 trademark dispute, see *Edison Papers* (reel 223, frames 478–485).

43. Richard Abel, *The Red Rooster Scare: Making Cinema American, 1900–1910* (Berkeley: University of California Press, 1999), 89, 232; Eckhardt, *King of the Movies*; and Balshofer and Miller, *One Reel A Week*, 5–9.

44. For a detailed account of the transition to story films that discussed the impact of copyright, see Musser, *Before the Nickelodeon*, ch. 8.

45. Letter, Frank Dyer to Thorvald Solberg (Oct. 6, 1905); letter, Solberg to Dyer (Oct. 11, 1905); *Edison Papers* (reel 323, frames 453–456).

46. *Biograph Co.* v. *Edison* (1905).

47. Patrick Loughney, "From Rip Van Winkle to Jesus of Nazareth: Thoughts on the Origins of the American Screenplay," *Film History* 9.3 (1997): 284.

48. Musser describes the negotiation over strongman Sandow's fee for performing in the Black Maria, in *Before the Nickelodeon*, 39.

49. Musser, *The Emergence of Cinema*, 193–200.

50. *Broder* v. *Zeno Mauvais Music Co.*, 88 F. 74 (C.C.N.D. Cal. 1898).

51. Segrave, *Piracy in the Motion Picture Industry*, 8; *Broder* v. *Zeno* (1898) ["Dora Dean"]; *Martinetti* v. *Maguire*, 16 F. Cas. 920 (C.C.N.D. Cal. 1867) [*Black Crook*]; *Glyn* v. *Weston Feature Films* (1 Ch. 261 1916); Edward S. Rodgers, "Copyright and Morals," *Michigan Law Review* 18.5 (Mar. 1920): 390–404; Jeanne Thomas Allen, "Copyright and Early Theatre, Vaudeville, and Film

Competition," in John Fell, ed., *Film Before Griffith* (Berkeley: University of California Press, 1983), 176–87. Even when vaudeville copyright cases were decided on different grounds, the question of moral censorship was always present; see, for example, *Barnes v. Miner*, 122 F. 480 (C.C.S.D.N.Y. 1903).

52. *Martinetti v. Maguire* (1867); Herbert Reynolds, "Aural Gratification with Kalem Films: A Case History of Music, Lectures and Sound Effects, 1907–1917" *Film History* 12.3 (2000): 427 (internal quotation marks removed).

53. *Fuller v. Bemis*, 50 F. 926 (C.C.S.D.N.Y. 1892).

54. Tom Gunning, "Now You See It, Now You Don't: The Temporality of the Cinema of Attractions," in Lee Grieveson and Peter Krämer, eds., *The Silent Cinema Reader* (New York: Routledge, 2004), 41–50.

55. Allen, "Copyright and Early Theatre, Vaudeville, and Film Competition."

56. On film and theater style from the period, see Ben Brewster and Lea Jacobs, *Theater to Cinema: Stage Pictorialism and the Early Feature Film* (New York: Oxford University Press, 1997).

57. David Bordwell, Janet Staiger, and Kristin Thompson, *The Classical Hollywood Cinema* (New York: Columbia University Press, 1985), 130.

58. "Dramatic Authors Ask for Protection," *New York Times*, Mar. 29, 1908, 8.

59. Ibid.

60. For example, Jessica Litman, *Digital Copyright* (Amherst, NY: Prometheus, 2001).

61. Letter, Frank Dyer to Thorvald Solberg (Mar. 22, 1909); Letter, Thorvald Solberg to Frank Dyer (Mar. 23, 1909), *Edison Papers* (reel 193, frames 172–173); Bordwell, Staiger, Thompson, *Classical Hollywood Cinema*, 132.

62. On the Berlin conference of 1908 and the Berne Convention, see Kamina, *Film Copyright in the European Union*, 18–21.

63. Vaidyanathan, *Copyrights and Copywrongs*.

64. Segrave, *Piracy in the Motion Picture Industry*, 47–48.

65. Both sides hired lawyers with long resumés in the field of literary, dramatic, and film copyright. Kalem's lawyers were John W. Griggs and Drury Cooper. Griggs had served as Attorney General under President William McKinley, and he had a long career in international policymaking and as a lawyer for media companies; he eventually became president of the Marconi Wireless Company. Cooper had represented Biograph in its first copyright case against Edison, which Biograph lost. *Biograph v. Edison* (1905). Klaw & Erlanger hired the firm and lawyer who had helped Augustin Daly forge dramatic copyright law in *Daly v. Brady*, 175 U.S. 148 (1899) and *Daly v. Webster*, 163 U.S. 155 (1896).

66. Brief of Kalem Company in *Kalem Co. v. Harper Bros.* (1911).

67. For a recent example of a case in which defendants unsuccessfully claimed that new technology was fair use because it increased sales, see *CleanFlicks of Colorado v. Steven Soderbergh*, 433 F. Supp. 2d 1236 (D. Col. 2006). For an example of a case in which a successful parody hurt the market for

the original but was still determined to be fair use, see *Elsmere Music, Inc.* v. *National Broadcasting Co.*, 482 F. Supp. 741 (S.D.N.Y. 1980).

68. Brief of Harper and Brothers, Henry Wallace, and Klaw & Erlanger in *Kalem* v. *Harper Bros.* (1911).

69. Ibid., 15.

70. *Kalem* v. *Harper Bros.*, 169 F. 61 (2nd Cir. 1909).

71. Brief of Klaw & Erlanger in *Kalem* v. *Harper Bros.* (1911), 16.

72. *MGM Studios, Inc.* v. *Grokster, Ltd.*, 545 U.S. 913 (2005).

73. Louis Menand, *The Metaphysical Club: A Story of Ideas in America* (Farrar, Straus, and Giroux, 2001), 342–43; Jeffrey Rosen, *The Supreme Court: The Personalities and Rivalries That Defined America* (New York: Times Books, 2006), 116.

74. *Bleistein* v. *Donaldson Lithographic Co.*, 188 U.S. 239 (1903).

75. In their respective histories of U.S. copyright law both Paul Goldstein and Siva Vaidhyanathan suggest that Holmes's view of copyright was, in part, immediate and personal as well as jurisprudential. In 1899, Holmes had lost a case before the Supreme Court involving his father's well-known story, *The Autocrat of the Breakfast Table*. The court found unanimously that the story had fallen into the public domain, because its copyright registration had not been renewed. As executor of his father's literary estate, Holmes lost all future profits from the sale of the story as well as the right to authorize translations, dramatizations, and, potentially, film adaptations. He clearly understood copyright law from the author's perspective. Goldstein, *Copyright's Highway*, 46, and Vaidhyanathan, *Copyrights and Copywrongs*, 95, 211n22.

76. *Kalem* v. *Harper Bros.* (1911).

77. Ibid.

78. *Harper Bros.* v. *Klaw & Erlanger*, 232 F. 609 (S.D.N.Y. 1916); *Report of the Register of Copyrights* (1912), 136–38; Patry, *Patry on Copyright*.

79. *United States* v. *Motion Picture Patents Co.*, 225 F. 800 (E.D. Pa. 1915); Janet Staiger, "Combination and Litigation: Structures of U.S. Film Distribution, 1896–1917," *Cinema Journal* (1983): 41–73.

80. Bordwell, Staiger, Thompson, *Classical Hollywood Cinema*, 132; Eckhardt, *King of the Movies*.

81. Bordwell, Staiger, Thompson, *Classical Hollywood Cinema*, 132; Eileen Bowser, *The Transformation of Cinema*, 1907–1915 (New York: Scribner, 1990), 227.

82. Patrick Loughney suggests that production companies started optioning plays even before the 1909 *Ben-Hur* decision; see "From Rip Van Winkle to Jesus of Nazareth," 285–86. Frances Taylor Patterson's advice can be found in *Cinema Craftsmanship: A Book for Photoplaywrights* (New York: Harcourt, Brace, and Howe, 1920), 81. Other books for screenwriters that contained copyright advice include Eapes Winthrop Sargeant, *The Technique of the Photoplay*, 2d ed. (New York: Moving Picture World, 1913).

83. Peter Decherney, *Hollywood and the Culture Elite: How the Movies Became American* (New York: Columbia University Press, 2005), ch. 2; Edward Azlant,

"The Theory, History, and Practice of Screenwriting, 1897–1920" (PhD diss., University of Wisconsin–Madison, 1980); Dana Polan, *Scenes of Instruction: The Beginnings of the U.S. Study of Film* (Berkeley: University of California Press, 2007), ch. 1.

84. *Mutual Film Corp.* v. *Industrial Commission of Ohio*, 236 U.S. 230 (1915).

2. HOLLYWOOD'S GOLDEN AGE OF PLAGIARISM

1. For criticism of copyright law's relation to originality, see the essays in Martha Woodmansee and Peter Jaszi, eds., *The Construction of Authorship: Textual Appropriation in Law and Literature* (Durham: Duke University Press, 1994) and James Boyle's great chapter, "I Got a Mashup," in *The Public Domain: Enclosing the Commons of the Mind* (New Haven: Yale University Press, 2008). For an introduction to the Hollywood studio system, see David Bordwell, Janet Staiger, and Kristin Thompson, *The Classical Hollywood Cinema* (New York: Columbia University Press, 1985) and John Belton's discussion of the star and genre systems in *American Cinema/American Culture*, 3d ed. (New York: McGraw Hill, 2008).

2. *International News Service* v. *Associated Press*, 248 U.S. 215 (1918) (Justice Brandeis dissenting); *Harper & Row* v. *Nation Enterprises*, 471 U.S. 539 (1985). Also see Yochai Benkler, "Free as the Air to Common Use: First Amendment Constraints on Enclosure of the Public Domain," N.Y.U. *Law Review* 74.354 (1999).

3. Peter Jaszi, "When Works Collide: Derivative Motion Pictures, Underlying Rights, and the Public Interest," *UCLA Law Review* 28.715 (1980): 729.

4. I use the word *plagiarism* in this chapter because Hollywood controlled borrowing through both legal and institutional means. But I also use the term *plagiarism* because it was the technical word used in court decisions throughout much of the twentieth century.

5. Kerry Segrave, *Piracy in the Motion Picture Industry* (Jefferson, NC: McFarland, 2003), 6, 15, 17, 18, 19.

6. Ibid., 17.

7. *Fuller* v. *Bemis*, 50 F. 926 (S.D.N.Y. 1892); Mary Louise Fuller, "Garment for Dancers," U.S. Patent 518347 (Apr. 17, 1894).

8. Loie Fuller, *Fifteen Years of a Dancer's Life* (Boston: Small, Maynard, 1913), 41–42, 55–56; Richard Nelson Current and Marcia Ewing Current, *Loie Fuller: Goddess of Light* (Boston: Northeastern University Press, 1997), 40–44, 62.

9. David Robinson, *From Peep Show to Palace: The Birth of American Film* (New York: Columbia University Press, 1996), 122.

10. *Thomas A. Edison Papers: A Microfilm Edition* (Frederick, Md.: University Publications of America, 1987–), reel 223, frames 810, 813.

11. For a great recent assessment of comedy and copyright, see Dotan Oliar and Christopher Sprigman, "There's No Free Laugh (Anymore): The Emergence

of Intellectual Property Norms and the Transformation of Stand-Up Comedy," *Virginia Law Review* 94.8 (Dec. 2008), 1787–1867.

12. *Daly v. Palmer*, 6 F. Cas. 1132 (S.D.N.Y. 1868).

13. *American Mutoscope & Biograph Co. v. Edison Manufacturing. Co.*, 137 F. 262 (D.N.J. 1905).

14. Charles Musser, *Before the Nickelodeon: Edwin S. Porter and the Edison Manufacturing Company* (Berkeley: University of California Press, 1991), 282.

15. Jay Leyda, "A Note on Progress," *Film Quarterly* 21.4 (Summer 1968): 28–33; Jay Leyda, "Waiting Jobs," *Film Quarterly* 6.2 (Winter, 1962–63): 29–33; Tom Gunning, "'Heard Over the Phone': *The Lonely Villa* and the de Lorde Tradition of the Terrors of Technology," *Screen* 32.2 (Summer 1991); Musser, *Before the Nickelodeon*, 424.

16. Rudolph Arnheim, "Chaplin's Early Films" (1929), rpt. in "Walter Benjamin and Rudolf Arnheim on Charlie Chaplin," trans. John MacKay, *Yale Journal of Criticism* 9 (1996): 312.

17. Theodore Huff, *Charlie Chaplin* (New York: Arno, 1972), 125; Walter Benjamin, "A Look at Chaplin" (1929), rpt. in "Walter Benjamin and Rudolf Arnheim on Charlie Chaplin," 310.

18. Siegfried Kracauer, "Two Chaplin Sketches," trans. John MacKay, *Yale Journal of Criticism* 10 (1997): 115–20.

19. Theodor W. Adorno, "Chaplin Times Two," trans. John MacKay, *Yale Journal of Criticism* 9 (1996): 57–61. Adorno's remarks about laughter appear in *The Dialectic of Enlightenment* and are quoted in MacKay's "Translator's Introduction," 57. MacKay points out that Adorno defended his admiration for Chaplin—and at the same time may have explained the soft approach reserved for this Hollywood star—with a personal anecdote: "Perhaps I may justify my speaking about him by recounting a certain privilege which I was granted, entirely without my having earned it. He once imitated me, and surely I am one of the few intellectuals to whom this happened" (Adorno, "Chaplin Times Two," 60).

20. Gilbert Seldes, *The Seven Lively Arts* (New York: Harper and Bros., 1924), 41–42. For more essays on Chaplin as artist, see Richard Schickel, ed., *The Essential Chaplin: Perspectives on the Life and Art of the Great Comedian* (Chicago: Ivan R. Dee, 2006).

21. Charles Maland, *Chaplin and American Culture: The Evolution of a Star Image* (Princeton: Princeton University Press, 1989), 10–11.

22. Kathy Merlock Jackson, "Mickey and the Tramp: Walt Disney's Debt to Charlie Chaplin," *Journal of American Culture* 26 (2003): 439–44.

23. John McCabe, *Charlie Chaplin* (Garden City, NY: Doubleday, 1978), 88–89; Joyce Milton, *Tramp: The Life of Charles Chaplin* (New York: Da Capo, 1998), 123–24.

24. Terry Ramsaye, *A Million and One Nights: A History of the Motion Picture Through 1925* (New York: Simon and Schuster, 1926), 732; Ulrich Ruedel, "Send in the Clones," The BFI Charles Chaplin Symposium (July 2005) (http://chaplin.bfi.org.uk/programme/conference/pdf/ulrich-ruedel.pdf).

25. See, for example, Susan McCabe, "'Delight in Dislocation': The Cinematic Modernism of Stein, Chaplin, and Man Ray," *Modernism/Modernity* 8 (2001): 429–52; Anthony Paraskeva, "Wyndham Lewis v. Charlie Chaplin," *Forum for Modern Language Studies* 43 (2007): 223–34; Austin Briggs, "Chaplin's Charlie and Joyce's Bloom," *Journal of Modern Literature* 20 (1996): 177–86; David Chinitz, T. S. *Eliot and the Cultural Divide* (Chicago: University of Chicago Press, 2003), 87–88, 101; Haim Finkelstein, "Dalí and *Un Chien andalou*: The Nature of a Collaboration," in Rudolf E. Kuenzli, ed., *Dada and Surrealist Film* (New York: Willis, Locker & Owens, 1987), 129–30; Paul Hammond, ed., *The Shadow and Its Shadow: Surrealist Writings on the Cinema*, 3d ed. (San Francisco: City Lights, 2000).

26. Matthew S. Witkovsky, "Surrealism in the Plural: Guillaume Apollinaire, Ivan Goll, and Devĕtsil in the 1920s," *Papers of Surrealism* 2 (2004): 1–14; Clare Cavanagh, "Rereading the Poet's Ending: Mandelstam, Chaplin, and Stalin," *PMLA* 109 (1994): 71–86; Susan Delson, *Dudley Murphy: Hollywood Wild Card* (Minneapolis: University of Minnesota Press, 2006), 60.

27. Milton, *Tramp*, 124; Maland, *Chaplin and American Culture*, 317.

28. Milton, *Tramp*, 124. Terry Ramsaye reports that the box-office receipts at the Crystal Hall dropped 50 percent when they showed Chaplin imitators rather than Chaplin himself. Ramsaye, *A Million and One Nights*, 732, 737.

29. See, for example, "Charlie Chaplin Protests," *Los Angeles Times*, Mar. 8, 1922; "Delay of Chaplin Suit," *Los Angeles Times*, Apr. 7, 1922; "Chaplin Papers Here," *Los Angeles Times*, Apr. 23, 1922; "Chaplin Injunction," *Los Angeles Times*, Jan. 5, 1924.

30. "Chaplin to Testify in Loeb Film Suit," *New York Times*, May 6, 1927, 20.

31. "Charlie Chaplin Sues Chaplin Imitator," *Los Angeles Examiner*, Feb. 20, 1925.

32. "Chaplin Garb Is Called Old," *Los Angeles Times*, Feb. 21, 1925, A1.

33. Ibid.; "Fears Monopoly in Acting," *Los Angeles Times*, Mar. 24, 1925, A10; "Aplin Will Call Chaplin," *Los Angeles Times*, Feb. 26, 1925, A1.

34. "Chaplin Pants Real Issue," *Los Angeles Times*, Feb. 25, 1925, A1.

35. *Charles Chaplin* v. *Western Features Productions*, 137 F. 262 (1925); "Chaplin Trial Ends Today," *Los Angeles Times*, Feb. 28, 1925, A11.

36. "Challenges Title of Film Comedian," *Los Angeles Times*, May 20, 1925, A1; "Chaplin Wins Suit to Protect Make-Up," *New York Times*, May 20, 1925, 8; "Chaplin Loses Fight on Exclusive Make-Up," *New York Times*, July 12, 1925, E2; "Chaplin Legally Unique," *Los Angeles Times*, July 12, 1925, B16; emphasis added.

37. "Chaplin Legally Unique," B16.

38. "Chaplin to Testify in Loeb Film Suit," 20; "Sues Chaplin For $100,000," *New York Times*, Nov. 15, 1928, 25; *Charles Chaplin* v. *Charles Amador*, 93 Cal. App. 358 (1928); *Kustoff* v. *Chaplin*, 120 F.2d 551 (9th Cir. 1941); and *Roy Export Company Establishment of Vaduz, Liechtenstein* v. *Columbia Broadcasting System*, 672 F.2d 1095 (2nd Cir. 1982).

39. *Chaplin* v. *Amador* (1928), 8.

40. Affidavit of Lee A. Ochs, *Chaplin* v. *Western Features* (1925).

41. See, for example, *Bert Lahr* v. *Adell Chemical Co.*, 300 F.2d 256 (1st Cir. 1962); and *Lone Ranger* v. *Cox*, 124 F.2d 650 (4th Cir. 1942).

42. *Nichols* v. *Universal Pictures Corp.*, 45 F.2d 119 (2nd Cir.1930); Robert C. Osterberg and Eric C. Osterberg, *Substantial Similarity in Copyright Law* (New York: Practicing Law Institute, 2004), ch. 5. Both the trial and appellate decisions carefully noted that Chaplin was "the first person to use the said clothes, as described herein and as described in the complaint, in his performing as an actor *in motion pictures*" (*Chaplin* v. *Amador* [1928], emphasis added). This is a dubious claim—there were many other screen tramps before Chaplin—but it also reveals the great advantage of performers adapting characters to a new medium.

43. The Marx Brothers copyright lawsuits include *Henry Barsha* v. *Metro-Goldwyn-Mayer*, 32 Cal. App. 2d 556, 90 P.2d 371 (1939); *Marx Bros.* v. *United States*, 96 F.2d 204 (9th Cir. 1938); and *Clancy* v. *Metro-Goldwyn Pictures Corp.* 37 U.S.P.Q. 406 (S.D.N.Y. 1938).

44. *Witwer* v. *Harold Lloyd Corp.*, 46 F.2d 792 (S.D.N.Y. 1930); Jeffrey Vance and Suzanne Lloyd, *Harold Lloyd: Master Comedian* (New York: Abrams, 2002), 126–27.

45. *Witwer* v. *Harold Lloyd* (1930); *Harold Lloyd Corp.* v. *Witwer*, 65 F.2d 1 (9th Cir. 1933); Tom Dardis, *Harold Lloyd: The Man on the Clock* (New York: Penguin, 1984).

46. *Witwer* v. *Lloyd* (1930) and *Lloyd* v. *Witwer* (1933).

47. See *White-Smith Music Publishing Co.* v. *Apollo Co.*, 209 U.S. 1 (1908); *Roe-Lawton* v. *Hal Roach Studios*, 18 F.2d 126 (S.D. Cal. 1927).

48. *Witwer* v. *Lloyd* (1930).

49. *Lloyd* v. *Witwer* (1933).

50. "Plagiarism Suit Lost by Lloyd" *Los Angeles Times* (Nov. 19, 1930), A9 (internal quotation marks omitted). See also "Finds Harold Lloyd Pirated Witwer Plot," *New York Times* (Nov. 19, 1930), 48.

51. *Bachman* v. *Belasco*, 224 F. 817 (2nd Cir. 1915); *Bachman* v. *Belasco*, 224 F. 815 (S.D.N.U. 1913); *London* v. *Biograph*, 231 F. 696 (2nd Cir. 1916).

52. *James O'Neill* v. *General Film Co.*, 171 A.D. 854 (N.Y. App. Div. 1916); *Roe-Lawton* v. *Hal Roach Studios* (1927); *Nichols* v. *Universal* (1930); *Barbadillo* v. *Goldwyn*, 42 F.2d 881 (S.D. Cal. 1930); *Shipman* v. *R.K.O. Radio Pictures, Inc.*, 100 F.2d 533 (2nd Cir. 1938); *Dellar* v. *Samuel Goldwyn, Inc.*, 150 F.2d 612 (2nd Cir. 1945).

53. Harry Carr, "The Lancer," *Los Angeles Times*, June 27, 1930, A1.

54. *Lloyd* v. *Witwer* (1933).

55. Ibid.

56. Ibid.

57. "Silent Star Heir Sues Disney," *BBC News Online* (Oct. 31, 2000); in 1976 a judge did accept the doctrine of unconscious or subconscious plagiarism in the case of *Bright Tunes Music* v. *Harrisongs Music*, 420 F. Supp. 177 (S.D.N.Y. 1976). In the case, Judge Owen asked how George Harrison could

have composed a song so similar to one by the Shiffons, and he concluded: "What happened? I conclude that the composer, in seeking musical materials to clothe his thoughts, was working with various possibilities. As he tried this possibility and that, there came to the surface of his mind a particular combination that pleased him as being one he felt would be appealing to a prospective listener; in other words, that this combination of sounds would work. Why? Because his subconscious knew it already had worked in a song his conscious mind did not remember. Having arrived at this pleasing combination of sounds, the recording was made, the lead sheet prepared for copyright and the song became an enormous success. Did Harrison deliberately use the music of He's So Fine? I do not believe he did so deliberately."

58. On *scènes à fair* see William F. Patry, *Patry on Copyright* (Eagan, MN: Thomson West, 2006).

59. Frank S. Nugent, "The Screen in Review," *New York Times*, Aug. 17, 1939, 23; Bosley Crowther, "The Dissenting Opinions," *New York Times*, Dec. 31, 1939, 89.

60. Leon Yankwich quoting Judge Lancombe, *James M. Cain v. Universal Pictures Co.*, 47 F. Supp. 1013 (S.D. Cal. 1942).

61. Patry, *Patry on Copyright*, 4–24.

62. Richard Fine, "Hollywood and the Profession of Authorship, 1928–1940" (PhD diss., University of Pennsylvania, 1979), 308–309; Richard Fine, *James M. Cain and the American Authors' Authority* (Austin: University of Texas Press, 1992), 70; Richard Maltby, "'To Prevent the Prevalent Type of Book': Censorship and Adaptation in Hollywood, 1924–1934," *American Quarterly* 44.4 (Dec. 1992): 559–60.

63. Maltby, "'To Prevent the Prevalent Type of Book,'" 559–60, 566; Lee Shippey, "The Lee Side O' L.A.," *Los Angeles Times*, July 18, 1935, A4; Murray Ross, *Stars and Strikes: Unionization of Hollywood* (New York: AMS Press, 1967), 49–54; T. J. Walsh, "Playwrights and Power," in Arthur Gerwitz and James K. Kolb, eds., *Art, Glitter, and Glitz: Mainstream Playwrights and Popular Theatre in 1920s America* (Westport, CT: Praeger, 2004); Tad Friend, "Credit Grab," *The New Yorker*, Oct. 20, 2003.

64. Philip K. Scheuer, "James M. Cain Takes Up Hapless Author's Cause," *Los Angeles Times*, June 2, 1946, C1.

65. Ibid.; Morris E. Cohen, "Literary Works: A Question of Ownership," *Hollywood Quarterly* 2.2 (Jan. 1947): 184–90; Fine, *James M. Cain and the American Authors' Authority*.

66. "'Cain Plan' Scored by Writers Group," *New York Times*, May 8, 1947, 14; "People Who Read and Write," *New York Times*, July 20, 1947, BR8; Byron Price, "Freedom of Press, Radio, and Screen," *Annals of the American Academy of Political and Social Science*, The Motion Picture Industry, 254 (Nov. 1947): 137–39; Fine, *James M. Cain and the American Authors' Authority*.

67. Ross, *Stars and Strikes*, 59.

68. "Film Held No Plagiarism," *New York Times*, Aug. 1, 1934, 14.

69. Siva Vaidhyanathan, *Copyrights and Copywrongs: The Rise of Intellectual Property and How It Threatens Creativity* (New York: New York University Press, 2001), 105.

70. *Stodart v. Mutual Film Corp.*, 249 F. 507 (S.D.N.Y 1917); *Stodart v. Mutual Film Corp.*, 249 F. 513 (2nd Cir. 1918); Ronald Cracas, "Judge Learned Hand and the Law of Copyright," *Copyright Law Symposium* 7.55 (1956).

71. *Stodart v. Mutual Film Corp.* (1917); Cracas, "Judge Learned Hand and the Law of Copyright."

72. *Nichols v. Universal Pictures Corp.*, 45 F.2d 119 (2nd Cir. 1930).

73. *Nichols v. Universal Pictures Corp.* (1930). My account of Learned Hand's influence on the idea/expression dichotomy and of the *Abie's Irish Rose* and *Letty Lynton* cases, in particular, is greatly indebted to Siva Vaidhyanathan's *Copyrights and Copywrongs* and Ronald Cracas's "Judge Learned Hand and the Law of Copyright."

74. Lou Taylor, *The Study of Dress History* (Manchester: Manchester University Press, 2002), 183–84; David Wallace, *Hollywoodland* (New York: St. Martin's, 2002), 110–12.

75. *Sheldon v. Metro-Goldwyn Pictures Corp.*, 81F.2d 49 (2nd Cir. 1936).

76. *Sheldon v. Metro-Goldwyn Pictures Corp.*, 309 U.S. 390 (1940); "Authors Win Half-Million on Film Piracy Charge," *Los Angeles Times*, May 10, 1938, 1; "Damages of $587,604 Fixed in Plagiarism," *New York Times*, May 10, 1938, 17; "Damage in MGM Copyright Suit," *Wall Street Journal*, May 10, 1938, 9; "Ruling on Plagiarism Upsetting," *Los Angeles Times*, July 31, 1939, 8; "High Court Limits Copyright Scope," *New York Times*, Mar. 26, 1940.

77. "Sues Over 'Road to Glory,'" *New York Times*, Nov. 10, 1939, 31; "Movie Writer Collapses at $1,000,000 'Piracy' Trial," *Washington Post*, Dec. 12, 1939, 11; *Sheets v. Twentieth Century Fox Film Corp.* (D.D.C. 1940).

78. Roland Flamini, *Thalberg: The Last Tycoon and the World of M.G.M.* (New York: Crown, 1994), 196, 202–203, 209.

79. *Universal Pictures Co., Inc. v. Harold Lloyd Corp.*, 162 F.2d 354 (9th Cir. 1947).

80. *Henry Barsha v. Metro-Godwyn-Mayer*, 32 Cal. App. 2d 556 (1939); *Barsha v. MGM* was not the Marx Brothers' first copyright suit nor even the only plagiarism suit leveled against *A Day at the Races*. The Marx Brothers were found guilty of infringement in a plagiarism suit the year before (*Marx Bros. v. Unites States*, 96 F.2d 204 [9th Cir. 1938]). They were acquitted in the other plagiarism suit involving *A Day at the Races*: *Clancy v. Metro-Goldwyn Pictures Corp.* 37 U.S.P.Q. 406 (S.D.N.Y. 1938).

81. Harry R. Olsson, "Dreams for Sale: Observations on the Law of Idea Submissions and Problems Arising Therefrom," *Law and Contemporary Problems* 23.1 (Winter 1958): 54–55.

82. *Victor Desny v. Billy Wilder*, 46 Cal. 2d 715 (Cal. 1956); Eric Hoyt, "The 'Fantastic, Unusual' Case of *Ace in the Hole*," *Cinema Journal* 50.2 (Winter 2011): 21–40.

83. *Julian Blaustein v. Richard Burton*, 9 Cal. App. 3d 161 (1970); *Buchwald v. Paramount Pictures Corp.* 13 USPQ 2d (BNA) 1497 (Cal. Sup. Ct. 1990); Pierce O'Donnell and William Lockard, "You Have No Idea," *Los Angeles Lawyer* (Apr. 2002). For more on idea protection, see Harry Warner, "Legal Protection of Program Ideas," *Virginia Law Review* 36.3 (Apr. 1950): 289–322, and Leon R. Yankwich, "Legal Protection of Ideas: A Judge's Approach," *Virginia Law Review* 43.4 (Apr. 1957): 375–95.

84. The Buchwald case also demonstrates another way that studios responded to awards given to writers in the post–*Letty Lynton* studio system. The court decided that Buchwald deserved his share of the film's profits because his ideas had been used. But when the court attempted to determine the size of the film's profits, it unearthed another strategy the studios had developed to keep writers as salaried craftsman. Although Buchwald's contract entitled him to a share in the film's profits, the Hollywood accountants calculated that this film, which had grossed over $280 million worldwide, did not turn a profit in the end. The studios' lawyers and accountants perfected a system for insulating themselves against the modest power that courts had bestowed on writers.

85. Pierce O'Donnell and Dennis McDougal, *Fatal Subtraction: The Inside Story of Buchwald v. Paramount* (New York: Doubleday, 1992).

86. See Friend, "Credit Grab," for a compelling account of the Writers Guild review process.

87. For a summary of the issues involved in protecting television formats, see Jay Rubin, "Television Formats: Caught in the Abyss of the Idea/Expression Dichotomy," *Fordham Intellectual Property, Media, and Entertainment Law Journal* 16.661 (Winter 2006): 663–708, and Warner, "Legal Protection of Program Ideas."

88. Robert W. Gilbert, "'Residual Rights' Established by Collective Bargaining in Television and Radio," *Law and Contemporary Problems* 23.1 (Winter 1958): 102–124.

89. Thomas F. Brady, "Hollywood Deals," *New York Times*, Feb. 1, 1948, X5.

90. Chris Anderson, *Hollywood TV: The Studio System in the 1950s* (Austin: University of Texas Press, 1994); Michel Hilmes, *Hollywood and Broadcasting: From Radio to Cable* (Urbana: University of Illinois Press, 1990); William Boddy, *Fifties Television: The Industry and Its Critics* (Urbana: University of Illinois Press, 1990).

91. *Warner Bros. Pictures Inc. v. Columbia Broadcasting System, Inc.*, 102 F. Supp. 141 (S.D. Cal, 1951); *Warner Bros. Pictures Inc. v. Columbia Broadcasting System*, 216 F.2d 945 (9th Cir. 1954), cert. denied 348 US 971 (1955).

92. *Warner Bros. Pictures Inc. v. CBS* (1954).

93. Ibid.

94. *Bevan v. Columbia Broadcasting System, Inc.*, 329 F. Supp. 610 (S.D.N.Y.1971).

95. Osterberg and Osterberg, *Substantial Similarity in Copyright Law*, ch. 5.

96. *Loew's Inc. v. Columbia Broadcasting System, Inc.*, 131 F. Supp. (S.D. Cal. 1955); *Columbia Pictures Corp. v. NBC*, 137 F. Supp. 348 (S.D. Cal. 1955).

97. *Loew's Inc. v. CBS, Inc.* (1955); *Columbia Pictures Corp. v. NBC* (1955).

98. *Loew's Inc.* v. *CBS, Inc.* (1955); *Columbia Pictures Corp.* v. *NBC* (1955).
99. *Loew's Inc.* v. *CBS, Inc.* (1955); "The Parody Defense to Copyright Infringement: Productive Fair Use after 'Betamax,'" *Harvard Law Review* 97.6. (Apr.
1984): 1402; *Saturday Night Live* defended its use of parody in *Elsmere Music,
Inc.* v. *National Broadcasting Co.*, 623 F.2d 252 (2nd Cir. 1980); *Luther R.
Campbell aka Luke Skyywalker* v. *Acuff-Rose Music, Inc.*, 510 U.S. 569 (1994);
Bruce P. Keller and Rebecca Tushnet, "Even More Parodic Than the Real
Thing: Parody Lawsuits Revisited," *Trademark Reporter* 94 (2004): 979–1016;
on Carroll Burnett's parody of *Gone with the Wind*, see *Metro-Goldwyn-
Mayer, Inc. et al* v. *Showcase Atlanta Cooperative Productions, Inc.*, 479 F.
Supp. 351, 357 (ND Ga. 1979).

3. AUTEURISM ON TRIAL: MORAL RIGHTS AND FILMS ON TELEVISION

1. *Fairbanks* v. *Winik*, 198 N.Y.S. 299, 299 (Sup. Ct. 1922); *Fairbanks* v. *Winik*,
201 N.Y.S. 487, 488 (App. Div. 1923).
2. *Fairbanks* v. *Winik*, 198 N.Y.S. 299, 299 (Sup. Ct. 1922); *Fairbanks* v. *Winik*,
201 N.Y.S. 487, 488 (App. Div. 1923).
3. The Chaplin case is discussed in the previous chapter.
4. *Curwood* v. *Affiliated Distributors*, 283 F. 223 (S.D.N.Y 1922).
5. On copyright and the Romantic idea of authorship, see Martha Woodmansee, "The Genius and the Copyright: Economic and Legal Conditions of
the Emergence of the 'Author,'" *Eighteenth-Century Studies* 17.4 (Summer
1984): 425–48, and Peter Jaszi, "Toward a Theory of Copyright: The Meta-
morphoses of Authorship," *Duke Law Journal* 455 (1991): 455–502. On the
marketing of auteurs, see Timothy Corrigan, *A Cinema Without Walls: Film
and Culture After Vietnam* (New Brunswick, NJ: A Cinema Without Walls,
1991).
6. Jane Ginsburg, "A Tale of Two Copyrights: Literary Property in Revolutionary France and America," *Tulane Law Review* 64.5 (May 1990): 991–1031.
7. On the development of the work-for-hire doctrine, see Peter Jaszi and Martha
Woodmansee, "Copyright in Transition," in Carl F. Kaestle and Janice A.
Radway, eds., *A History of the Book in America*, vol. 4: *Print in Motion: The
Expansion of Publishing and Reading in the United States, 1880–1940* (Chapel Hill: University of North Carolina Press, 2009), 90–101.
8. The Creative Commons has made it much easier for authors to give away
some or all of their rights by providing free licenses; see www.creativecom-
mons.org.
9. Pascal Kamina, *Film Copyright in the European Union* (Cambridge: Cambridge University Press, 2002), 285.
10. Act of Mar. 3, 1891, 51st Cong., 2d sess., 26 Stat. 1106. On the history of Berne,
see Kamina, *Film Copyright in the European Union*, and William F. Patry,
Patry on Copyright (Eagan, MN: Thomson West, 2006).

11. The bill would have made it easier for Hollywood studios to bypass play producers and negotiate film rights directly with authors, and it would have allowed Hollywood to prosecute even inadvertent copyright infringers. Play producer William Brady, who had always been an active copyright lobbyist, attacked the bill as the creation of Hollywood, and the Famous Players–Lasky Company (later Paramount) in particular. Paul J. Sherman, "The Universal Copyright Convention: Its Effect on United States Law," *Columbia Law Review* 55.8 (Dec. 1955): 1137–75.

12. "International Copyright Protection and the United States: The Impact of the UNESCO Universal Copyright Convention on Existing Law," *Yale Law Journal* 62.7 (June 1953): 1065–1096; "Says Movie Interests Wrote Copyright Bill," *New York Times*, May 20, 1930, 22; "Vestal Bill Vexes Dill," *Spokesman Review* (Jan. 24, 1931): 7.

13. Joining Berne did not necessarily entail adopting moral rights. Great Britain joined the 1928 Berne Convention without adopting moral rights; instead, the U.K. argued that other areas of British law offered equivalent protection for authors and artists, as the United States would when it finally joined Berne in 1989. "Copyright Reform and the Duffy Bill," *Yale Law Journal* 47.3 (Jan. 1938): 433–50; Philip K. Scheuer, "News of Film and Play Productions," *Los Angeles Times*, Apr. 5, 1936, B4.

14. "Movies Seek Change in Copyright Pact," *New York Times*, July 11, 1939, 24. Determining the moral rights holder in the collaborative medium of film is extremely difficult, and different countries have found different solutions. One solution would be to ask whose personality (or artistic vision) would be harmed by the violation of the bundle of protections under a moral rights regime. In the end, when the United States did finally relent and sign an international copyright treaty, they signed the UNESCO Universal Copyright Convention in 1952, which left moral rights to national discretion. The United States eventually joined the Berne Convention as well, but not until 1989, sixty years after the 1928 revision. In response, Congress passed very limited moral rights legislation, the Visual Artists Rights Act of 1990 or VARA. But even VARA allows artists to waive their moral rights, which again is tantamount to nullifying them.

15. See Thomas M. Pryor, "Film Writer Seeks to End RKO Suit," *New York Times*, June 5, 1952, 39.

16. For more on *Iron Curtain* see Daniel J. Leab, "*The Iron Curtain* (1948): Hollywood's First Cold War Movie," *Historical Journal of Film, Radio, and Television* 8.2 (1988): 153–88; Solomon Volkov, *Shostakovich and Stalin: The Extraordinary Relationship Between the Great Composer and the Brutal Dictator*, trans. Antonia W. Bouis (New York: Knopf, 2004), ch. 6; Per Skans, "The 1948 Formalism Campaign," in Ian MacDonald, *The New Shostakovich*, rev. and ed. Raymond Clarke (London: Pimlico, 2006).

17. Volkov, *Shostakovich and Stalin*; *Dmitry Shostakovich v. Twentieth Century-Fox Film Corp.*, 80 N.Y.S.2d 575 (N.Y. Sup. Ct. 1948), aff'd, 87 N.Y.S.2d 430 (N.Y. App. Div. 1949).

18. *Shostakovich* v. *Twentieth Century-Fox* (1948).

19. *Soc. Le Chant de Monde* v. *Soc. Fox Europa,* Cour d'appel [CA] [regional court of appeal] Paris, 1e ch., Jan. 13, 1953, Gaz. Pal. 1953, 191, note Ancel (Fr.).

20. Marshall McLuhan, *Understanding Media: The Extensions of Man* (New York: McGraw-Hill, 1964), 8.

21. By the early 1950s, the studios had become so stubborn about releasing their films that the Justice Department sued Hollywood (ultimately unsuccessfully), claiming that its unmovable hold on its films amounted to monopolistic behavior. Michel Hilmes, *Hollywood and Broadcasting: From Radio to Cable* (Urbana: University of Illinois Press, 1990); William Lafferty, "Feature Films on Prime-Time Television," in Tino Balio, ed., *Hollywood in the Age of Television* (London: Unwin Hyman, 1990), 235–56; William Boddy, *Fifties Television* (Urbana: University of Illinois Press, 1990); Chris Anderson, *Hollywood TV: The Studio System in the 1950s* (Austin: University of Texas Press, 1994).

22. *Autry* v. *Republic Prods., Inc.,* 104 F. Supp. 918 (S.D. Cal. 1952), aff'd, 213 F.2d 667 (9th Cir. 1954).

23. Thomas M. Pryor, "Roy Rogers Suing on Video Problem," *New York Times,* July 24, 1951, 21.

24. He accused the studio of violating antitrust and labor laws by forcing actors to give away television rights when they signed new film contracts. Talent should be allowed, he argued, to negotiate rights for different media separately. "Autry Sues Studio Over Films for TV," *New York Times,* Oct. 31, 1951, 31.

25. *Autry* v. *Republic* (1952).

26. Thomas M. Pryor, "TV-Movie Tie-Ins Remain Confused," *New York Times,* May 15, 1952, 39.

27. *Autry* v. *Republic* (1954), emphasis added; *Republic* v. *Roy Rogers* (1954); Frank Chesley, "Homer Truett Bone," *HistoryLink.org* (Dec. 28, 2003), see www.historylink.org/essays/output.cfm?file_id=5628.

28. Locke's relevant theory of property can be found in John Locke, *Two Treatises on Government,* ed. Peter Laslett (Cambridge: Cambridge University Press, 1992). To be fair, Locke was equally concerned about the rights of readers when it came to intellectual property; see Ronan Deazley, *Rethinking Copyright: History, Theory, Language* (Northampton, MA: Edward Elgar, 2006), 143.

29. Walter Ames, "Republic Sells Autry, Rogers Films to Video; Pair Happy in Musicals," *Los Angeles Times,* Mar. 22, 1955, 26.

30. Boddy, *Fifties Television,* 71.

31. See Douglas Gomery, *The Hollywood Studio System: An Introduction* (London: British Film Institute, 2005); Thomas Schatz, "The New Hollywood," in Jim Collins, Hilary Radner, and Ava Preacher Colli, eds., *Film Theory Goes to the Movies* (New York: Routledge, 1993), 8–36; Geoff King, *New Hollywood Cinema: An Introduction* (New York: Columbia University Press, 2002).

32. Jon Lewis, *Hollywood v. Hardcore* (New York: New York University Press, 2000); Peter Biskind, *Easy Riders, Raging Bulls: How the Sex-Drugs-and-Rock'n'Roll Generation Saved Hollywood* (New York: Simon and Schuster, 1998).

33. On Sarris's influence, see Robert Stam, *Film Theory: An Introduction* (Malden, MA: Blackwell, 2000), 89–90, and Peter Wollen, review of Andrew Sarris's *You Ain't Heard Nothin' Yet*, in *Sight and Sound* 8.11 (1998): 20–25.

34. Joyce Haber, "Otto Preminger Likes and Earns His Reputation," *Los Angeles Times*, July 19, 1970, R13.

35. Philip K. Scheuer, "Otto's Midas Touch Pays Off," *Los Angeles Times*, Mar. 30, 1965, C9; *Preminger v. Columbia Pictures Corp.*, 267 N.Y.S.2d 594 (Sup. Ct. 1966).

36. *Stevens v. National Broadcasting Company*, 76 Cal. Rptr. 106 (Ct. App. 1969); "Writ to Keep Film Off TV is Refused," *New York Times* (October 14, 1965), 53; *Preminger v. Columbia* (1966)

37. Peter Bart, "N.B.C.-TV Is Sued by Film Director," *New York Times*, Oct. 27, 1965; "TV Commercials Play Knock-Knock," *Los Angeles Times*, Nov. 18, 1965, D16; *Stevens v. National Broadcasting Co.* (1969).

38. "TV Commercials Play Knock-Knock," *Los Angeles Times*, Nov. 18, 1965, D16.

39. Walt Dutton, "Television-Movie Tiff Shaping Up," *Los Angeles Times*, Feb. 18, 1966, C16.

40. Ben Gross, "Artistic Last Laugh May Be on Hollywood," *Los Angeles Times*, Feb. 8, 1966, C13.

41. For a discussion of contracts that involve rights to publication using future technologies see, for example, Rhonda Baker, *Media Law: A Users Guide for Film and Programme Makers* (London: Routledge,1995), and *New York Times Co. v. Tasini*, 533 U.S. 483 (2001).

42. Jeremy Braddock and Stephen Hock, eds., *Directed By Alan Smithee* (Minneapolis: University of Minnesota Press, 2001). In his directorial debut, the *New York Times* noted that *Death of a Gunfighter* "was sharply directed by Allen Smithee." Howard Thompson, "Screen: Tough Western: 'Death of a Gunfighter' Stars Widmark," *New York Times*, May 10, 1969, 34.

43. John G. Cawelti, "*Chinatown* and Generic Transformation," *Mystery, Violence, and Popular Culture* (Madison: University of Wisconsin Press, 2004), 193–209.

44. Will Brooker, *Using the Force: Creativity, Community, and "Star Wars" Fans* (New York: Continuum, 2002), 164.

45. Tom Shales, "Viewpoint," *Los Angeles Times*, Sept. 24, 1978, P7; Dale Pollock, *Skywalking: The Life and Films of George Lucas*, updated edition (New York: Da Capo, 1999), 197.

46. Pollock, *Skywalking*, 198; Kirk Honeycutt, "Are TV Films 'Ripping Off' Hollywood?" *New York Times*, May 18, 1980, D41.

47. *Sid & Marty Krofft Television Prods., Inc. v. McDonald's Corp.*, 562 F.2d 1157, 1167 (9th Cir. 1977); Siva Vaidhyanathan, *Copyrights and Copywrongs:*

The Rise of Intellectual Property and How It Threatens Creativity (New York: New York University Press, 2001), 114–15; *Twentieth Century-Fox Film Corp.* v. *MCA, Inc.*, 209 U.S.P.Q. (BNA) at 201; Dennis McDougal, *The Last Mogul: Lew Wasserman, MCA, and the Hidden History of Hollywood* (New York: Da Capo, 2001), 426.

48. "FVI: What You Didn't Know," Montoro interview by Jim Bertges, *The Unknown Movies* (n.d.); see www.badmovieplanet.com/unknownmovies/reviews/fvi.html.

49. *Smith* v. *Montoro*, 648 F.2d 602, 603 (9th Cir. 1981).

50. *Warner Bros. Inc.* v. *Film Venture International*, 403 F. Supp. 522 (C.D. Cal. 1975). While the court denied the injunction enjoining the film, they did enjoin FVI from using advertisements that resembled *The Exorcist's* ads.

51. *Universal* v. *Film Venture International* (1982).

52. Les Brown, "B.B.C.'s 'Monty Python' Surprise Hit on Public TV," *New York Times*, Mar. 15, 1975; Thomas Meehan, "And Now for Something Completely Different," *New York Times*, Apr. 18, 1976, 159; Hendrik Hertzberg, "Onward and Upward with the Arts: Naughty Bits," *The New Yorker*, Mar. 29, 1976.

53. Dick Adler, "Python Objects to ABC Editing," *Los Angeles Times*, Dec. 18, 1975, H31; Hertzberg, "Naughty Bits," 70, 72.

54. Marcia Landy, *Monty Python's Flying Circus* (Detroit: Wayne State University Press, 2006), 28.

55. See Peter Jaszi, "When Works Collide: Derivative Motion Pictures, Underlying Rights, and the Public Interest," *UCLA Law Review* 28.715 (1980), for a discussion of the contract issues in the case.

56. Adler, "Python Objects," H31; Robert Hewison, *Monty Python: The Case Against* (New York: Grove Press, 1981), 46. Note that the term "mutilation" had been used in different contexts in earlier copyright cases. See, for example, Robert Spoo, "Copyright Protectionism and Its Discontents: The Case of James Joyce's *Ulysses* in America," *Yale Law Journal* 108.3 (Dec. 1999): 633–67.

57. Michael Palin, *Diaries, 1969–1979: The Python Years* (New York: St. Martin's, 2006), 275–78; Hertzberg, "Naughty Bits," 82.

58. Hertzberg, "Naughty Bits," 78; Hewison, *Monty Python*, 53.

59. Hertzberg, "Naughty Bits," 72, 84; Palin, *Diaries*, 275–78.

60. "U.S. Judge Upholds ABC-TV Showing of Monty Pythons," *New York Times*, Dec. 25, 1975, 43; "Judge Allows ABC to Air Its Monty Python Special," *Wall Street Journal*, Dec. 26, 1975, 3; Palin, *Diaries*, 278; Hertzberg, "Naughty Bits," 86.

61. Hertzberg, "Naught Bits," 86; Hewison, *Monty Python*, 54.

62. Hertzberg, "Naught Bits," 87.

63. Ibid. Michael Palin comments on the Pythons' friendship with Hertzberg in Palin, *Diaries*, 271.

64. *Gilliam* v. *ABC*, 538 F.2d 14 (2d Cir. 1976), list of supporting case law removed.

65. *Gilliam* v. *ABC* (1976); Gene Autry had also used a Lanham accusation in his case (*Autry* v. *Republic* [1954]).

66. Hewison, *Monty Python*, 56.

67. John J. O'Connor, "TV: Emmy Ceremonies, Efficient but Rather Dull," *New York Times*, May 19, 1976, 60.

68. Palin, *Diaries*, 355; Susanne Ault, "'South Park' Creators Prove Python Charmers," *Variety*, Oct. 11, 1999. On the Pythons' decision to upload clips to YouTube, see Chris Anderson, *Free: The Future of a Radical Price* (New York: Hyperion, 2009), 1–2. Terry Gilliam again ran into trouble when his film *Brazil* (1985) was significantly edited to be aired on television, although he chose not to sue.

69. Timothy M. Casey, "The Visual Artists Rights Act," *Hastings Communication and Entertainment Law Journal* 85 (1991–92): 89.

70. Michael Cieply, "Movie Classics Transformed to Color Films," *Wall Street Journal*, Sept. 11, 1984, 37. For detailed treatments of the colorization debates, see Eric J. Schwartz, "The National Film Preservation Act of 1988: A Copyright Case Study in Legislative Process," *Journal of the Copyright Society of the USA* 36.2 (Jan. 1989): 138–59; Stuart Klawans, "Rose-Tinted Spectacles," in Mark Crispin Miller, ed., *Seeing Through Movies* (New York: Pantheon, 1990), 150–85; Anthony Slide, *Nitrate Won't Wait* (Jefferson, NC: McFarland, 1992), ch. 9; Craig A. Wagner, "Motion Picture Colorization, Authenticity, and the Elusive Moral Right," *New York University Law Review* 64 (1989): 628–724.

71. Slide, *Nitrate Won't Wait*, 123; Woody Allen, "The Colorization of Films Insults Artists and Society," *New York Times*, June 28, 1987, A1.

72. "A Colorful Copyright Campaign," *Los Angeles Times*, Oct. 17, 1986, M1; Klawans, "Rose-Tinted Spectacles," 157–58.

73. Slide, *Nitrate Won't Wait*, 124.

74. Stam, *Film Theory*, 89.

75. Senate Subcommittee on Patents, Copyright, and Trademarks, *The Berne Convention: Hearing on S. 1301 and S. 1971 Before the Subcommittee on Patents, Copyrights, and Trademarks of the Senate Committee on the Judiciary*, 100th Cong., 2d sess. (1988), 482 (prepared statement of George Lucas).

76. Senate Subcommittee, *The Berne Convention* (prepared statement of Steven Spielberg), 509. (Ironically, *Jaws* producer David Brown argued against the directors.) See also "Final Say Over Films at Issue," *New York Times*, Mar. 4, 1988, C18; Serge Guilbaut, *How New York Stole the Idea of Modern Art*, trans. Arthur Goldhammer (Chicago: University of Chicago Press, 1983); Frances Stonor Saunders, *The Cultural Cold War: The CIA and the World of Arts and Letters* (New York: The New Press, 2000); Peter Decherney, *Hollywood and the Culture Elite: How the Movies Became American* (New York: Columbia University Press, 2005), ch. 6.

77. Schwartz, "The National Film Preservation Act"; Klawans, "Rose-Tinted Spectacles"; Ronald Brownstein, *The Power and the Glitter: The Hollywood Washington Connection* (New York: Random House, 1990), 218.

78. National Film Preservation Act of 1988, Pub. L. No. 100-446, 100th Cong., 2d sess. (September 27, 1988), 102 Stat. 1774, 1782, renewed by Act of June

26, 1992, Pub. L. No. 102-307, tit. II, 102d Cong., 2d sess., 106 Stat. 264, 267; Schwartz, "The National Film Preservation Act."

79. Kara Swisher, "House Takes Steps on Colorization," *Wall Street Journal*, June 25, 1988; Irvin Molotsky, "Film-Color Panel Seeks Meaning of 'American,'" *New York Times*, Jan. 24, 1989, C19; Andrew L. Yarrow, "Action but No Consensus on Film Coloring," *New York Times*, July 11, 1988, C13.

80. Comments of Professor John Belton on Behalf of the Society for Cinema Studies (now the Society for Cinema and Media Studies) and Comments of Professor Peter Jaszi Before the Copyright Office in the Public Hearing on New Technology and Audiovisual Works, United States Copyright Office (Sept. 8, 1988).

81. *Turner Entertainment* v. *Huston*, CA Versailles, civ. ch. (Dec. 19, 1994). A translation of the *Turner* v. *Huston* decision is published in the *Entertainment Law Reporter* 16.10 (Mar. 1995); Elizabeth Kolbert, "A Turner Channel Seeks Carriers," *New York Times*, Apr. 11, 1994, D5; Lawrie Mifflin, "Clash of the Old-Movie Titans," *New York Times*, Mar, 19, 1995, H38.

82. Drew Clark, "Bowdlerizing for Columbine," *Slate.com* (Jan. 20, 2003); Directors Guild of America, Press Release, "DGA Denounces Lawsuit Filed Against 16 Directors by Two Entities Engaged in Unauthorized Editing of Films" (Aug. 29, 2002).

83. Clark, "Bowdlerizing;" Michael Apted: "We had, as a guild, a legal obligation to protect the work of our members. But what I was also saying is that we have a moral obligation to do so as well. . . . It was a very well-planned and orchestrated campaign from the beginning, but it was made much stronger once the studios joined us. There was not just good legal basis, in my mind; there was a very strong moral claim, and that is what I thought was so important and exciting that we took that stand." Peter Kiefer, "Dialogue with Michael Apted," *The Hollywood Reporter*, Aug. 18, 2003; Directors' Parties Motion for Leave to File Sur-reply, *Huntsman* v. *Soderbergh*, No. 02-M-1662 (MJW) (D. Colo. Jan. 7, 2004).

84. Comment of Jack Valenti in Motion Picture Association of America, Press Release (Sept. 20, 2002), see www.dga.org/news/pr_mpaaasupportsdgastance. php3; Randall Picker, "CleanFlicks and Digital Rights Management," *University of Chicago Law School Faculty Blog* (July 1, 2006).

85. Orrin Hatch served as chairman of the Judiciary Committee from 1995 to 2001 and from 2003 to 2005. In one speech, for example, Hatch reveled his position on copyright when he remarked, "There are many who do not understand that ideas, inventions, artistic works, and other commercially-viable products created out of one's own mental processes deserve the same protection under the law as any other tangible product or piece of real estate. . . . As I hope you can tell, the protection of intellectual property has been and is one of my top priorities in the Senate." Orrin G. Hatch, Remarks at the International Confederation of Societies of Authors and Composers World Copyright Summit (June 9, 2009), available at http://msl1.mit.edu/furdlog/docs/usgov/ Speech_Hatch_WCS.pdf ; Family Entertainment and Copyright Act of 2005, 119 Stat. 218.

86. [Part 1] Artists' Rights and Theft Prevention Act of 2005, Pub. L. 109–9, §
102, 119 Stat. 218; [Part 2] Family Movie Act of 2005, Pub. L. 109–9, § 202, 119
Stat. 223. 309. Id. 310; [Part 3] National Film Preservation Act of 2005, Pub.
L. 109–9, § 302, 199 Stat. 224.

87. *CleanFlicks of Colo., LLC* v. *Soderbergh*, 433 F. Supp. 2d 1236 (D. Colo.
2006).

4. HOLLYWOOD'S GUERRILLA WAR: FAIR USE AND HOME VIDEO

1. H.R. Rep. No. 1476, 94th Cong., 2nd sess. (Mar. 1967), 66.

2. For some examples of the influence of gatekeepers on fair use, see Patricia
Aufderheide and Peter Jaszi, *Untold Stories: Creative Consequences of the
Rights Clearance Culture for Documentary Filmmakers* (Washington, D.C.:
Center for Social Media, 2004); Fred von Lohmann, "Fair Use as Innovation
Policy," *Berkeley Technology Law Journal* 23.1 (2008); and the International
Communication Association's report, *Clipping Our Own Wings Copyright
and Creativity in Communication Research* (Mar. 2010).

3. Garret the Copyright Ferret made his debut in the comic book "Copyright
Crusader to the Rescue," a supplement to *Weekly Reader* 4 (1995); "L.A. Boy
Scouts Get Award Patch for 'Respecting Copyrights,'" *Foxnews.com* (Oct.
23, 2006); the Electronic Frontier Foundation's education site can be found
at www.teachingcopyright.org. See also Tarelton Gillespie, "Characterizing
Copyright in the Classroom: The Cultural Work of A just nti-Piracy Campaigns," *Communication, Culture, & Critique* 2.3 (Sept. 2009): 247–318.

4. *Berlin* v. *E. C. Publications Inc.*, 329 F.2d 541 (2d Cir. 1964); *Rosemont Enterprises* v. *Random House*, 366 F.2d 303 (2d Cir. 1966); *Time Inc.* v. *Bernard Geis
Assocs.*, 293 F.Supp. 130 (D.C.N.Y. 1968).

5. *Williams & Wilkins Co.* v. *United States*, 420 U.S. 376 (1975); Lawrence Lessig, *Free Culture: How Big Media Uses Technology and the Law to Lockdown
Culture and Control Creativity* (New York: Penguin, 2004), 59–61.

6. Stephen Breyer, "The Uneasy Case for Copyright: A Study of Copyright in
Books, Photocopies, and Computer Programs," *Harvard Law Review* 84.2
(1970): 337; Benjamin Kaplan, "An Unhurried View of Copyright: Proposals
and Prospects," *Columbia Law Review* 66.5 (May 1966): 843.

7. H.R. Rep. No. 92-487, 92d Cong., 1st sess., 3 (1971).

8. Lee Edson, "Lone Inventor with a Genie Complex," *New York Times Magazine*, Dec. 17, 1967, 29, 80–87; Frederic Wasser, *Veni, Vidi, Video: The Hollywood Empire and the VCR* (Austin: University of Texas Press, 2001), 60;
James Lardner, *Fast Forward: Hollywood, the Japanese, and the Onslaught of
the VCR* (New York: Norton, 1987), 115.

9. Wasser, *Veni, Vidi, Video*, 63.

10. Lloyd Boardman, "'Disk-Television': Some Recurring Copyright Problems in
the Reproduction and Performance of Motion Pictures," *University of Chicago Law Review* 34.3 (Spring 1967): 703.

11. "Agreement on Guidelines for Classroom Copying in Not-for-Profit Educational Institutions with Respect to Books and Periodicals," H.R. Rep. No. 94-1476, pp. 68–70 (1976) and "Guidelines for Educational Uses of Music," H.R. Rep. No. 94-1476, pp. 70–71 (1976); all in 127 Cong. Rec. 18 (1981) 24,048-49. See also Kenneth D. Crews, "The Law of Fair Use and the Illusion of Fair-Use Guidelines," *Ohio State Law Journal* 62 (2001), and Ann Bartow, "Educational Fair Use in Copyright: Reclaiming the Right to Photocopy Freely," *University of Pittsburgh Law Review* 60 (Fall 1998).

12. "Off-Air Taping for Educational Use: Hearings Before the House Subcommittee on Courts, Civil Liberties, and the Administration of Justice," 96th Cong., 1st sess. (1979), p. 32; "Guidelines for Off-Air Recordings of Broadcast Programming for Educational Purposes," Cong. Rec. 127 (1981) 24048-49 (remarks of Rep. Robert W. Kastenmeier).

13. The fair use section of the copyright statute reads, in part:

    [T]he fair use of a copyrighted work, including such use by reproduction in copies or phonorecords or by any other means specified by that section, for purposes such as criticism, comment, news reporting, teaching (including multiple copies for classroom use), scholarship, or research, is not an infringement of copyright. In determining whether the use made of a work in any particular case is a fair use the factors to be considered shall include—
    (1) the purpose and character of the use, including whether such use is of a commercial nature or is for nonprofit educational purposes;
    (2) the nature of the copyrighted work;
    (3) the amount and substantiality of the portion used in relation to the copyrighted work as a whole; and
    (4) the effect of the use upon the potential market for or value of the copyrighted work.
    (17 U.S.C. §107)

14. Lucas Hilderbrand, *Inherent Vice: Bootleg Histories of Videotape and Copyright* (Durham, N.C.: Duke University Press, 2009), 129–30.

15. Ibid., 140–54.

16. U.S.C. § 108(f)(3) (1978); Hilderbrand, *Inherent Vice*, ch. 3.

17. *Encyclopaedia Britannica Educational Corp.* v. *Crooks*, 447 F. Supp. 243 (W.D.N.Y. 1978), 542 F. Supp. 1156 (W.D.N.Y. 1982), and 558 F. Supp. 1247 (W.D.N.Y 1983); William Patry, *Fair Use in Copyright Law* (Washington, D.C.: Bureau of National Affairs, 1985), 195–200.

18. *Bruzzone* v. *Miller Brewing Co.*, 202, U.S.P.Q. 809 (N.D. Cal. 1979).

19. *New Boston Television, Inc.* v. *ESPN, Inc.*, 215 U.S.P.Q. 755 (D. Mass. 1981).

20. Lardner, *Fast Forward*, 21–22.

21. On Disney and TV/home video, see Douglas Gomery, *The Hollywood Studio System: An Introduction* (London: BFI, 2005), and Douglas Gomery, *Shared Pleasures: A History of Movie Presentation in the United States* (Madison: University of Wisconsin Press, 1992).

22. Robert Metz, "Market Place," *New York Times*, May 13, 1977, 81, and Gomery, *Shared Pleasures*, 278–79.

23. *Sony Corp. v. Universal City Studios, Inc.*, 480 F. Supp. 429 (C.D. Cal. 1979).

24. *Sony Corp. v. Universal City Studios* (1979); Steve Wozniak tells the story of the blue box in *iWoz: Computer Geek to Cult Icon: How I Invented the Personal Computer, Co-Founded Apple, and Had Fun Doing It* (New York: Norton, 2007), ch. 6.

25. *Stanley v. Georgia*, 394 U.S. 557 (1969); *Sony Corp. v. Universal City Studios*, 659 F2d 963 (9th Cir. 1981).

26. *Home Recording of Copyrighted Works: Hearing on H.R. 4783, H.R. 4794, H.R. 4808, H.R. 5250, H.R. 5488, and H.R. 5705, Before the Subcommittee on Courts, Civil Liberties, and the Administration of Justice of the House of Representatives Committee on the Judiciary*, 97 Cong., 2d sess. (1982) (comments of Jack Valenti, president of the Motion Picture Association of America).

27. Roy Rosensweig, *Eight Hours for What We Will: Workers and Leisure in an Industrial City, 1870–1920* (Cambridge: Cambridge University Press, 1983); Andrew Pollack, "Video Recorder Sales Go On," *New York Times*, Oct. 21, 1981, D5; Eric Gelman, Janet Huck, Connie Leslie, Carolyn Friday, Pamela Abramshon, Michael Reese, "The Video Revolution," *Newsweek*, Aug. 6, 1984. For a complete history of the video store business, see Joshua M. Greenberg, *From Betamax to Blockbuster: Video Stores and the Invention of Movies on Video* (Cambridge: MIT Press, 2008).

28. Eugene Secunda, "VCRs and Viewer Control Over Programming: An Historical Perspective," in Julia R. Dobrow, ed., *Social and Cultural Aspects of VCR Use* (Hillsdale, NJ: Lawrence Erlebaum, 1990), 17, 21; Gomery, *Shared Pleasures*, 280.

29. Kathryn Harris, "Copyright Expert Looks Beyond Court Decision in Betamax Case," *Los Angeles Times*, Nov. 1, 1981, H3; Kathryn Harris, "Hollywood Wages Battle Over Videocassette Rentals," *Los Angeles Times*, Oct. 17, 1982, F1. The MPAA also commissioned a report from Harvard law professor Lawrence Tribe on the constitutionality of home taping. *Home Recording of Copyrighted Works* (comments of Jack Valenti); Stephen Prince, *A New Pot of Gold: Hollywood Under the Electronic Rainbow, 1980–1989* (New York: Scribner's, 2000), 100.

30. Charles Schreger, "A Concatenation of Clinkers," *Los Angeles Times*, Mar. 19, 1980, I7; Lardner, *Fast Forward*, 207.

31. Secunda, "VCRs and Viewer Control," 19; Bruce Apar, "Home Videotaping Hurts No Copyrights" (letter), *New York Times*, Nov. 9, 1981, A20; Ernest Holsendolphs, "Legislative Plan to Tax Video Recording Gear," *New York Times*, Mar. 12, 1982, A30; Lardner, *Fast Forward*, 213, 294; Penny Pagano, "Video Battle Will Now Go to Congress," *Los Angeles Times*, Jan. 18, 1984, F1; "Video Cassette Debate Off," *New York Times*, Feb. 23, 1984, C22; Laura Landro, "Movie Studios' Cuts in Videocassette Prices Stir Battle with Retailers on Video Rentals," *Wall Street Journal*, Sept. 23, 1983, 33.

32. Janet Wasko, *Hollywood in the Information Age* (Austin: University of Texas Press, 1995), 128.

33. Lardner, *Fast Forward*, 207; Jon Pareles, "Royalties on Recorders and Blank Audio Tapes," *New York Times*, Nov. 21, 1985, C34.

34. *Sony Corp. v. Universal Studios, Inc.*, 464 U.S. 417 (1984); Prince, *A New Pot of Gold*, 101; Jonathan Band and Andrew J. McLaughlin, "The Marshall Papers: A Peek Behind the Scenes at the Making of *Sony v. Universal*," *Columbia-VLA Journal of Law & the Arts* 17.427 (1993): 433; Pamela Samuelson, "The Generativity of *Sony v. Universal*: The Intellectual Legacy of Justice Stevens," *Fordham Law Review* 74.4 (Mar. 2006): 1831–76; Jessica Litman, "The Story of *Sony v. Universal Studios*: Mary Poppins Meets the Boston Strangler," in Jane C. Ginsburg and Rochelle Cooper Dreyfess, eds., *Intellectual Property Stories* (New York: Foundation Press, 2006), 358–94; Jessica Litman, "The Sony Paradox," *Case Western Reserve Law Review* 55 (2005): 917–62.

35. The MPAA continued to work toward a legislative change. In fact, in Jack Valenti's public response to the Supreme Court's Sony decision, he focused largely on Congress. "It is Congress," he told reporters on the day the decision was released, "who must decide if copyright protection is real, or whether it is mush." Valenti, quoted in Pagano, "Video Battle Will Now Go to Congress," F1.

36. Leslie Berger, "A Social Event," *Los Angeles Times*, Aug. 13, 1981, H10; *Columbia Pictures Industries, Inc. v. Redd Horne, Inc.*, 749 F.2d 154 (3rd Cir. 1984); *Columbia Pictures Industries, Inc. v. Aveco, Inc.*, 800 F.2d 59 (3rd Cir. 1986); *Columbia Pictures Industries, Inc. v. Professional Real Estate Investors, Inc.*, 866 F2d 278 (9th Cir. 1989); "Ban Upheld on Stores' Renting Screening Rooms," *New York Times*, Sept. 8, 1986, C18; "Video Rental Rooms Fought," *New York Times*, Aug. 20, 1984, D1.

37. "Twelve Movie Firms Sue 10 Video Retailers, Charging Film Piracy," *Wall Street Journal*, Sept. 15, 1982, 56; "2 Charged with Stealing Films, Selling Copies," *Los Angeles Times*, July 16, 1979, E15; Prince, *A New Pot of Gold*, 95–96; Kerry Segrave, *Piracy in the Motion Picture Industry* (Jefferson, NC: McFarland, 2003), 106–108; "McDowell Films Seized in Piracy Investigation," *New York Times*, Jan. 18, 1975, 31.

38. Frank Lovece, "Fast Forward," *Billboard*, Oct. 11, 1986, 64.

39. There was, however, a brief dip in ticket sales in 1985. Gomery, *Shared Pleasures*, 276; Gelman et al., "The Video Revolution."

40. See Gomery, *Shared Pleasures*, ch, 14, and Prince, *A New Pot of Gold*, ch. 3.

41. Andrew Pollack, "A Battle Over Video Cassettes," *New York Times*, Dec. 11, 1981, D1; Laura Landro, "Film Studios' Plans to Lease Videocassettes Bring Big Outcry from Squeezed Retailers," *Wall Street Journal*, Jan. 18, 1982, 25.

42. Lardner, *Fast Forward*, 197; Greenberg, *From Betamax to Blockbuster*, 119.

43. Gomery, *Shared Pleasures*, 283–85; Edward Jay Epstein, *The Big Picture: The New Logic of Money and Power in Hollywood* (New York: Random House, 2005), 65–74.

44. *Harper & Row, Publishers, Inc.* v. *Nation Enterprises*, 471 U.S. 539, 566 (1985).

45. *Loews Inc.* v. *CBS Inc.*, 131 F. Supp. (S.D. Cal. 1955); *Columbia Pictures Corp.* v. *National Broadcasting Company*, 137 F. Supp. 348 (S.D. Cal. 1955).

46. *Elsmere Music, Inc.* v. *National Broadcasting Co.*, 623 F.2d 252, United States Court of Appeals, Second Circuit (June 9, 1980).

47. Pierre N. Leval, "Toward a Fair Use Standard," *Harvard Law Review* 103.1105 (1990) (internal footnotes omitted; emphasis added).

48. *Campbell*, v. *Acuff-Rose Music*, 510 U.S. 569 (1994).

49. Scott MacDonald, *A Critical Cinema 3: Interviews with Independent Filmmakers* (Berkeley: University of California Press, 1998), 202.

50. Ibid., 41.

51. David Thompson and Ian Christie, eds., *Scorsese on Scorsese*, rev. ed. (New York: Faber and Faber, 2003), 21. Completing the circle of misinformation, composer Phil Spector briefly considered seeking an injunction against *Mean Streets* because the Ronettes cover his song "Be My Baby" on the soundtrack, although it isn't exactly clear what he thought the infringement was. John Anderson, "In Documentary, Wall of Sound Meets Wall of Law," *New York Times*, June 25, 2010.

52. Scott MacDonald, "From Underground to Multiplex: An Interview with Todd Haynes," *Film Quarterly* 62.3 (Spring 2009): 57.

53. Andrea Chase, interview with Todd Haynes, PRX Radio (Mar. 25, 2011); see www.prx.org/pieces/60842-mildred-pierce-todd-haynes-on-his-five-part-hbo.

54. See Hilderbrand, *Inherent Vice*, ch. 4.

55. Naomi Klein, *No Logo: No Space, No Choice, No Jobs* (New York: Picador, 2009), 181; Andrea Chase, interview with Todd Haynes (PRX Radio); Kembrew McLeod, *Freedom of Expression* ®: *Overzealous Copyright Bozos and Other Enemies of Creativity* (New York: Doubleday, 2005), 144; Carrie McLaren, "Illegal Art: Freedom of Expression in the Corporate Age," at www.illegal-art.org/index.html.

56. Francesca Coppa, "Women, *Star Trek*, and the Early Development of Fannish Vidding," *Journal of Transformative Works* 1 (2008); Clive Young, *Homemade Hollywood: Fans Behind the Camera* (New York: Continuum, 2008).

57. Letter from Morgan Griffin (Mar. 1, 2010).

58. Rebecca Tushnet, "Legal Fictions: Copyright, Fan Fiction, and a New Common Law," *Loyola of Los Angeles Entertainment Law Journal* 17 (1997): 672–73; Coppa, "Women, *Star Trek*, and the Early Development of Fannish Vidding"; Jennifer Granick, "Cyber Rights Now: 'Scotty: Beam Down the Lawyers,'" *Wired*, Oct. 9, 1997.

59. Dale Pollock, *Skywalking: The Life and Films of George Lucas*, updated edition (New York: Da Capo, 1999), 220; David A. Cook, *Lost Illusions: American Cinema in the Shadow of Watergate and Vietnam, 1970–1978* (Berkeley: University of California Press, 2000), 48; Tamara Nunn, "Smashing Home Video?" *Orange Coast Magazine* (Feb. 1982): 125.

60. Irv Broughton, *Producers on Producing: The Making of Film and Television* (Jefferson, NC: McFarland, 1986), 88–90; Young, *Homemade Hollywood*.

61. Will Brooker, *Using the Force: Creativity, Community, and "Star Wars" Fans* (New York: Continuum, 2002), 164–68; Tushnet, "Legal Fictions," 674n113; Leanne Stendell, "Fanfic and Fan Fact: How Current Copyright Law Ignores the Reality of Copyright Owner and Consumer Interests in Fan Fiction," *Southern Methodist University Law Review* 58 (Fall 2005); Granick, "Cyber Rights Now."

62. Henry Jenkins, *Convergence Culture: Where Old and New Media Collide* (New York: New York University Press, 2006), 154.

63. Ibid.; Brooker, *Using the Force*, 177.

64. Chris Hegedus's remarks are archived on the website of Duke University's Center for the Study of the Public Domain; see www.law.duke.edu/framed.

65. "A Professor's Class Video Runs into an MTV Protest," *New York Times*, May 18, 1991, 146; Patricia Aufderheide and Peter Jaszi, *Reclaiming Fair Use: How to Put Balance Back in Copyright* (Chicago: University of Chicago Press, 2011), 37.

66. Fiona Morgan, "A Conference at Duke Law School Looks at How Filmmakers and Musicians Get in Trouble with the Law," *Independent Online* (Apr. 7, 2004); Tom Zeller, "Permissions on Digital Media Drive Scholars to Lawbooks," *New York Times*, June 14, 2004); The Society for Cinema and Media Studies, "Statement of Best Practices for Fair Use in Teaching for Film and Media Educators," *Cinema Journal* 47. 2 (2008); Peter Jaszi and Patricia Aufderheide, "Untold Stories: Collaborative Research on Documentary Filmmakers' Free Speech and Fair Use," *Cinema Journal* 46.2 (Winter 2007): 133–39

67. Jaszi and Aufderheide, "Untold Stories," 137.

68. Lessig, *Free Culture*, 187; Jenkins, *Convergence Culture*; Lawrence Lessig, *Remix: Making Art and Commerce Thrive in the Hybrid Economy* (New York: Penguin, 2008). Another group that has advocated for fair use to be supplemented by exemptions is the Copyright Principles Project. See Pamela Samuelson and Members of the Copyright Principles Project, "The Copyright Principles Project: Directions for Reform," *Berkeley Technology Law Journal* 25 (2010): 1175–1245.

5. DIGITAL HOLLYWOOD: TOO MUCH CONTROL AND TOO MUCH FREEDOM

1. For the legislative history of the DMCA, see Jessica Litman, *Digital Copyright* (Amherst, NY: Prometheus, 2001), and Bill D. Herman and Oscar Gandy Jr., "Catch 1201: A Legislative History and Content Analysis of the DMCA Exemption Proceedings," *Cardozo Arts & Entertainment Law Journal* 24 (2006): 121–90.

2. Paul C. Spehr, "Unaltered to Date: Developing 35mm Film," in John Fullerton and Astrid Söderbeergh Widding, eds., *Moving Images: From Edison to the Webcam* (Sydney: John Libby. 2000).

3. Janet Staiger, "Combination and Litigation: Structures of U.S. Film Distribution, 1896–1917," *Cinema Journal* (1983): 41–73.

4. Douglas Gomery, *The Coming of Sound: A History* (New York: Routledge, 2005), ch 1.

5. Ibid., and Donald Crafton, *The Talkies: American Cinema's Transition to Sound* (Berkeley: University of California Press, 1997), 129–30.

6. James Lardner, *Fast Forward: Hollywood, the Japanese, and the Onslaught of the VCR* (New York: Norton, 1987), 119–20.

7. Hans Fantel, "Tangles in the Anti-Copying Thicket," *New York Times*, Aug. 30, 1987; Paul McDonald, *Video and DVD Industries* (London: British Film Institute, 2007); Frank Lovece, "Fast Forward," *Billboard*, Oct. 11, 1986: 64–65; "How to Get the Most from Your VCR," *Popular Mechanics*, Nov. 1983, 154.

8. Bill Holland, "RIAA Chief Expresses Fears on DAT," *Billboard*, Aug. 16, 1986; Will Crutchfield, "Next Home Stereo Advance: Digital Tape Cassettes in 1987," *New York Times*, Oct. 24, 1986, A1; Joel L. McKuin, "Home Audio Taping of Copyrighted Works and the Audio Home Recording Act of 1992: A Critical Analysis," *Hastings Communication & Entertainment Law Journal* 16 (2994).

9. S. 506 (1987), H.R. 1384 (1987); S. 2358 (1990). For the legislative history of the AHRA, see Judiciary Committee, S. Rep. No. 102–294 (1992).

10. Peter Jaszi, "Intellectual Property Legislative Update: Copyright, Paracopyright, and Pseudo-Copyright," talk delivered at the Association of Research Libraries Conference, Eugene, OR (May 1998), available at www.arl.org/resources/pubs/mmproceedings/132mmjaszi.

11. Lawrence Lessig, *Remix: Making Art and Commerce Thrive in the Hybrid Economy* (New York: Penguin, 2008), 111–12.

12. Herman and Gandy, "Catch 1201," 212–90; Litman, *Digital Copyright*, 144, and Katherine Sender and Peter Decherney, "Defending Fair Use in the Age of the Digital Millennium Copyright Act," *International Journal of Communication* (2007): 1–7; all of the documents relating to the rulemakings can be found at www.copyright.gov/1201.

13. Electronic Frontier Foundation, Press Release, "DMCA Triennial Rulemaking Failing Consumers Completely: EFF Bows Out of Broken Process" (Dec. 1, 2005).

14. Comments and testimony can be found at www.copyright.gov/1201. Also see Mark Gray, "A 'Casual Nexus of Harm': DMCA Circumvention and Rulemaking" (Senior thesis, Princeton University, Apr. 5, 2011).

15. For an excellent account of the rulemaking process and the 2009 rulemaking in particular, see Rebecca Tushnet, "I Put You There: User-Generated Content and Anticircumvention," *Vanderbilt Journal of Entertainment and Technology* 12 (2010): 889–946.

16. Sales data come from Apple's press releases, available at www.apple.com/pr/.

17. Steve Jobs interviewed by Daniel Morrow for the Smithsonian Oral History Project (Apr. 20, 1995), see http://americanhistory.si.edu/collections/comphist/sj1.html; Steve Wozniak, *iWoz: Computer Geek to Cult Icon: How I Invented the Personal Computer, Co-Founded Apple, and Had Fun Doing It* (New York: Norton, 2007); Alex Soojung-Kim Pang, ed., *Making the Macintosh:*

Technology and Culture in Silicon Valley (website), see http://library.stanford. edu/mac/; Danial Cohen, "Review of *Making the Macintosh*," *History Matters* (June 2002), see http://historymatters.gmu.edu/d/5551/.

18. Gates's comments are reported in Andy Hertzfeld, "A Rich Neighbor Named Xerox" (Nov. 1983); see folklore.org. The court agreed that, "Apple cannot get patent-like protection for the idea of a graphical user interface, or the idea of a desktop metaphor." *Apple Computer, Inc. v. Microsoft Corp.*, 35 F.3d 1435 (9th Cir. 1994).

19. Owen W. Linzmayer, *Apple Confidential 2.0: The Definitive History of the World's Most Colorful Computer* (San Francisco: No Starch Press, 2004), 248; Scully's comments appear in the film *Triumph of the Nerds: The Rise of Accidental Empires* (1996).

20. Linzmayer, *Apple Confidential 2.0*, 248, 250.

21. Steve Jobs, Macworld Keynote Address, Boston, 1997, archived at www.youtube.com/watch?v=WxOp5mBY9IY; World Wide Developers Conference Keynote, June 7, 2010, at www.apple.com/apple-events/wwdc-2010/.

22. Press Release, "Apple Reports Fourth Quarter Results" (Oct. 13, 2004), at www.apple.com/pr/library/2004/oct/13results.html; Katie Marsal, "iPod: How Big Can It Get?" *Apple Insider* (May 24, 2006).

23. Robert X. Cringely, "Masters Tournament" I, *Cringley* (blog) (Apr. 9, 2010), at www.cringely.com/2010/04/masters-tournament/; Steven Johnson, "Rethinking a Gospel of the Web," *New York Times*, Apr. 9, 2010.

24. Miguel Helft and Ashlee Vance, "Apple Passes Microsoft as No. 1 in Tech," *New York Times*, May 26, 2010.

25. Comments of Electronic Frontier Foundation submitted in the *Exemption to Prohibition on Circumvention of Copyright Protection Systems for Access Control Technologies: Hearing Before the Copyright Office*, Library of Congress, No. Docket No. RM 2008–8 (2008).

26. Some 26 percent of U.S. homes had internet access in 1998; see National Telecommunications and Information Administration, "Falling Through the Net II: New Data on the Digital Divide" (July 28, 1998); Lev Manovich, "What Is Digital Cinema?" (1995), at www.manovich.net/TEXT/digital-cinema.html.

27. Peter H. Lewis, "Prodigy Seen Opening Doors in Cyberspace," *New York Times*, May 11, 1995.

28. *Religious Technology Center v. Netcom On-Line Communication Services, Inc.*, 907 F. Supp. 1361 (N.D. Cal. 1995); *Playboy Enterprises, Inc. v. Frena*, 839 F. Supp. 1552 (M.D. Fla. 1993); *Sega Enterprises Ltd. v. MAPHIA*, 948 F. Supp. 923 USPQ2d (BNA) 1705 (N.D. Cal. 1996).

29. 47 U.S.C. § 230.

30. Barney Frank, 144 Cong. Rec. H7092 (daily ed. Aug. 4, 1998).

31. 17 U.S.C. § 512(c); Fred von Lohmann, "Fair Use, Film, and the Advantages of Internet Distribution," *Cinema Journal* 46.2 (Winter 2007): 128–33.

32. "YouTube Serves Up 100 Million Videos a Day Online," *USA Today*, July 16, 2006.

33. Henry Jenkins, "What Happened Before YouTube?" in Jean Burgess and Joshua Green, *YouTube: Online Video and Participatory Culture* (Cambridge: Polity Press, 2009), 109–125.

34. *Code of Best Practices for Online Video* (Washington, D.C.: Center for Social Media, American University, June 2008).

35. Stan Schroeder, "Can Free Content Boost Your Sales? Yes it Can," *Mashable.com* (Jan. 23, 2009); Burgess and Green, *YouTube: Online Video and Participatory Culture*, 31–32; David Kravets, "Accusations Fly in Viacom, YouTube Copyright Fight," *Threat Level Blog*, Wired.com (Mar. 18, 2010); Ben Fritz and Steve Zeitchik, "Viacom Gets Vexed," *Daily Variety* (Mar. 14, 2007); Memorandum of Law in Support of Defendants," Motion for Summary Judgment, *Viacom International* v. *YouTube, Inc.*, Case No. 1:07-cv-02 103 (S.D.N.Y. 2010); Gretchen Morgenson, "Bidder Beware," *New York Times*, July 2, 2010.

36. Frederic Lardinois, "It's Complicated: Warner Music Comes Back to YouTube," *Read Write Web* (blog) (Sept. 29, 2009).

37. Chilling effects.org; *Reporter's Shield Legislation: Issues and Implications: Hearing Before the S. Judiciary Comm.*, 109th Cong. (2005) (testimony of William Safire, *New York Times*); Jennifer Urban and Laura Quilter, "Efficient Process or 'Chilling Effects'? Takedown Notices Under Section 512 of the Digital Millennium Copyright Act," *Santa Clara Computer & High Technology Law Journal* 22 (May 2006): 621–93; David F. Gallagher, "New Economy: A Copyright Dispute with the Church of Scientology Is Forcing Google to Do Some Creative Linking," *New York Times*, Apr. 22, 2002.

38. Fred von Lohmann, "Public Interest Cyber-Lawyering on the Electronic Frontier," lecture delivered at New York University Law School, Feb. 23, 2009.

39. *John Doe (aka Brian Sapient)* v. *Uri Geller*, Order to Dismiss, No. C. 07–2478 VRW (N.D. Cal. 2008). To make matters more complicated, Geller claimed that because he was in the U.K., the British fair dealing standard and not the fair use standard applied.

40. Siva Vaidhyanathan, *The Googlization of Everything* (Berkeley: University of California Press, 2011); Johnny Mango, "'Lost' Police Incident Report . . . Is This What Heather Wilson 'Lost' 13 Years Ago?" *albloggerque* (blog) (Oct. 19, 2006), at http://albloggerque.blogspot.com/2006/10/lost-police-incident-reportis-this.html.

41. Letter, Trevor Potter (McCain-Palin, General Counsel) to Chad Hurley (YouTube CEO), Zahavah Levine (YouTube General Counsel), and William Patry (Senior Copyright Counsel, Google) (Oct. 13, 2008). See also Center for Democracy and Technology, "Campaign Takedown Troubles: How Meritless Copyright Claims Threaten Online Political Speech" (Sept. 2010), at www.cdt.org/report/campaign-takedown-troubles-how-meritless-copyright-claims-threaten-online-political-speech.

42. Sarah Lai Stirland, "Stifled by Copyright, McCain Asks YouTube to Consider Fair Use," *Threat Level Blog*, Wired.com (Oct. 14, 2008).

43. Corynne McSherry's quote appears in the introduction to the Electronic Frontier Foundation's webpage archiving documents relating to *Lenz v. Universal*, at www.eff.org/cases/lenz-v-universal.

44. *Lenz v. Universal*, 572 F. Supp. 2d 1150 (N.D. Cal. 2008); Ben Sheffner, "Expect to See Greater Clarity on the Legality of Fan-Created Music Videos," Billboard.com (Jan. 23, 2010).

45. Calvin Reed, "Ellison, AOL Battle Over DMCA 'Safe Harbor,'" *Publishers Weekly*, Apr. 15, 2002; Bob Goodbey, "When the Harbor Is No Longer Safe — AOL and Repeat Infringers," *Hawaii Business* (June 2004); *Io Group, Inc. v. Veoh Networks Inc.*, 586 F. Supp. 2d 1132 (N.D. Cal 2008); *UMG Recordings. Inc. v. Veoh Networks. Inc.*, 620 F. Supp. 2d 1081 (C.D. Cal . 2008); *UMG Recordings. Inc. v. Veoh Networks Inc.*, 665 F. Supp. 2d 1099 (C.D. Cal. 2009); Liz Gannes, "Universal Follows through on Video Lawsuit Threats," *GigaOm* (Oct. 17, 2006).

46. Memorandum of Law in Support of Viacom's Motion for Partial Summary Judgment on Liability and Inapplicability of the Digital Millennium Copyright Act Safe Harbor Defense, *Viacom International v. YouTube, Inc.*, Case No. 1:07-cv-02 103 (S.D.N.Y. 2010).

47. See Zack Shenaz, "Content ID and Fair Use," *Google Public Policy Blog* (Apr. 23, 2010).

48. CBS, et al., "Principles for User Generated Content Services," (2007), and Electronic Frontier Foundation, et al., "Fair Use Principles for User Generated Video Content," (2007).

CONCLUSION: THE COPYRIGHT REFORM MOVEMENT

1. Jessica Litman, *Digital Copyright* (Amherst, NY: Prometheus, 2001), 194.

2. Campaign contributions and lobbying efforts are tracked by OpenSecrets. org.

3. The library organizations and the Digital Future Coalition were largely responsible for the adoption of the triennial rulemaking process through which the Library of Congress creates exemptions to the DMCA. This dynamic process, which seemed like a large concession in 1998, has proven to be a significant check on the reach of the anticircumvention measures of the DMCA.

4. Joe Trippi, *The Revolution Will Not Be Televised: Democracy, the Internet, and the Overthrow of Everything* (New York: HarperCollins, 2004).

5. Robert W. McChesney and John Nichols, "Our Media, Not Theirs: Building the U.S. Media Reform Movement," *In These Times* (Apr. 2003).

6. Cecilia Kang, "Net Neutrality's Quiet Crusader," *Washington Post*, Mar. 28, 2008.

7. For Lawrence Lessig, see *Code and Other Laws of Cyberspace* (New York: Basic Books, 1999), *The Future of Ideas: The Fate of the Commons in a Connected World* (New York: Random House, 2001), *Free Culture: How Big Media*

Uses Technology and the Law to Lock Down Culture and Control Creativity (New York: Penguin, 2004), and *Remix: Making Art and Commerce Thrive in the Hybrid Economy* (New York: Penguin, 2008); and for Siva Vaidhyanathan, see *Copyrights and Copywrongs: The Rise of Intellectual Property and How It Threatens Creativity* (New York: New York University Press, 2001), and *The Anarchist in the Library: How the Clash Between Freedom and Control Is Hacking the Real World and Crashing the System* (New York: Basic Books, 2004).

8. Eric J. Schwartz and Matt Williams, "Access to Orphan Works: Copyright Law, Preservation, and Politics," *Cinema Journal* 46.2 (Winter 2007): 139–45.

9. Creative Commons tracks the number of Creative Commons licenses at http://wiki.creativecommons.org/Metrics. On Creative Commons in China, see Bingchun Meng, "Articulating a Chinese Commons: An Explorative Study of Creative Commons in China," *International Journal of Communication* 3 (2009): 192–207.

10. Bill Herman, "The Battle Over Digital Rights Management: A Multi-Method Study of the Politics of Copyright Management Technologies" (PhD diss., University of Pennsylvania, 2009).

INDEX

FILM AND CULTURE A SERIES OF COLUMBIA UNIVERSITY PRESS Edited by John Belton